Online Community Management

FOR

DUMMIES®

by Deborah Ng

WILEY

John Wiley & Sons, Inc.

Online Community Management For Dummies®

Published by
John Wiley & Sons, Inc.
111 River Street
Hoboken, NJ 07030-5774

www.wiley.com

Copyright © 2012 by John Wiley & Sons, Inc., Hoboken, New Jersey

Published by John Wiley & Sons, Inc., Hoboken, New Jersey

Published simultaneously in Canada

For general information on our other products and services, please contact our Customer Care Department within the U.S. at 877-762-2974, outside the U.S. at 317-572-3993, or fax 317-572-4002.

For technical support, please visit www.wiley.com/techsupport.

Wiley publishes in a variety of print and electronic formats and by print-on-demand. Some material included with standard print versions of this book may not be included in e-books or in print-on-demand. If this book refers to media such as a CD or DVD that is not included in the version you purchased, you may download this material at http://booksupport.wiley.com. For more information about Wiley products, visit www.wiley.com.

Library of Congress Control Number: 2011941692

ISBN 978-1-118-09917-9 (pbk); ISBN 978-1-118-18276-5 (ePDF); ISBN 978-1-118-18277-2 (eMobi); ISBN 978-1-118-18278-9 (ePub)

Manufactured in the United States of America

10 9 8 7 6 5 4 3 2 1

WILEY

About the Author

In addition to working in the past as a community manager and professional blogger for several online brands, **Deborah Ng** also grew a small writing blog into the No. 1 online community for freelance writers before selling in 2010. Currently, Deb works for BlogWorld and New Media expo helping to find speakers and content for their events. When she's not oversharing on the social networks, Deb blogs at `Kommein.com` and enjoys time with her extremely handsome husband and brilliant son.

Dedication

Online Community Management For Dummies is dedicated to Linda Lindsay, who I miss every single day.

Author's Acknowledgments

Many, many years ago, probably before many of you were born, my family noticed my enjoyment of writing and encouraged me to go beyond school essays and research reports and consider a career as a writer. It took a while, but eventually it happened. Even before I saw it myself, my mother and father encouraged me to write, and I'm so extremely grateful to them.

I'm even more grateful to my husband Bert and son Timothy for putting up with all the days and nights spent parked in front of my laptop, instead of spending time with them. They not only encouraged my dream but put up with crankiness and my absence as I opted to meet deadlines over going on family hikes or spending time with them in the pool.

In addition to my family, four people deserve the bulk of my thanks because I can honestly say this book never would have happened if my BlogWorld bosses, and true friends Rick Calvert, Dave Cynkin and Patti Hoskings, along with my very dear blogging friend Chris Garrett, didn't take me to a John Wiley & Sons, Inc. party in Austin, Texas to introduce me to Ellen Gerstein. Ellen didn't dig my original idea, but the introduction led to several pitches, and my idea for *Online Community Management For Dummies* is the one that stuck.

I'd also be remiss if I didn't thank the rest of my BlogWorld team, because they were so encouraging and supportive through the whole book writing process — even if I was late with work stuff. Thank you for your kind words and friendship Allison Boyer, Lara Kulpa, Nikki Katz, Dani Goren, Chris Castro, and the rest of our growing team. I have the best job in the world, and it's such an honor to work with the most amazing gosh-darned group of people ever. Ever.

My brothers and sisters are also a big part of who I am today. Perhaps we don't see eye to eye on everything, and, yeah, there's been some family drama, but they're a wonderful support group and a heck of a lot of fun. Thank you for putting up with all my talking, singing, and Donny Osmond worship, Donald Dederick, Diana Hayes, Desiree Pacuk, Doug Dederick, and Dawn Vota. I love you all.

Before I start with the big list of thank you's, I also have to single out Andy Hayes. A girl couldn't ask for a better person to have on her side. Andy cracked the whip to make sure I was working on my book over wasting time fooling around and was always there whether to talk about serious stuff or just share a little gossip. Everyone needs an Andy Hayes in their corner.

There are so many more people to thank, it would take a much bigger book to tell you who and why. I hope the following people know what an impact they've made in my life and how much their friendship means to me: Thank you for your friendship, kindness, and support Jodee Redmond, Aliza Sherman, Tereece Clarke my White Meadow friends especially Anne Sickles, Robbin Seidel and Sarah Brake, Mike Stelzner, Joe DeCarli, Celina Pellicane, Jennifer Hoffman, Amy Porterfield, Tommy & Julie Tilert, Joel Durham, Jr., Jonathan Fields, Jonathan Magrid, Deb Dorchak, Wendi Kelly, Wendy Piersall, Becky McCray, David Crawford, Yury Polnar, Eddie Vallee, Kurt & Kate Ernst, Kelby Carr, Heather Solos, John Hewitt, Vanessa VanSciver, Alex Manger, Renee Kaestner, the Ng family (including all the millions of cousins and spouses), and so many other people who I will probably regret not naming here. Also, a special thanks to Chris Cella for all his help with my book proposals.

Finally, I'd like to thank my editors who put up with more than one missed deadline because of one calamity or another: Amy Fandrei, Ellen Gerstein, and Kelly Ewing, thank you. I hope this is a long, beautiful relationship.

Publisher's Acknowledgments

We're proud of this book; please send us your comments at `http://dummies.custhelp.com`. For other comments, please contact our Customer Care Department within the U.S. at 877-762-2974, outside the U.S. at 317-572-3993, or fax 317-572-4002.

Some of the people who helped bring this book to market include the following:

Acquisitions and Editorial

Project Editor: Kelly Ewing

Acquisitions Editor: Amy Fandrei

Copy Editor: Kathy Simpson

Technical Editor: Andrea Vahl

Editorial Manager: Jodi Jensen

Editorial Assistant: Amanda Graham

Sr. Editorial Assistant: Cherie Case

Cover Photo: © iStockphoto.com / zudy-box

Cartoons: Rich Tennant
(`www.the5thwave.com`)

Composition Services

Project Coordinator: Nikki Gee

Layout and Graphics: Claudia Bell, Samantha K. Cherolis, Corrie Socolovitch

Proofreaders: Laura Albert, BIM Indexing & Proofreading Services

Indexer: Potomac Indexing, LLC

Publishing and Editorial for Technology Dummies

Richard Swadley, Vice President and Executive Group Publisher

Andy Cummings, Vice President and Publisher

Mary Bednarek, Executive Acquisitions Director

Mary C. Corder, Editorial Director

Publishing for Consumer Dummies

Kathleen Nebenhaus, Vice President and Executive Publisher

Composition Services

Debbie Stailey, Director of Composition Services

Contents at a Glance

Table of Contents

Introduction

*E*very business has fans or people who are so passionate about a product, a service, or the people who make up the brand that they want to take the relationship beyond that of the buyer/seller. Thanks to the Internet, you can connect with the people who appreciate your brand in many different ways. People who like your brand on Facebook, follow you on Twitter, and comment on the corporate blog are more than just customers; they're a community.

About This Book

Online Community Management For Dummies helps you cultivate, foster, and manage an online community. It also helps you provide a good customer experience by providing a great community experience. You discover why all these Facebook pages, tweets, forum posts, and blog comments are so important, and most of all, you find out why mutual respect is your most important customer service tool.

This book is a practical guide to community management. If I did my job properly, you won't have to hunt for the dictionary after every word. Instead, you'll spend your time learning the importance of community, and why an online community manager is the most important job in your place of business.

You discover

- ✔ Why people want to be part of your online community
- ✔ Why it's important for you to be a regular presence in your online community
- ✔ How to communicate with the members of your online community
- ✔ The perks of joining an online community
- ✔ The different types of negativity affecting most online communities
- ✔ The different types of online communities
- ✔ The importance of organizing offline community events
- ✔ How to evaluate the success of your online campaigns

Online Community Management For Dummies isn't a technical manual. Instead, it offers useful tips for fostering and interacting with your online community as well learning what they're looking for in a brand.

Foolish Assumptions

Though this book falls under the *For Dummies* umbrella, I'm assuming that that majority of my readers are anything but. As I was writing this book, I assumed the following:

- ✔ You're either working as or hoping to work as an online community manager.
- ✔ You know a thing or two about the various social networks.
- ✔ You know what a blog is.
- ✔ You enjoy interacting with others.
- ✔ You're more interested in professional community management than being a hobbyist.
- ✔ You have basic Internet knowledge.
- ✔ You know that customer service is more than an 800 line.

Mostly, I assumed that you enjoy a good conversation and understand the value of reaching out to those who believe in your brand.

Conventions Used in This Book

When I wrote this book, I tried to be consistent about it, so I set a few conventions:

- ✔ Any word I'm defining appears in italics.
- ✔ When I recommend a website or online application, I provide the URL.

For the most part, it's all pretty self-explanatory. Headings and subheadings separate chapters and sections, photos are referenced and captioned. And just like my blogging and writing online, I rock the bullets throughout this book when I feel information needs to be broken down into easy-to-understand, bite-sized bits of conversation.

What You Don't Have to Read

I have a confession to make. I hope you'll read this whole book because I truly enjoyed writing it for you. However, I know you're busy with your online communities, and the last thing you want to do is spend your time reading a reference book like this one. I get it.

Online Community Management For Dummies isn't a cliffhanger. It's not an edge-of-your-seat thriller, nor is it a vacation-time page turner. It's a reference book. In fact, you don't have to read *Online Community Management For Dummies* in any particular order. You can start reading this book anywhere and stop anywhere, choosing only those topics that interest you most.

How This Book Is Organized

Online Community Management For Dummies is made up of seven parts. Here's a peek into what you can look forward to for each part.

Part 1: The Basics of Online Community Management

This part is an overview of a community manager's duties as well as the importance of fostering community within a brand. Knowing why people join online communities in general is just as important as learning why members are joining your community. Part I defines online community, covers the reasons folks join communities, and discusses the important tasks you'll have to undertake in your role as community manager.

Part II: Embracing the Community Manager's Role

Your job has many different layers and levels. In Part II, I get more in depth about those layers and levels and discuss best practices for successful online community management. Whether it's handling the different types of negativity that comes with this gig, thinking up fun promotions, or positively interacting with your community, I cover the basics — and even some of the not-so-basics.

Part III: Building a Productive Online Community

Successful communities work and grow together. Part III touches on the ways your community helps you — and vice versa. You find out how to use your community for feedback and also how to create promotions that will drive sales and help create a word-of-mouth marketing campaign.

Part IV: Growing Your Community

The most successful communities have a steady influx of members, but they don't mosey in on your own. They find your community through searches, promotions, and recommendations from your existing members. Part IV covers all the things you need to know to bring in and welcome new members.

Part V: Assessing the Health of Your Community

Your community is up and running. So how are things going? In this part, I tell you how you can see how your community is faring, using both subjective indicators and cold, hard numbers.

Part VI: Taking Your Community Offline

You may think as a community manager that all your work is done on a desktop computer or laptop. You'd be wrong. In fact, offline work is just as important. In this part, you find out everything you need to know about attending conferences, holding classes, hosting meetups and tweetups, and more.

Part VII: The Part of Tens

No *For Dummies* book is complete without the famous Part of Tens. These staples include quick but vital lists of things you need to know and do to be a successful community manager.

Icons Used in This Book

As you use *Online Community Management For Dummies*, you'll probably notice little pictures in the margins. These icons are there to catch your eye and lead you to important information. Here's a breakdown of the different icons and what you can expect from them:

This icon marks the places where I share an idea or practical advice for managing your online community.

Whenever you see this icon, know that the information is something you'll want to keep in mind.

This icon warns you of some negative things to look out for.

You don't have to read text marked with this icon. It gives you more information that you don't have to know to complete the task at hand.

Where to Go from Here

You can read this book in any order you like. My recommendation is to browse the Table of Contents or index and look for the chapters, sections, and topics that resonate most with the role you play as online community manager for your brand.

If you already understand the role and responsibilities of an online community manager is, skip the overview in Chapter 1. If want to find out how to understand your online traffic patterns, head on over to Part V.

It's my hope you'll refer to this book when you have questions regarding your job as a community manager and some of the issues you'll encounter.

Occasionally, we have updates to our technology books. If this book does have technical updates, they will be posted at `dummies.com/go/online communitymanagementfdupdates`.

Part I
The Basics of Online Community Management

The 5th Wave   By Rich Tennant

"I don't care what your online community friends in Europe say, you're not having a glass of Chianti with your bologna sandwich."

In this part . . .

In this part, I take you on a tour of online communities. You discover exactly what they are and why they're important. I also take a look at the role of an online community manager and your relationship with both your community members and your brand.

Chapter 1

Fostering an Online Community

In This Chapter

▶ Getting the inside scoop on how online communities work

▶ Benefitting from online communities

▶ Digging into the community manager's job

*T*ribe, clique, group, network, club, collective, collaborative, and clan are just a few of the words used to describe *online communities,* or places where groups of like-minded people converge on the Internet. You probably even belong to a few online communities yourself. It doesn't matter if you're a gamer, a knitter, or someone who creates video, the people you share and interact with over the Internet are your online community.

Online communities start out slowly, with a few tentative members at a time. Sooner or later, personalities emerge, friendships and alliances form, and cliques and heated discussions follow. If left to their own devices, online communities can become free-for-alls. However, properly managed online communities flourish into a positive experience for all involved.

In this chapter, you discover what it means to be a part of an online community and why a community manager is the backbone of both the community and the brand. You find out why online communities are important, how community members benefit from the brand, and how the brand benefits from the community. Finally, this chapter discusses your role as an online community manager and how online communities absolutely can't flourish without you.

Understanding What an Online Community Is

A *community* is a group of people interacting, sharing, and working toward a common goal. This definition works for all communities, whether it's an offline neighborhood, online collective, or colony of ants.

An online community takes these groups and moves the interaction to the Internet. Whereas neighbors may converse in their yards, in an online community, they interact via social networks, such as Twitter, Facebook, and the newest kid on the block, Google+. They also share in forums, e-mail groups, and even in the comments sections of blog posts and news articles. Members of online communities talk about the same things with their online friends as they do their offline neighbors, but they also rally around a specific topic, product, or cause to share ideas, offer tips, or act as mentors. Online community members are made up of customers, fans, or hobbyists who share a passion for a product, topic, or pastime. Many times, they join communities because people at home in the offline world don't share similar passions. So they come online to talk at length with the folks who "get it."

Online communities are no longer primitive forums where hobbyists discuss their crafts. Now marketing teams for household brands are creating Facebook pages and YouTube accounts specifically to sell products. And it's working.

While members still visit online communities to talk about their passion, thanks to social media and conversational marketing, online communities are now also seen as places to discuss products, receive feedback, and begin word-of-mouth marketing campaigns.

Online communities are best explained by exploring offline "real life" neighborhood communities. Close-knit neighbors not only socialize, but they also help each other. They borrow tools and bring in the mail. They make dinner for sick parents and trade off watching kids. They also maintain common interests — for example, working together to keep common areas attractive and productive.

Just like offline neighborhoods, members of online communities work together to ensure that their haven is safe and tidy and suits the best interests of everyone. Both offline and online communities

- ✔ **Share:** Perhaps the members of online communities aren't going next door for a cup of sugar, but they're sharing in other ways. They turn each other on to tips, links to resources, advice, commiseration, and secrets to success. They share ideas, swap stories, and answer questions.

- ✔ **Teach:** In offline neighborhoods, the woman across the street shares her gardening expertise, and the accountant down the road offers over-the-fence tax advice. Communities have teachers. Many of them don't set out to teach; to them, it's all part of the conversation. The same holds true online. In conversation, the members of online communities teach and learn.

- ✔ **Discuss:** Tight-knit neighborhoods flourish because individual members stay apprised of the issues that affect their area. They talk among themselves and decide as a united body what changes need to be made. They also discuss common interests. Though united for a common interest, off-topic discussions also take place. Both online and offline communities are places to interact, converse, and cultivate relationships.

✔ **Entertain:** At home, you probably enjoy community life. You might attend parties and barbecues at each other's homes, put together block parties, Easter egg hunts, and parades and make sure that there's more to where you live than houses and stores. Regular participants in online communities also do so because of their entertainment value. Sure, you also learn and make important connections, but if you didn't enjoy participating in the events and discussions there, you wouldn't come back.

✔ **Assist:** Online communities may not experience a barn-raising or rummage sale, but members often receive support in other areas. For example, members who participate at web design forums often collaborate on design ideas and learn new techniques thanks to the generosity of other members of their communities.

✔ **Work toward a common goal:** Neighbors band together for the common good. Perhaps they form a PTA to help out with school, rally around a sick or injured neighbor, or raise funds for a veteran's garden. Online groups do these deeds as well. They raise funds for charities, bring awareness to causes, and contribute toward the good of the community.

✔ **Beautify:** One dingy home brings down the property value of an entire block. A decrepit downtown keeps people from moving or investing into a neighborhood. Ditto a decrepit online community. If a forum or social network is outdated and riddled with spam and vulgarity, members are going to stay away. It's in everyone's best interest to make sure that their online hangouts are as beautiful as their offline communities.

✔ **Patrol:** The safest neighborhoods are patrolled by police and Watch organizations who keep an eye out for unsavory types. Community management and members stay vigilant to make sure online communities remain positive, productive places to network.

Similarities between online and offline communities abound. Members vote on issues, organize safety patrols, and carry on casual conversation. Like offline communities, online neighborhoods work together harmoniously for a common cause. Online communities cast the same positive vibe and sense of belonging.

Exploring the Types of Online Communities

Many different types of online communities exist, but the mechanics and inner workings are similar. Although the focus of each online community may be unrelated, the personality types are universal. After a while, these personality types are easy to identify, even if you've moved on to another community.

Online communities are hosted on a variety of platforms, with different purposes each. In fact, platform and purpose are the two most important determining factors before starting an online community. For example, if a community platform is the corporate blog, the purpose may be to offer news and updates to the community while receiving feedback in return. So before you start your online community, think about why you're bring a community together and what platform you want to use to host your community discussions.

Before deciding your community's function, think about what type of community you're looking to host. Knowing how each type of online community works and the benefits of each will eventually help you decide what role your community should play in your business.

Online communities take several different forms. Some brands have a presence on all the different social networks, while others choose the one or two platforms that will best represent what their trying to achieve. For example, they may have a corporate blog for updates, news, and niche-related tips, but also a Facebook page for conversation that isn't so deep. You don't have to have a presence on all the social networks, but you do want to be where the people are, so it's best to visit each of the different platforms to see what works best for you. Over time, you may find that one platform works while another yields no results, so it's better to work on something that's working than to beat a dead horse. Try a variety of different social media tools, take them for a spin, and see which ones yield the best results.

Blogs

Blogs are no longer personal online journals. Many businesses and individuals start blogs in order to bring in business and even make money. For example, a cosmetics brand might use a beauty blog to write short articles called *blog posts* to share beauty tips and techniques. Blogs are also a terrific way to showcase product news and information.

Because blogs are content heavy, they catch the attention of search engines like Google or Bing. In order to rank high on the search engines and bring in new readers, most bloggers have to research traffic-building techniques in addition to community management techniques.

A blog's community grows over time as more readers tune in, usually as a result of their own online research. Community happens when readers participate in the day's blog topics. By commenting, readers are able to share their views and take part in an intelligent discussion (see Figure 1-1). The only place to take part in topic talks is the comment section at the bottom of each blog post, but that doesn't stop readers from having a lively and productive chat.

Figure 1-1:
Comments
and Share
buttons turn
a blog from
an article
into an
interactive
community.

Moderating a blog's community is also relatively easy. Each blog platform comes with a comment moderation system that allows the blogger or community manager to delete spam messages or abusive comments, keeping the atmosphere positive and productive. Because comments are specific to each day's discussion topic, commenters more or less have to stay on topic.

Facebook pages

Though a social network, Facebook deserves a place of its own on this list. Many businesses are now inviting customers to Like them on Facebook fan pages (see Figure 1-2). Friends and family see those Likes, which are linked, and follow them to the fan pages from which they originated. Once there, they may be inclined to Like the page as well. These individual Likes soon become a community of participants. Because any page updates appear on the Facebook user's status page, members don't even have to log into a separate website to participate.

Facebook pages, also known as Facebook fan pages, are a breeze to set up and maintain. These communities are among the simplest to maintain because they require only a few updates, and members abide by Facebook's rules. Heavy moderation isn't needed, and your biggest issue is spam, which is easy to remove.

Unlike forums where members hold many different conversations at the same time, your Facebook members don't want to receive Facebook updates from brands in their statuses all day. Otherwise, a member's own Facebook status page is nothing but brand updates. One to three daily conversation starters spread out throughout the day is a good rule, but don't forget to come back and respond to members who comment after your updates. When you post too many status updates on your Facebook page, members get tired of seeing nothing but you on their status pages or newsfeeds and "unlike" so they're better able to see updates from friends and family.

Figure 1-2:
Use
Facebook
pages to
share news
and updates
with your
community.

The amount of updates you post on the social networks is a key difference between a forum, which members can visit at their leisure and update as often as they like, and a Facebook or Twitter stream, where members hope to see a variety of updates from all their friends and not just a barrage from a single brand.

TIP

Facebook pages aren't to be confused with Facebook groups. The pages are made-up updates from you on behalf of the brand and comments from fans who wish to receive updates from brands or celebrities in their Facebook statuses. Facebook groups, on the other hand, are discussions created mostly by individuals who wish to talk about a particular topic. For example, a Facebook group called "Community Manager, Advocate and Evangelist" features discussion topics of interest to community managers. Though there are some public groups, most are private and require that members opt in to participate. Instead of clicking the Like button as you would a fan page, members *join* the group as they would join a club.

Brands can create discussion groups on Facebook. However, most companies find that it's easier and more conducive to their business to create a fan page where they can drop one or two discussion topics in a day over more deep discussion groups. Most people who join Facebook brand pages aren't necessarily there for a deep conversation; they simply want to show support for the brand.

Forums

Online forums are websites or subdomains dedicated to community discussions (see Figure 1-3). In fact, most early online forums were created strictly for their conversational element and not to sell products or build name awareness. As businesses and brands realized the potential of communities, more forums were created. Various interest groups and support groups also created forums in order to mentor or commiserate.

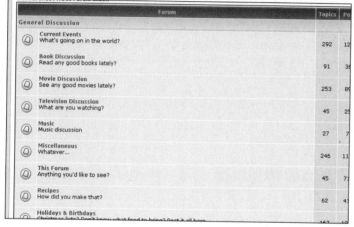

Figure 1-3: If you have the knowledge, you can use forums to foster online discussions.

Most forums are made up of topic folders, with different discussions in each folder. They're "threaded" into easy to follow conversations so new members can read the discussion from the very beginning — even if they're coming in at the end.

Forums do require a bit of technical expertise to install and keep running properly, but they're not difficult to manage. If not moderated properly, forums are magnets for spammers, trolls and other negativity. Still, forums foster loyal communities with members who look forward to participating each and every day.

E-mail groups

Community discussions also take place via e-mail or through Yahoo! or Google's group options. The most popular e-mail communities are both a blessing and a curse in that they send e-mails to members' accounts for every response to a discussion topic. So if a member asks a question and 100 people respond, he can expect 101 e-mails for that one specific topic.

Participants do have the option of receiving a single *digest* e-mail with a set number of messages to defray this overload, but heavy discussions can still be cumbersome. That isn't to say that e-mail groups don't have their benefits because they're useful tools and a convenient way to participate in discussions without having to visit websites and social networks.

The re-using and recycling organization Freecycle is an example of a very successful Yahoo! Group community. In fact, Freecycle has individual e-mail groups for regions all over the world.

Moderators can opt to have *closed* or *open communities,* and type determines whether or not to approve new members and comments. A *closed* community indicates members need approval before they can join. The moderator looks at the potential member's information to determine whether she is a good fit, and also to keep out spammers. *Open* communities allow anyone to sign up without approval, although these communities are the most inundated with spam.

Unmoderated e-mail groups become a spammer's paradise, driving away members.

Social networks

Twitter, YouTube, Facebook, and LinkedIn are a few familiar examples of social networks. These communities provide a way for members to discuss or comment on other members' contributions. Most of these types of groups don't require an elaborate setup, but they may offer the ability to customize your profile and sidebar to reflect your brand.

You may find most of your members participate in more than one social networks. Many of the same people who participate on Facebook also use Twitter, a social network where members share brief 140 character updates with each other. Job seekers also use LinkedIn, which is more than an online resume; it also has discussion areas and places for members to interact. You Tube allows members to share videos and comment on the videos. If you're looking to build your community base, the different social networks are a good place to start.

Social networks aren't necessarily topic specific. Thousands of conversations take place each day among the different cliques and sub communities. Businesses and individuals have the opportunity to establish groups and/or pages within these networks, and many do.

The problem with having groups and accounts spread across all the different social networks is that it can drive traffic and conversation away from the main website, and keeping up with dozens of different networks can prove challenging.

Still if you're looking to grow a personal or business brand or drive traffic to a website, it's a good idea to have active accounts with many of the larger social networks, such as Twitter, Facebook, and LinkedIn.

Knowing Why Communities Need Management

If you've ever watched a television debate, you've noticed a moderator sitting neutrally behind a desk asking questions and making sure that no one hogs up too much air time. The moderator also makes sure that discussions don't lead to arguments or arguments to fights. If not for the moderator, a debate could become a battle of *snark,* where members "politely" insult each other, and anarchy can ensue, making an uncomfortable situation for everyone in attendance.

A *community manager* is similar to a moderator but with more cowbell because community management involves more than moderating a conversation. A community manager advocates for both the member and the brand, while ensuring that discussions are positive and productive. Without such a person at the helm, the community can become a hotbed of negativity, attended only by people who crave drama and nastiness.

Understanding how people socialize online

Participants in online communities don't always set out to socialize when using the Internet. Many times, they're researching a hobby, product, or topics of interest and become intrigued after landing upon a particularly interesting conversation. After a few days of lurking or watching discussions unfold, they're hooked and begin participating. They check in every day to see who responds to their comments and look forward to taking part in new discussions. Sometimes online communities become an addiction, and participants check back often, more than several times a day even. There are always a few who appear to be present the entire day.

Not only are members passionate about their communities, but they're also passionate about their beliefs. This passion is especially reflected in how they respond in comments. For some, it means pleading for other members to see their side of the story, and for others, it means becoming abusive and calling names and questioning morals and integrity.

If you spend enough time in online communities, the various personalities and behaviors of the members become predictable and familiar:

- ✔ **The shy person who finds her voice:** Quiet or shy people are often surprised by how outgoing they are online. They find it easier to talk to people behind a computer screen than face to face. Sometimes they're so emboldened by their participation that they begin to speak up offline as well.

- ✔ **The brutally honest person who turns mean:** People who pull no punches in the real world might turn downright abusive online. They're dealing with people whom they don't know, without serious repercussion, and may respond with snark or insults.

- ✔ **Members who fall into friendships and cliques:** Just like your own offline community, those who participate in online groups also form alliances, friendships, and cliques. They respond to each other's comments and defend each other when discussions turn heated.

- ✔ **The voice of reason:** Every community has a mother hen or voice of reason. When arguments happen or discussions turn into debates, this person steps in as unofficial moderator and attempts to keep the peace. Sometimes community members are cooperative, and sometimes the voice of reason is shouted down.

- ✔ **The pile-on:** As cliques form, personalities form and sometimes members of a clique act as one. As members become empowered by both their anonymity and their new online friends, they may take issue with anyone who disagrees and band together to shut down an opposing view.

- ✔ **The chronic malcontent:** Have you ever noticed that there's one person in your group or neighborhood who simply isn't happy? Nothing goes right for this person, or everyone is out to get him. He complains about everything from gas prices to faulty service, but never has anything nice to say. Online communities often have at least one chronic malcontent. Most participants tend to avoid this person after a while.

- ✔ **The person who questions authority:** Every now and then, someone comes along who doesn't agree with or even approve of management. This person publicly questions every move a community manager makes and confuses comment moderation with censorship.

I'm not suggesting that all online communities are hotbeds of negativity where members nitpick and fight. However, this tendency does show the need for management and moderation. If no one in authority is present, eventually the only people participating are the ones who can yell the loudest. Communities with the right management are positive, productive, enjoyable places to visit.

Guiding community members in the right direction

An online community is not a set-it-and-forget-it website. Members, whether they agree or not, need guidance and direction. They can't just show up and think, "Now what?" It's up to community management to keep a positive conversation flowing and to ensure that the members are interacting and enjoying each other's company. Here are a few good practices to put into place so everyone feels welcome:

- ✓ **Make new members feel at home.** Many new members, or *newbies,* enjoy introducing themselves and saying a little about who they are and what they do. Community members do what they can to welcome newbies and invite them to participate in discussion topics. Many community managers like to remember certain details about participants' expertise and knowledge, inviting them to share their points of view in conversations.

- ✓ **Choose topics for discussion.** Community managers engage. They ask questions and respond to comments, making sure that members have a reason to return each day.

- ✓ **Ensure that discussions stay on topic.** Most online communities focus on a specific subject, practice, or brand. For example, a forum for knitters may feature discussions regarding stitches, materials, and patterns, so talking about monster truck races wouldn't be appropriate. Some forums do have folders for off-topic discussions, but most visit to learn about and talk about their passion.

- ✓ **Discourage negativity.** If a discussion turns into an argument or inappropriate language comes into play, the community manager steps in to get things back on track. This responsibility may mean soothing hurt feelings or reminding members of the community's comment policy. (I get to in Chapter 4.)

It's up to you as community manager to make sure that everyone is happy, entertained, and achieving their purpose for being on your community. You don't have to nag, lecture, and force your way into every community interaction. Instead, sit back and observe. Watch how members interact and step in when necessary. Your community should be able to function while you're away, but its members should know enough about the policies that they're respectful and positive even when you're not watching.

A Manager Does More Than Moderate

Think an online community manager only keeps conversation flowing? Think again. Moderating discussions is only a small part of a community manager's job. You're also expected to provide outreach to other communities, while providing support and acting as an advocate for both community members and your employer. As a community manager, you provide customer support, respond to questions and inquiries, and monitor the web to see what is being said about the businesses you work for. You act as spokesperson and ambassador for your company.

Online community management encompasses many departments, so some businesses are confused about which department their community managers should report to. "Community manager" also tends to be a sort of catchall title for someone who deals with the people who use a particular product or brand. Usually, the job evolves with the brand.

Keeping the lines of communication open

If members are joining a business or brand's community, they're doing so because they believe in the product, service, or whatever it is they're selling or promoting. Members join to discuss the best ways to use said product or service, receive discounts, and learn of news and updates.

The business or brand hosting the online community also has a vested interest. It wants to discover its customers' opinions, how they use its products or services, drive sales, and hopefully foster word-of-mouth marketing.

As a result, the community manager has to ensure a two-way street, ensuring that members are offering feedback to the brand while the brand is keeping members apprised of news and updates.

The community manager is the mouthpiece of the organization. You ensure that both members and management are learning as much as they can about each other. In some cases, you need to add updates on the community's discussion page. It also means sending out newsletters, writing blog posts, articles, and press releases, and making announcements on Twitter and Facebook. You then report the resulting comments, both positive and negative, to the proper channels.

Attracting new members

Members of online communities are transient. Many stick around only until they achieve a certain goal. Others lose interest and find new hangouts. Thus, without a regular influx of new members, communities die out.

Going through all the trouble of putting up a place for folks to interact only to let it turn into a virtual ghost town seems like a waste. Encouraging new membership is one of the key duties of a community manager. A good manager really rocks the people skills and is friendly, inviting, and welcoming. A good manager is also active in many other online communities and networks, in hopes of driving traffic and raising awareness, and uses a variety of methods to keep folks coming in:

- ✔ **Participates in social networking:** Community managers often share news and events on social networks, such as Twitter and Facebook.
- ✔ **Cross-promotes with other communities:** Many community managers join forces for contests and discussion among like-minded communities.
- ✔ **Offers perks and discounts:** New members are drawn to coupons, discount codes, freebies, and other perks.
- ✔ **Attends conferences and meet-ups:** Community managers often attend conferences and meet-ups among same-interest groups in order to raise awareness and bring in new members.

Focusing on goals and policies

If you're entering into community management thinking you'll be spending all your time on Facebook and Twitter, you're in for a rude awakening. The gig entails way more than hanging out on the social networks. In fact, social networking is only a small part of the community manager's focus. Online communities are created for a purpose. Groups hosted by a business are usually there to drive sales, bring in new customers, provide customer satisfaction, build buzz, and create an effective word-of-mouth campaign.

A company typically gives a community manager a set group of goals, which may entail anything from achieving a dollar amount in sales, a percentage of community growth, a positive word-of-mouth marketing campaign, or higher rankings on the search engines.

The challenging part is to achieve those goals while still following company policies and guidelines, especially among those businesses that are reluctant to embrace social media tools, such as Twitter or Facebook. Many such businesses are hush-hush about the inner workings of their organizations and don't want their community managers talking about them on the networks. Some businesses even insist upon approving every single tweet or status update. Even businesses that are more transparent about operations have policies and procedures to follow regarding the community manager's jobs, goals, and responsibilities.

Although the community manager is, indeed, an advocate for her community, her real loyalty is toward her place of employment. Before beginning as a community manager, you'll want to get a clear overview of all goals, policies, and procedures in writing so that no mistakes or miscommunications occur.

Evaluating Member Participation and Community Health

Have you ever stumbled upon a company Twitter account where the last tweet is over two years ago? How about a once-lively forum that receives maybe one or two posts per year? Have you ever been turned off from joining or staying with a Facebook group because the members do nothing but insult each other? If so, this section is dedicated to you.

When I discuss *community health,* it's in regard to membership and participation. Healthy communities are vibrant and active. Members are helpful and enthusiastic. Unhealthy communities aren't updated often and the members appear to be there only to promote their own causes or interests. Sometimes these communities aren't updated at all.

As a community manager, you can't set up a community and hope for the best. You have to take the necessary steps to keep it going regularly and positively.

Figuring out how members are using the community

Determining whether you're meeting your goals has more to do with watching what's going on than crunching numbers and checking stats. You also need to observe your community to determine why folks are coming back each day (or why they're not!) and what they do when they're visiting.

Your members are offering important clues as to how successful your community is. How they comment, how often they comment, and what they're saying gives you the ammunition you need to create topics, as well as help create the types of promotions that will drive both membership and sales.

How do your members use the community? See whether you recognize these different types of conversations:

- ✔ **Company or self-promotion:** Not everyone who visits an online community does so to engage in chat or learn about a new hobby. Plenty of people join up because they feel it's a great way to promote their personal or professional brand. Most promotion is subtle. For example, blogs and forums allow signature lines in every post where members can post links to their blogs, websites, or sales pages. However, some people get a little more "in your face." Most obvious promoters are called on their actions by other members of the community, moderators or community managers No one likes to participate in a social network and receive spam instead of conversation.

- ✔ **Community engagement:** How do members respond to discussion topics? Are they commenting or lurking? Is the discussion free flowing? Do they need you to hold their hands to keep the topic flowing? While you're there to help keep things moving along, the healthiest communities can function even in your absence. In fact, in the best communities, the community manager is one who is active, but not so much that he's the dominant force. The members should be front and center, not the community manager.

- ✔ **Shared resources:** Like a neighborhood, members of a healthy community work together to achieve a common goal. If the goal is find out more about a certain topic, members work together to achieve that knowledge and share tips, advice, and online resources. While all communities do have a self-centered member or two, the healthiest communities feature members who aren't all out for themselves and do what they can to help each other.

- ✔ **Responses to promotions:** You know what isn't fun? Throwing a party where no one shows up. So if you offer coupon codes, discounts, prizes, or freebies to your community, you want to monitor the response. A healthy community will have plenty of takers. You won't receive 100 percent interest, but if a good percentage of your most active members and even many of your inactive members participate, your community efforts are a success.

Encouraging community participation

How does a community come together, anyway? All this talking and sharing on online communities doesn't happen overnight, and it certainly doesn't happen on its own. Setting up a place to meet is nice, but an online community can sometimes resemble a high school dance, with everyone shyly hanging off to one side waiting for the first person to get started.

In essence, the community manager is the first person up to dance. She encourages everyone onto the floor, regardless of skill or expertise. She doesn't make them feel inept, but rather teaches them the latest steps. Soon, all the chairs are empty, and the dance floor is full.

The community manager is also the host. She stands at the door and says "Hello" and "Welcome" to all guests, paying special attention to the newcomers. She puts everyone at ease and makes sure that each person has someone to talk to. If the conversation isn't happening, she gets it started. If a newcomer is finding it difficult to keep up with the conversation or discussion topic, she finds a mentor to help. She never makes anyone feel self-conscious or ineffective, but encourages everyone to have a voice.

Fostering a community all sounds good in theory, but an online community isn't a party or high school dance. It's a forum or social networking group where people come to interact. Though the community manager doesn't even have to get up out of her chair, getting others to participate is sometimes challenging. However, regardless of the reason for the community, the members joined to benefit from talking to others. Therefore, members shouldn't need a whole lot of encouragement, and most don't. However, there are still people who aren't very comfortable with interacting with others online or aren't sure how to use an online community, and they need some help coming out of their shells.

Pinpointing areas of concern

Knowing how to identify a positive, productive community is only half the job. Community managers also have to identify problem areas and take necessary action. Sometimes, a problem that isn't handled properly or swiftly escalates into something major. Sweeping something under the rug never helps. Keeping an eye out for these behaviors and situations will save you from a massive headache later:

- ✔ **Cliques:** Cliques aren't necessarily a bad thing, but you'll want to keep an eye on them because they imply exclusivity. Sometimes when a community clique forms, members band together against other members or authority figures. Most of the time, though, they're a group of friends socializing online. When they begin banding together to "take over" the community, if they have to monopolize every discussion and pile on, or band together to belittle anyone who disagrees with a member of your clique, they're a problem. (You can find out more about creating a positive user experience in Chapter 4.)

✔ **Arguments:** There's a big difference between fights, arguments, insults, and respectful disagreements. Disagreement is good; it means folks are speaking their minds. When disagreements turn into fights and insults, chaos can ensue. Community managers need to monitor conversations and steer things in the right direction if they seem to be headed into negative territory. In Chapter 4, I talk about the difference between respectful disagreement and personal attacks.

✔ **Bad buzz:** Is someone using the social networks to talk about your business in a negative manner? In this age of transparency, don't sweep anything under the rug. Find out what is being said and by whom and discuss the proper course of action with your team.

✔ **Lack of cooperation:** Your idea of running an online community may be different from someone else's idea of running an online community. For example, you may want to be more transparent with your members, while your superiors don't want you talking about anything besides community business. If your community doesn't feel you're being honest or upfront with them, it may lead to a difficult situation. This topic is important, and you have to discuss it with your team.

✔ **Lack of response:** If members aren't responding to discussion topics or promotions, you have to determine why. There's no sense even fostering a community if no one is participating. Perhaps you're not talking about topics or doing things that interest them. Polls and surveys can help you pinpoint problem areas and move things to a more positive level.

✔ **Members feeling excluded:** Not only are communities like a high school dance, but they're also like the high school cafeteria. Members feel jealous if the most popular people are always singled out or if their concerns aren't addressed. Take care to include all and create the kinds of programs that include everyone.

Don't let an issue that seems like a minor problem escalate out of control. Identify issues early and take the necessary action. If dealt with effectively, members don't even know situations exist.

Taking Care of Business

Most people don't often look at community managers as business people or representatives of their brand. Rather, they tend to think of them more as community members because they're so outgoing. Behind the scenes community managers are attending meetings, planning events and promotions, handling some customer service issues and doing a lot of unglamorous, business-y, non-community type things.

Knowing your responsibility to the brand

Brand advocacy is the community manager's most important responsibility. Everything you do online under the brand umbrella is reflective of the brand. Though you may be tempted to let your hair down and cut loose on the social networks, it's not a good idea while using the brand accounts.

You may want to have two separate accounts on social networks, such as Twitter and Facebook, so that you can do some personal, off-the-record online socializing. However, this isn't to say that there aren't repercussions for acting inappropriately on your personal account either. Some members may still see you as representing the brand, even when you're off the clock. (Please see Chapter 7 for more details on dealing with personal negativity.)

So how do you represent the brand in a responsible manner?

✓ **Maintain an authoritative presence.** One reason community management is such a desirable field right now is because it looks so darn fun. What other jobs allow you to hang out on the social networks and chat up people all day? The problem with this attitude is that you can get a little too comfortable with socializing and with community members. You can have a good time, but members need to know who is in charge and show respect for the rules and regulations those in authority are there to enforce. If your members see you as one of the guys, retaining control can be hard, and the brand may look like it has an unruly community.

✓ **Behave in a matter befitting the brand.** Community managers who embarrass their employers don't last long, and other brands are reluctant to hire them. Keep the cursing, innuendo, and other inappropriate language at bay, even if you're just joking. Save the salty talk for when you're not on company time. Also be careful cutting loose while representing your place of employment at conferences, professional events, meet-ups, and tweetups. (For more information, see Chapter 7.)

✓ **Be very careful when doing things off the record.** As painful as it is for me to say, not everyone who interacts online is completely trustworthy. Be sure not to give away any company secrets or speak off the record, even to participants you feel you can trust. You may have made some friends among the community, but your loyalty is to your employer.

✓ **Don't get personal.** Certain personal details are okay to discuss. For example, if you're managing a parenting community, it's fine to talk about some of the things you do with your family as they relate to the topic. However, talking about your dating or sex life and sharing too much information in general doesn't reflect well upon the brand.

When a community manager feels relaxed among her "tribe," it's a good sign things are going right. But be careful that comfort doesn't lead to too much familiarity. Stay relevant and on topic and keep your personal life personal. Remember, everything you do or say is an extension of your place of business.

Knowing who to answer to

Probably the biggest source of confusion for any business starting an online community is what to do with the community manager. Because you fill so many different roles, no one is quite sure where to put the community manager's cubicle. There's no simple answer to this dilemma because different communities have different goals. Also, many community managers help out many different departments:

- **Social media:** If your business has a social media team, this area is where you'll find the community manager hanging out most of the time. Because you spend so much time interacting with the community via the social networks and using social media tools to create campaigns, you're an integral part of a company's social media strategy.

- **Marketing:** Because the community manager spends so much time with the people who make up the community, you know the most about your company's target audience. Being involved in marketing and promotional campaigns only makes sense.

- **Customer service:** Community managers monitor the social networks, e-mails, and other channels to ensure customer happiness. When things aren't working out for members, you make sure that they're concerns are taken care of.

- **Editorial:** Many community managers handle the company blogs and newsletters. If there's an editorial department, you'll occasionally meet with it to help plan content.

As you can see, the community manager's role is hard to define because you wear so many hats. Though it may be confusing at first, having a community manager answer to one department only may be a mistake. Communication with all involved departments is essential for good community and employee relations.

You also need to consider something else. If other people are handling campaigns or services that directly affect the community, and you aren't involved in any of the discussions or decision-making, resentment may occur. Plus, not involving the community manager can lead to unsuccessful campaigns run by people who don't have the community's best interests at heart.

Setting realistic expectations

It may seem as if so much is expected of a community manager, you may be expecting a super hero cape to come with your employee manual. Just be careful not to give the impression you can do it all. For sure, you have to achieve certain goals, but don't set yourself up for failure. If you say you can grow your community by a certain percentage, be sure you can do so. Ditto claiming to be able to drive a certain dollar amount in sales. If you can't do what you say you can, you'll look as if you're someone who makes lots of promises but doesn't come through.

For many businesses, online community is a hard sell. The muckety-mucks in the big offices want to see numbers and know that they're getting a good return on their investment (ROI.). Their goals for you may even be loftier than the ones you're setting for yourself. The thing is, you can't throw out or agree to any numbers without knowing enough about the community and the brand.

Don't make any decision regarding sales or growth until you've taken enough time to observe the following:

- ✔ **Past records:** View past reports to see how much the business and community has grown, or not grown , in the past. See how the people who were in a similar position before you achieved the same goals. If your business had a community manager in the past, you'll most likely have access to his records and accounts. If you're the first community manager, you'll have to find out how online campaigns were handled in the past and take it from there.

- ✔ **Stats:** View website data, analyze traffic, review the amount of activity and comments left by community members in the past, and check out sales and social media campaigns.

- ✔ **Notes and messages:** Read through all the notes and messages from your company's social media accounts. If someone complained on Twitter, how was it handled? Did your predecessor reach out to bloggers to foster good relations? What can you change about the handling of the Facebook page?

- ✔ **Other community managers:** You'll find the community of online community managers to be very helpful. If you're not sure how to set realistic goals, ask. They may not have the exact answer, but they'll be able to guide you in the right direction.

If you're new at your job, it's common to want to prove yourself. Setting the bar too low or too high will set the wrong expectations. Research your community and past campaigns as well as the campaigns put out by similar communities before throwing out any numbers.

Fostering Relationships Beyond the Community

The beautiful part about community is how other communities in the same vein or genre can act as an extension of yours. Sure, competition occurs between brands, but smart community managers see colleagues and collaborators over competitors.

Here's an analogy for you. People who read blogs don't read only one blog and call it a day. They have a roster of blogs they like to enjoy on a regular basis, especially blogs with a similar theme. A writer enjoys reading different writing blogs to discover a variety of tips. Fisherman read different fishing blogs to become aware of the latest techniques and products. Readers may be most loyal to one particular blog, but they still read and comment on other blogs.

Most online communities have similar stories. Their members might like a variety of brands on Facebook or participate in more than one forum. You read more than one book and watch more than one movie, so it only makes sense that you participate in a variety of different communities. Community managers pinpoint the favorite haunts of their community members and work out promotions and campaigns to bring everyone together and drive cross-promotional traffic.

It may seem as if a community is a single enclave. The truth is, many communities have thousands of members and include other communities. A good manager can harness the energy and power of all these communities and turn his own online community into something truly awesome.

Chapter 2

What You Have to Know about Online Communities

In This Chapter

▶ Seeing reasons to socialize online

▶ Gaining the benefits of community membership

▶ Getting to know some common personality types

*O*nline communities come in as many types as there are reasons to join them. For some people, joining an online community is a way to stave off loneliness. For others, it's a way to discuss topics of interest, such as politics, books, religion, parenting, or movies, with like-minded people.

Online communities can be as serious as they are lively. In some communities, the members share tips for hobbies or careers, while in others, they want to find out more about a topic that interests them. Some online communities even exist simply to have a light-hearted conversation with others. You can't pinpoint a single reason for joining a community because the reasons are just as personal and individual as the community members themselves.

Why People Join Online Communities

In order to manage a community, you have to know as much as you can about why members are there. As a community manager, how much do you know — I mean, truly *know* — about your online community? I'll even go as far as to say that you can't adequately run a community unless you understand the reasons people are there.

Some communities are more than a place to come each day and share a few words. For the members, they're a place to belong. Die-hard community members see their communities as a home away from home, even if it's only a virtual home. They share, discuss, and commiserate.

Over time, you'll come to know your members almost as well as you know your own family or coworkers. Getting to know your members different personalities and reasons for joining gives you better insight into the people you're managing.

If you ask ten people why they participate in online conversations, you'll get ten different answers, but all of them participate because they receive something of value in return. Whether it's information or interaction, members participate in online communities because they're welcoming and entertaining.

Meet with like-minded people

Joining a group online is kind of like joining a group offline. Someone may attend a book club because she enjoys books, for example, or play on a baseball team because she loves the sport. The people with whom she interacts during those activities are doing the same things for the same reasons. Similarly, online communities let people talk about the things they love with other people who love the same thing.

Also, some people are so passionate about a topic or idea that they don't want to talk about anything else. The people they see every day, however, probably don't want to hear them talking about their jobs or hobbies all the time. Online communities are safe havens — little enclaves where the members can talk at length about a shared passion, free of unwilling, eye-rolling listeners. Fisherman, knitters, writers, and scrapbookers all have somewhere to interact without worrying about boring anyone else.

Socialize without going out

Some people are more outgoing online than in the real world. Thanks to a phenomenon called *keyboard courage,* a wallflower type can come out of his virtual shell and make some real friends. In fact, much of the socializing that happens in online communities leads to deeper relationships. Online friends take it private and have more in-depth conversations via e-mail, private messages, phone calls, and instant messages. Some of these relationships blossom into offline friendships and even into romances.

Many shy people are surprised by how much easier they can communicate online than in person. They're not embarrassed to take part in a conversation because they're laptop to laptop, not face to face. In fact, many active community members often remark, "I'm actually quite shy offline."

Also, people who spend a large portion of time confined to their homes no longer feel lonely when they can communicate online. Though communicating online isn't the same as having friends to talk to every day, an online community helps take the edge off loneliness.

Get the job done

Researchers gather data by asking questions or viewing behaviors, so it's natural that online communities often harbor researchers, most of whom let the community members know their intentions. Although researchers come to do a job, they also participate and enjoy the atmosphere of the communities.

In addition, online communities are welcome distractions for home-based workers and telecommuters. Many of them miss the camaraderie that an outside place of employment has to offer, so they go to their favorite online communities to enjoy conversation throughout the day.

These communities also work well for people who are passionate about or want to know more about their business. Accountants, marketing people, and even wait staff all have places to interact online. They like knowing that other people are experiencing the same things and that they're not alone.

Have a place to belong

Not everyone is the popular kid with dozens of friends to hang out with and a place to go after work or school. Unlike some real ones, online communities are very accepting. As long as members aren't abusive, they're welcome. Some members feel as though they're finally fitting in somewhere.

Communities give members a safe, welcoming place to hang out and talk about their interests, even if those interests are "uncool" subjects that cause snickering at school or at the office. Forums and newsgroups are available for almost every topic. Participants find these communities by accident, usually while they're looking for information about the topics they enjoy. As they find discussion groups, they may lurk for a while and then eventually become members.

Communities are also safe places to talk about personal issues that many other people may not understand. Expert communities have people who can help sort out problems and refer members to sources of professional help, if necessary.

The beautiful thing about online communities is that people no longer have to feel that they have no one to turn to or anywhere to go. Online, people can be anyone they want to be.

Promote a product or service

Internet marketers and traditional salespeople are discovering that there's money to be made online. If a company wants to promote a lemonade brand, for example, it may try to build a presence on Facebook — not because it expects folks to do nothing but discuss lemony beverages, but because a Facebook presence can draw people in to have a conversation.

Marketers don't even need to create their own communities to drive sales, however. They're happy enough to participate in existing groups and networks. This participation isn't necessarily a bad thing. The best online salespeople are low-key, productive pillars of the community. They drive sales because members trust them.

Bloggers and other online authors also like to use online communities for marketing or promotional purposes, but they have a different reason: They want to drive traffic to their websites and create awareness for their names, their blogs, and even their businesses. Many highly trafficked blogs and websites earn the bulk of their income through advertising and product sales, so it's essential for them to bring in new traffic each day.

Dig online communities for other reasons

Fitting in and selling aren't the only reasons why folks are converging online. Whether it's to talk politics, do research, or discover more about an interesting topic, members are finding value in online communities every single day. Here are a few other benefits:

- ✔ **Unwinding with friends:** Online friendships may be just as important as offline relationships. Members care about what their virtual peers think of them, and they look forward to talking with the people in their cliques. Whether community members are reading the day's Facebook statuses, enjoying conversations on Twitter, or sharing news in a forum, they're spending their spare time with people whose company they enjoy.

- ✔ **Receiving freebies, discounts, and perks:** Bargain hunters love receiving and sharing opportunities to save money. Entire communities are devoted to free stuff: coupons, contests, and more.

- ✔ **Exchanging knowledge:** Students and teachers are helping with homework in various communities, and professionals are sharing the secrets of their success. Recipes, fashion tips, and links to interesting articles and fun websites are also freely exchanged in online communities.

- ✔ **Honing a craft or hobby:** Crafters and hobbyists can share their passion to their heart's content, discussing tools, tricks, tips, safety, and sources for everything they need.

- ✔ **Mentoring:** Some people simply want to help. Perhaps they're joining professional communities to coach job seekers, or maybe they're giving tips to new parents. They enjoy helping others and seek nothing in return.

- ✔ **Reminiscing:** Many people are online simply to connect with their pasts. They're joining Facebook or school alumni groups to talk with people they never thought they'd hear from again. The Internet is reuniting old neighborhoods and elementary-school classes.

Knowing members' habits and reasons for participation is the first step in keeping things interesting. After you know that, you can think about what will keep members coming back for more.

Recognizing the Value of Online Communities

Engaging community members goes beyond just sharing discounts or polling members for feedback. The company that sells lemonade, for example, no doubt realizes that people show approval of the brand by joining its social network, but it also realizes that to keep members interested, entertaining stuff has to happen, too. How fun would it be to host a lemonade recipe contest, for example, or have members make up limericks involving the use of citrus fruits?

Engaging community members is more than sharing discounts or polling members for feedback. The value of a community isn't in the content of a lemonade page, for example. It's in how the brand chooses to interact with the community and what each member receives in return.

Creating personal or business brand awareness

Companies aren't the only entities that are interested in enhancing their online presence; many community members are looking to do so as well. Thanks to social media, lots of folks are using the Internet to get their names out there. They want to be recognized as experts or authorities in their chosen fields, and online communities allow them to do so. They want themselves or their businesses to be recognizable brands. The Internet is the perfect place to grow both a reputation and a brand.

Personal branding is the buzz phrase for the art of promoting one's self and one's name. *Professional branding* is the same thing for a business. Good personal and professional branding means networking with all sorts of communities, both online and off. Though seeing and being seen are big parts of branding, it's more about making others aware of the brand and seeing it as something important. It's making the name synonymous with the niche.

Many people in the offline world aren't aware that each community has "famous" people: well-known bloggers, popular social-media professionals, renowned public-relations professionals, and so on. They're famous mostly within their own groups, but their fame may spill over into other communities as well. Top marketing professionals are now being seen as top names in blogging and social media. Famous offline radio announcers are crossing over into the world of podcasting and Internet video. Other people are making names for themselves by sharing instructional videos on cooking or cards.

What's even more interesting about online up-and-comers is how many of them discard the communities that helped promote their names after they've achieve their end results. For example, I used to own an online community for freelance writers. Some members were very obvious in their self-promotion, and after they raised awareness of their own communities or interests, they moved on. Also, the more "famous" some folks become online, the more likely they are to hang out with the in crowd instead of those participating in a lesser known community. They use some online communities simply as springboards.

Still, online communities are perfect for growing a personal or professional brand. Members can hone their skills, share their expertise, and get advice from experts. They may become friendly with the movers and shakers in their field and even collaborate with them or land employment opportunities.

Getting schooled

In today's age, you can find answers to anything you want online. This quest for knowledge goes beyond Googling for answers, however. Online communities can be knowledge bases where participants come to share their know-how and walk away with something far more valuable:

   ✔ **Professional expertise:** Professional online communities are out there for everything from dog walking to chimney sweeping. Members are using the virtual world to promote their businesses, for sure, but they're also joining these networks to trade experiences. People do tasks differently in different regions, for example, and online communities allow them to meet and share their knowledge.

✔ **Answers to common questions:** Some people call it laziness, and others call it *crowdsourcing,* but people are now finding getting answers to their questions simply by asking online. Rather than consult a thesaurus, writers are using Twitter to ask for synonyms, moms are using Facebook to ask their friends how to remove grass stains from baseball uniforms, and customer service personnel are tossing out "What would you do?" situations.

✔ **Coaching:** Virtual friends can help community members prep for job interviews and speaking engagements, as well as advise them on legal issues. Though members have to be sure that they're accepting advice from true professionals, the community can help them advance their careers, brands, and lives in ways that were impossible 20 years ago.

To be sure you're receiving advice from someone who knows his stuff, check his member profile to see whether he has a few words detailing his background. Also, don't be afraid to give him a Google to be sure he is who he says he is. Sometimes well-intentioned people offer what they feel is sound advice, but they're not necessarily speaking from experience.

✔ **Redirection:** Maybe no one in a community has the answer to a specific question, but more than a few members can help members find what they need by sending them in the right direction. If you're hunting in the wrong place, they'll help you get back on track. If you're headed in the right direction, they'll get you there quicker.

✔ **Practical advice and how-to information:** Do-it-yourselfers and hobbyists can receive valuable step-by-step instructions that help them complete their projects.

✔ **Homework help:** Safe social networks for students provide tutoring, homework help, and encouragement.

✔ **Recommendations:** Looking for book or movie recommendations? Want to find the best Mexican or seafood place in your area? Your local online community can help.

Sharing knowledge

Online communities truly shine when it comes to sharing. Though a few members are obviously there to profit or to promote something, most participants are generous and kind. The helpfulness of those who make up online communities may be surprising to newbies, but anyone who spends a lot of time socializing on the web knows that online sharing isn't a rare occurrence.

Why people share online

Many people are mistrustful of those who do good deeds, wondering what's in it for them. This mistrust sometimes occurs in virtual communities, but most members share simply because they want to. There are as many reasons why people share as there are things being shared:

- ✔ **They want to feel good.** Sharing is good juju. Folks share because they get all warm and fuzzy about it. Sharing is more about doing a good deed than about getting something in return.

- ✔ **They're giving back.** People share because they want to pay forward a kindness.

- ✔ **They know things that other people don't.** People share to give answers or enlighten.

- ✔ **They see an easier way to do something.** Online friends love to share tips and shortcuts.

- ✔ **They're know-it-alls.** Some people appear to share because they want to show how smart they are, sometimes in a way that makes them feel superior.

- ✔ **They found something useful and hope that others do as well.** Something made life easier for them, and they want to spread the word.

- ✔ **They're promoting something.** People sometimes share to promote a business or online content. Perhaps they're promoting a cause, a recall, or a news event.

- ✔ **They're establishing trust.** Trust is an important factor in the online world, especially for those who are growing a personal or business brand. (Refer to "Creating personal or business brand awareness," earlier in this chapter.) If members trust shared information, they're likely to trust the person who shared it.

How people share online

Online sharing goes way beyond just providing links to news articles and YouTube videos. People often go to great lengths to research items that they feel are of interest to others, and they use a variety of methods to do so:

- ✔ **Blogs:** The beauty of blogging is that it involves sharing more than just links. The person who's blogging is sharing more in-depth information, such as news, videos, or roundups of online resources.

- ✔ **Informational websites:** The lines that differentiate blogs and websites are getting blurrier. Websites used to be more static, with no owner/ visitor interaction. This situation changed when blogs began gaining popularity, thanks to conversational writing and the ability of a community to interact. Now, even news-related websites offers ways for visitors to comment and share information.

- ✔ **Instructional videos:** Video bloggers and many subject-matter experts share what they know online. In most cases, this information is free, though many of today's experts also host *pay-to-play* online informational communities, which require you to pay a subscription fee to be a member.

- ✔ **Twitter chats:** Tools such as Tweet Chat allow people to cut through the noise and participate in online conversations by using hash tags and keywords. (Two popular examples are #blogchat and #speakchat.) In these chats, a moderator asks participants to share tips and advice.

- ✔ **Facebook fan pages:** Fan pages aren't only for brands or celebrities. Bloggers use them, too, as do professional groups, clubs, and offline communities.

- ✔ **E-mail:** Newsletters are important tools for many businesses. They're terrific ways to share news and fun stuff.

- ✔ **Social bookmarking sites:** Bookmarking networks, such as StumbleUpon or Delicious, not only allow an individual share, but also let others pick up the share and spread it to their own networks.

- ✔ **Share buttons:** Share buttons are everywhere these days. Look at articles, blog posts, videos, and images, and you'll find small icons inviting readers to share with friends on Facebook, Twitter, LinkedIn, and other networks.

Use Share buttons, such as the ones pictured in Figure 2-1, so that your community can also share your content with others.

Making important personal and business connections

If you're old enough to remember the olden days of power networking, you may recall putting on a business suit matched with some uncomfortable shoes and heading out to stuffy meetings where attendees handed out business cards and gave *elevator pitches* — brief sales pitches to either promote a product or a person who is hoping to land a job or client. Though these networking events still happen, online networking and communities now give people the opportunity to meet important people without even having to dress up.

Figure 2-1:
Share but-
tons not
only let your
community
follow your
content, but
also lets
them share
your content
with others.

Professional networks abound. Whatever a person does for a living, she can find a place to talk about it online. Even better, many of these groups are visited, at least occasionally, by some of the power players in the field. The best part of online networking is the interaction of "ordinary" people with both the high-ranking and the up-and-comers. Brand executives, chief executive officers, and potential clients are all online. Even people who aren't necessarily there to do businesses can offer important references.

Suppose that a web designer is spending time on Twitter. He may talk web design now and then, but most of his interaction involves conversations about many things. He may talk about what he had for dinner or how he's going to a ball game over the weekend, but folks will also remember what he does for a living. This recognition will come in handy when someone approaches his online friends, looking for a recommendation for web design. They'll probably remember him and make the introduction.

Like your community's members, you never know how many important people you're socializing with online. The man who you discuss baseball with every day may be someone who's in a position to hire someone like you. All online interactions, regardless of where they're happening, are with potential clients or employers, even if you're not looking for work at the moment.

Online friendships always have the potential to be something more. Some people associate with only those members who have a high count of Twitter followers or who are major names in the blogosphere because they want to be associated with the company they keep. The people in your online communities are the same people who might review your books or send traffic to your websites. Every connection you make online is important, even if you don't realize it at the time.

Getting feedback

Online communities provide peace of mind. Even if members' friends and relatives don't totally get what they're doing, their online friends do. They're the ones who say, truthfully, whether a dress makes you look fat. They critique designs and proofread writing and say exactly what they think.

Many online communities are created so that people who have the same interests or career choices can commiserate, swap ideas, and share new ways to do things. They beta-test products and tools, comment on blogs and news items, and review books, products, and services.

 Members have to have truly thick skins when they request feedback, however. Although most participants are gentle with their criticisms, every community has at least one member who's rather blunt with feedback, and sometimes hurt feelings can ensue. Still, despite the rare bit of negativity, online networks and professional groups are valuable tools. Through them, members know what they're doing wrong — or right — and can tweak their projects accordingly.

Receiving support

Community members can also receive support on a personal level. Parents who are struggling through a discipline or medical issue, for example, can find other parents online who are going through the same thing. Now they can swap stories and tips and know that they're not alone.

People who don't have supportive family members or coworkers also have a place to go online where they can receive the backing they're looking for.

 Many times, the online world provides something that's missing in the offline world.

Meeting Community Members

Simply put, a community is nothing without its members. No matter how good your community management is, if a group doesn't have plenty of willing participants, it simply isn't going to last.

Sometimes you have to look at each member as an individual rather than view all members as a collective unit. For example, the shy person who is afraid to share with the community for fear of being laughed at may be able to use your help to come out of her shell. Someone who has never been a part of an online community and is overly enthusiastic may benefit from some gentle guidance (over a strict recitation of the rules). Get to know your members and find out why they're there so that you're better able to enhance their online community experience.

Knowing about your members individually also provides insight into why they're interested in your brand. If you're a business, knowing who your customers are and why they use your product or service is essential for both brand and community growth.

In Part IV, I discuss various ways to bring in new members and keep them active. In this section, I concentrate on the types of community members and why they hang around.

Recognizing the types of community members

The online world isn't too different from the offline world. Though many people try to reinvent themselves online, their true selves eventually emerge. Anyone who spends a lot of time in online communities can easily recognize the different personalities and hierarchies within the group. Knowing how the different personalities work together and interact can help you manage a community properly.

Popular personality types

A few personality types are so easy to spot that you'll recognize them in any community. Here are a few of the recognizable community member types.

- ✓ **The Lurker:** You rarely hear from the Lurker. She likes to read all the conversations and takes what she needs from each discussion, but she rarely participates. Maybe she's shy, lacks confidence, or is more interested in observing than in participating. Every now and then, she surprises everyone by voicing an opinion, but most of the time, you don't even know she's there.

✔ **The Newbie:** *Newbies* (new members) often don't know where to start. Newbies may introduce themselves to the group and then do their best to find ways to fit in. Their participation may range from tentative while they find their bearings to very active as they respond to every message posted within the past few weeks. Most members welcome newbies and do what they can to make them feel at home.

✔ **The Regular:** The Regular is a familiar personality in the online community. Everyone knows her face or recognizes her *avatar* — the image she uses to portray herself online. Because the Regular is so active, other community members may feel that they know her and trust her judgment — most of the time. Sometimes, a Regular is rather outspoken or gives bad advice, so other members take what she says with a grain of salt. Suffice it to say, The Regular is a familiar face, someone who you will see every day at your favorite online haunts.

✔ **The Leader:** Whether self-appointed or through mutual respect, the Leader is someone who has been with the community for years and truly knows his stuff. When he offers his two cents, people listen. Sometimes, the Leader is someone that the community has chosen; at other times, the Leader is a legend in his own mind.

✔ **The Elder:** As a pillar of the online community, the Elder isn't necessarily active anymore, but she's held in high esteem. When she does participate, members hang on to her every word. The Elder has been with the community since day one. Not every member may agree with or even like the Elder, but no one will say a disparaging word about her.

✔ **The Expert (aka the Know-It-All):** Every group has an Expert — someone who knows everything about everything. The Expert has been everywhere and seen everything. He did it all long before the other members did and thinks that he did it better, stronger, and faster. The Expert doesn't have many friends but doesn't seem to notice.

✔ **The Elite:** Forums and communities that rank their members by how long they've been around or how often they participate have a clique of Elite members. Though an Elite member mingles with the newer members now and then, she keeps pretty much to herself.

Potentially negative people

Possibly one of the most difficult tasks of a community manager is dealing with negative personalities. Being able to spot them early on can help prevent a bad or uncontrollable situation.

Beware the community bully, according to Lara Kulpa, community manager for Blogworld & New Media Expo. If not kept in check, negative people sometimes morph into a stronger personality type — the community bully — and the target isn't only members, but also the community manager. "They try to make it difficult for you," Kulpa says, "because while they often provide loads of good content, they behave like they're superior or entitled over other members and tend to drive people away." Kulpa adds that if you don't deal with them swiftly, the community bullies take over, and soon, the community is made up only of members of their own clique.

You may not be happy about getting to know some negative personality types, but the more you find out about them, the better equipped you are when it comes to handling each different situation. Keep a look out for these common negative personality types; they all have the potential to cause discontent within your community:

- **The Malcontent:** This community type goes way beyond a bit of crankiness. The Malcontent finds fault with everything, especially with the way that the community is run. He complains about everything from the hosting to management and never has anything positive to say. His comments often lead to arguments within the community because the regulars get fed up with his constant complaining.

- **The Heckler:** Though the Heckler doesn't always behave in a negative manner, her antics can be equally as unfavorable as the Malcontent. She doesn't criticize so much as question everything that everyone talks about. She's not even there to disagree; mostly, she's there to show her own superiority or to make others look bad.

- **The Rabble Rouser:** Beware the Rabble Rouser because he's the one who can turn a community against its management. Perhaps he doesn't like some of the community rules. Instead of discussing it privately or even in a quiet, respectful manner, the Rabble Rouser gets up on his podium and incites the community to riot. He knows that there are better ways to go about things, but he's not interested in being subtle.

- **The Troll:** The anonymity of the Internet gives the Troll the keyboard courage to be cruel to other members. She doesn't use her own name as she leaves mean, profane, and abusive comments. The good news is that although trolls cause arguments and even stress within the community, the troll's lifecycle isn't a long one as most community managers ban them soon after they join the community.

I talk more about dealing with Trolls and other haters in Chapter 9. For now, suffice it to say that negativity never has to escalate. You have ways of dealing with bullies and abusive members effectively without turning your community into a hotbed of negativity. Take swift action in the beginning, and you'll earn the respect of your community.

When you're identifying and dealing with the different personality types in your community, keep in mind most members are there because they believe in and support the community. Keeping the atmosphere positive and upbeat will ensure a happy, productive online network of friends, fans, and followers.

Knowing why some community members last longer than others

Online communities host transient members. Though they have are some long-term participants, most members leave after a while for a variety of reasons. Often times, their departure has nothing to do with the community itself, but rather that it's their time to move on:

- **Nothing new to gain:** Many people join online communities to receive and share information, and after they've taken everything they can from the group, they move on. Their leaving isn't an affront or insult; they just feel that they've benefited all they can from that particular network.

- **Too much negativity:** If bullies, trolls, and malcontents take over a community, they're going to drive everyone away. Keeping a community positive helps ensure a positive mix of both old and new members.

- **No time to participate:** Many people join online communities with the best of intentions but find that they just don't have the time to participate. Either they check in only sporadically, or their membership declines to nothing at all.

- **Same old, same old:** The same people talking about the same things all the time doesn't make for a very interesting community. Introducing fresh topics and new members can keep existing members coming back for more.

- **Too much change:** In some communities, longtime members often miss the "good old days" and don't relate well to new members, who may come in with new management. Longtime members who are set in their ways aren't always open to change, so be careful not to change too many things at once, or you may drive away some of the regulars. Also, roll out new rules and changes a little at a time. Abrupt changes throw people off.

- **Poor management:** When negative members prevail or spam is left up for days, members begin to feel that management doesn't care, and they move on.

The communities that have the most long-term, active members are those that remain positive and introducing with fresh new topics and ideas often. Making changes is okay, but be sure that you know your members well so that you can monitor how they'll react to any changes. Long-term members understand that change is good; they just don't want to feel as if you've forgotten about them.

Part II
Embracing the Community Manager's Role

In this part . . .

Part II is about you and your job as online community
manager. Some people think community managers
do little more than post Facebook or Twitter updates.
This part dispels that myth and shows there's much more
to managing a community.

Chapter 3

Becoming an Online Community Manager

In This Chapter

▶ Wearing lots of hats

▶ Promoting your community and your brand

▶ Seeing why your job matters

As far as jobs go, being an online community manager is one of the most enjoyable career choices. Think about it: You get to spend lots of time online, enjoying the social networks and chatting up new friends. Of course, there's more to the job than just trolling Twitter and updating Facebook, though. Community managers undertake a variety of tasks, some more enjoyable than others.

For the most part, though, there's never a dull moment. In this chapter, I describe the many responsibilities of an online community manager.

Wearing the Many Hats of a Community Manager

Defining your role as a community manager is difficult because you do so many different things. On one hand, you're advocating for the customer. On the other hand, your loyalty is to your brand. You answer to many different people and departments and perform a variety of tasks.

Fortunately, most of an online community manager's duties are enjoyable. They allow for creativity, and an outgoing nature can shine through. Other duties aren't so fun and exciting, but they're important nonetheless.

Make no mistake — despite the friendly nature of the job, community management is a huge responsibility. As the most public person in the company, you have to present an image befitting the brand. A major portion of the job is making sure that the customers and the community members are happy with the brand, the product, and the image.

I hope you like hats because you're going to be wearing a lot of them, and all of them have to fit. The job of community management is for you if you truly rock the people skills and handle negativity with humor and grace, but are strong enough to handle public criticism and not give in to adversity.

 There's more to being a community manager than a little social networking. You need a thick skin, a pleasant personality, and the ability to organize and prioritize.

Leader

Community managers aren't necessarily appointed because of their sparkling wit, although a sense of humor goes a long way in this job. The best community managers are leaders, not only in the sense of being able to handle a community discussion, but also in guiding community members.

There's a reason why a brand chooses to host an online community. Whether that reason is sales, web traffic, a word-of-mouth marketing campaign, or awareness of a cause, it's up to a community manager to lead participants in the right direction.

 Being a successful leader is kind of a delicate thing, though. No one wants to be preached or pitched to. People mostly want to come to an online community to let down their hair. Even if they know the reasons behind the community, members don't want to be made to feel as though they have to buy something or donate to a cause. Community members want to make these types of decisions on their own. You, as community manager, have to lead the proverbial horses to water without forcing them to drink — but get them to drink nonetheless.

Reach out

Part of leading a community is in generating interest in bringing people into your community, and you have to do so without getting out your bullhorn and making your quest for new members obvious. Community managers commonly search social networks looking for people who are having conversations having to do with their brands or subjects relating to their brands. Oh, and you have to reach out to them without looking like a spammer.

If your company sells lemonade and you notice on Twitter that someone is looking for some interesting beverages to serve at a barbecue, reach out with some recipes. This contact may inspire the other person not only to follow your brand's Twitter account, but maybe even to buy your brand of lemon-ade to make those recipes.

Likewise, if someone on the same social network is complaining about a poor experience with your brand, don't just ignore the complaint. Reach out to see how to make things right. Offer to call or e-mail the other person to help. The issue may not even be your department, but unhappy customers are always the community manager's department.

Even if you can't fix the situation, it's up to you to introduce the unhappy person to the person who can help and then follow up to make sure it's been done.

Offer guidance

Online community managers offer guidance to both community members and the brands they represent. By gauging the wants and needs of the commu-nity, they're putting their product and business development and marketing teams in a better position to give the people what they want. With a commu-nity manager's guidance, the brand is truly able to put out a product people are asking for.

Community members look to the community manager for guidance as well. In addition to wanting to know the best ways to use the brand's product or ser-vice, they see a community manager as someone who is wise and can steer them in the right direction, whatever direction that may be.

Answer questions

Though some questions from community members are difficult to answer, community managers do best not to avoid them. Don't sweep anything under the rug or put off responding to e-mails. Instead, tackle the issue. If you're not set up to answer the question or if you'd rather not step on someone else's toes, find the person who can and be sure to follow up until it's resolved.

Unresponsive community managers don't help the brand's cause at all. Instead, they're seen as being inaccessible and gain a reputation for not caring about their customers. Provide honest answers in a positive manner, even if you're not giving very good news.

Ask for feedback

The reason many leaders fail is because they don't respond well to feedback. Community managers know that the best way to improve or grow is to ask questions, request feedback, and respond to that feedback. Brands can no longer assume that they know what's best for their customers. By asking questions or using surveys to request feedback, community managers are able to pass on valuable information to the brand.

Content developer

Everything posted online is content, including text, video, and audio. Community managers tend to be the keepers of the content. They maintain the company blogs, post to the social networks, and even plan videos or company podcasts.

The most successful community managers are creative types. They have a way with words and never run out of things to talk about.

Choosing forms of content

Content creation for an online community can fill a *For Dummies* book all on its own, but for brevity's sake, I'll condense it down to a section or two.

Content comes in many forms:

- ✔ Blogs
- ✔ Newsletters
- ✔ Webinars
- ✔ Website articles
- ✔ Updates to the social networks
- ✔ Forum entries
- ✔ Video

Discuss the type of content your community needs with your team. If your company has an editorial department, it may help shape and edit your content. As the person who is to be the brand's most active web presence, however, you provide most content.

This isn't to say that you'll have to write fresh articles and blog posts every day, unless that's part of your agreement. Community content may also come in the form of frequently asked questions (FAQs), comment policies, community guidelines, and other more official types of writing.

Most community managers put a plan together listing the best ways to reach out to the community and stick to it on a regular schedule. A weekly customer newsletter, twice- or thrice-weekly blog posts, and lots of social networking or forum updates will ensure that customers are kept in the know. (See Chapter 6 for a more in-depth discussion of communicating with your community.)

Writing and editing content

If you never took editorial classes and don't have an English degree, you may be worried about being expected to write and edit content for the company website or blog. Don't worry too much. When you're writing for your community, it's more about using conversational language than about following a strict format. Without dumbing things down, write in a manner that's easy to understand and that comes naturally for you.

When writing for an online community, keep the following pointers in mind:

- **Write how you speak.** Use a conversational tone. Customers and community members are more responsive when they understand what you're saying and your content isn't filled with jargon. Be mindful of slang and avoid profanity, but don't be afraid to use humor to get your point across. That isn't to say that you should be slapstick, but people do relate best to a light tone.

- **Be mindful of typos and errors.** Even if you didn't attend journalism school, you likely have a good grasp of the basic principles of grammar and can spot typos. Always double-check your work before making it public to be sure that it's clean.

  Your content is a reflection of your community. If it's poorly written and filled with typos, it reflects poorly on your brand, and people will think you don't care.

- **Take care not to offend.** Things that may seem small to you may seem major to someone else. Be careful not to offend anyone in your community. Avoid stereotypes and don't poke fun at different groups or ethnicities. Don't bring up politics or religion unless you belong to a political or religious community, and even then, be careful what you're putting out there. Also be careful when pushing the envelope. You may think that edgy or swear words are hip, but not everyone reacts to them the same way.

- **Remain neutral.** Community managers are Switzerland. There's no taking sides. Even if you personally feel strongly about a particular issue, you can't take sides. Community managers are neutral parties and must always remain neutral regardless of personal preference.

Moderator

The most notorious part of a community manager's job is moderating community comments. This task gets a bum rap because

- You may have to delete comments.

- You may have to remind participants to play nice.

- You may have to ban abusive members or regular offenders.

- You can't choose sides.

- You have to remain positive even when others are baiting you or doing their best to stir up controversy.

- You deal with many personality types.

Moderating comments

Possibly the most-talked-about aspect of online community management is moderating comments because it often causes the most controversy. Although comment moderation is only a small aspect of the job, if a member of your community doesn't appreciate that you asked him to edit or delete a comment, or if you deleted a comment or banned a member for inappropriate comments, your action can be a source of discourse online. Sometimes community managers spend a lot of time defending their decisions to edit or delete comments outright.

Chapter 10 goes into comment moderation in much more detail. Keep in mind, though, that community negativity isn't something that happens every day and is more prevalent in poorly moderated or nonmoderated communities. The only reason you hear so much about it is because disgruntled members love to take their gripes public, and there's nothing a negative person dislikes more than being asked to keep his negativity in check.

Now, not every comment is going to be negative, but it's the unfavorable comments that are going to catch your attention. Very few people respond in a negative manner to a positive comment. Positive comments don't cause people to get turned off and leave the community forever nor are they likely to stir up strong emotions. So it's the off-color or heated comments that you're most likely to have to "deal" with.

Keep in mind that respectful disagreement isn't negativity and not every discussion has to be sunshine and puppy dogs. Still, you're there to keep things on the right track, ensuring participants stay on topic without a lot of sniping at each other.

You're also online to monitor the social networks to see what others are saying about your brand. Reach out and join the conversation. If the brand is being discussed in a positive light, say "thank you" and ask what they love the most about it. If you find negative comments, ask about the bad experience and take it private if necessary.

Moderating comments isn't issuing smackdowns to naysayers or deleting content. It's making sure that content flows in a positive and productive manner, even if sometimes folks don't agree.

Refereeing and mediating arguments

One of the most unattractive hats worn by community managers is in refereeing arguments among community members. When you're content-heavy, whether that content is in the form of a blog post or tweet, you're inviting folks to comment. Although this is exactly what you want, you also have to enter into it with the understanding that everyone doesn't feel the same way. Sometimes the most innocent posts can lead to flame wars and out-and-out fights.

It's up to you, as community manager, to make sure that folks stay on topic and keep the caps on their poison pens. Respectful disagreement is encouraged and leads to thought-provoking conversations. On the other hand, arguments can put a damper on the vibe.

Getting things back on track in a diplomatic manner is sometimes a challenge, but for the most part, you'll find people are receptive. Let them know you appreciate their passion, but remind them it's a community discussion. You may need to throw out a question or subtopic to get things back on track.

As a neutral party, you can't take sides, but you can encourage all parties to respectfully present their best arguments. In a heavy discussion, it's very rare that either side will give in and agree with the person he was arguing with. You're not going to resolve the matter 100 percent, but you can get each side to listen and then move on. Without being condescending, allow all involved to agree to disagree, and move on to the next discussion.

Community advocate

Community evangelists look out for their people. Acting in their best interests ensures trust in the brand. It means having their backs even though it might lead to an uncomfortable situation in the workplace. It shouldn't come to that, however. You'll find that for the most part, the brand is interested in learning the needs of the community and establishing trust by providing a positive user experience. The last thing they want is bad buzz or animosity. They hired you to create trust in the brand and to keep the channels of communication open, and here's how you can do just that:

- **Handle complaints.** As community manager, you'll sometimes feel as if you're a dumping ground for customer nitpicks and complaints. Most of the time, these are things you can handle on your own. Perhaps someone didn't receive a refund or a product didn't show up in the mailbox on time. These are easy fixes either by you or another person in your company. Other times, complaints aren't so cut-and-dried but are still deserving of a solution. Community managers not only find help, but also follow up to ensure that the matter has been resolved. (I discuss this topic in more detail in the next section.)

- **Pass on concerns.** Community members who care about a brand also become concerned when reading negative press or having a negative experience. Not only does a community manager help to rectify these issues, but she also makes sure that those beyond the customer service department know about them. The reason many executives seem ignorant of situations is because they often are. It's only when things escalate out of control that they learn that a product is inferior or people are bad-mouthing them all over Twitter. The community manager passes on concerns before they reach the breaking point so that they can be handled effectively and positively.

✔ **Monitor the channels.** It's up to the community manager to learn what's being said online about the brand. You can monitor the channel in several ways. By using keywords and setting up Google Alerts, you'll receive notices in your mailbox every time someone mentions your company on a blog, website, or social network. (For more on Google Alerts, see Chapter 12.)

You can also monitor the chatter on Twitter with applications such as TweetDeck, Seesmic, or HootSuite. When you type search terms or keywords in the search function of these apps, you'll receive notice every time your brand is mentioned.

It's incredibly important to not only know what's being said, but to reach out to the people who are saying it, whether it's positive, negative, or neutral. If someone is relating a negative experience, reach out to them and ask whether you can discuss it at length in a phone call, e-mail, or text chat. If someone is saying something nice, say thank you and ask questions about the user's experience. When your community knows you're watching, listening and reacting in kind, they feel confident in the brand.

✔ **Have good communication.** Keeping the channels open goes beyond Twitter. As community manager, you're going to receive plenty of e-mails, and with the exception of spam or abusive messages, you'll have to respond to each and every one. This may mean you'll have to suck up to a customer who had a bad experience or simply drop a line to say that a matter is being looked into. The important thing is to never leave anyone hanging.

The last thing you want is to have a reputation for not responding to customer queries or complaints. So it's good practice to answer every e-mail, even if only to say, "I forwarded your complaint to John in Customer Service, and he'll take it from here."

Also, don't write off angry complaints as being trollish or abusive. There's validity in anger. Many people write heated letters after a bad experience, and although most have second thoughts after sending, to write off those letters you receive is to minimize the issue. Don't brush off the issue or the anger and respond in a kind manner.

When good communication occurs between the company and the brand, customers believe in the brand and remain loyal.

✔ **Fight for the needs of the community.** Because the community manager has her finger on the pulse of the community, she's also the one who knows what's best for them. At times when she has to be vocal about some things she might think are a bad fit or unfair. If a product or service is about to roll out, and it's out of the price range of most of the community, the community manager might press for a lower price.

Sometimes these things are a hard sell, which means she'll have to present her team with well-thought-out arguments as to why something won't work. Presenting ideas in a respectful manner goes a long way in getting your point across.

Sometimes community managers feel their teams are unreceptive and not really in tune with their communities. That's exactly why they hired someone to manage their customers and fans. They're not unreceptive as much as they need their community managers to set them on the right track.

Mediator

There's debate as to whether community managers belong in the customer service department. No matter which department the role ends up in, you do spend a lot of time fielding customer issues. Because you're the most visible person, people are going to reach out to you when they need something. It doesn't matter if you're equipped to handle the situation; you still need to be gracious and see each item through until it's resolved.

Something else to consider is that when you're in a public role, people take things public. So if you reached out to a community member who was complaining about your brand on Twitter, and you failed to deliver, she might take her public outrage back to the social-media streets and complain about you.

Dealing with complaining customers requires a bit of finesse, patience, and (though you won't always feel it) good cheer:

- **Do treat every complaint as if it's urgent.** Customers and community members don't like to be made to feel silly or insignificant. Make sure that they know you take their concerns seriously and that you're giving the matter your full attention.

- **Don't ridicule complainers on the social networks.** Even if a complaint seems trite, don't make fun of anyone who has a concern, and especially don't make fun in public. Mocking complainers will turn off anyone who is in the vicinity and make folks think twice about doing business with you.

- **Do respect your members' privacy.** If a customer has a complaint, it's no one's business but the customer and the people who are working to resolve said complaint. Don't discuss anyone's personal business with anyone.

- **Don't keep putting it off.** As soon as you learn of a complaint, get the ball rolling to resolve it. Introduce the complainer to the person who is helping or begin making inquiries. If you put it off until later, you're more likely to forget.

- **Do follow up.** Don't assume a matter is resolved simply because you passed it on to someone else. Check back with both the customer and the person handling the issue. Only after the issue has been resolved to the customer's satisfaction should you let it go.

- **Don't assume this is an isolated incident.** Many times when a single customer has a complaint, other people are experiencing the same thing. Do a little investigating. If it's not an isolated incident, take the necessary action.

For more in-depth information on defusing difficult situations, see Chapter 7.

Analyst

How do you know all your programs and outreach efforts are working? You're expected to report the outcome of all your community outreach efforts, whether they're successful or not. To do this report, you'll need some analytical tools in place.

Your company will no doubt have a stats or analytics program or app available for you to use. These programs enable you to see a variety of experiences.

When you evaluate your programs and efforts, consider the following questions:

- ✔ Where is traffic coming from?
- ✔ How are current promotions doing?
- ✔ Which pages are getting the most response?
- ✔ What older content is doing well?
- ✔ What products and services work, and which need work?
- ✔ What are people doing when they're on your website?
- ✔ Which tags and keywords are getting the best response?
- ✔ Which discussions and discussion topics are the most popular?
- ✔ In what towns, cities, states, and countries do your community members live?
- ✔ What are people searching on before landing on your blog, website, or forum?
- ✔ Who is linking to you, and what are they saying?
- ✔ Which content, product, or service is getting the most lackluster response?

The more you know about your community, the better you'll be able to provide them the conversations, products, or services they're looking for. You can't assume you know people just because you tweeted back and forth a couple of times.

I get more into stats and numbers in Chapters 12 and 13.

Promoting Products, Brands, and Services

So your community is now gathered around and hanging on your every word. They're interacting and feeling good about the brand. What are you going to do to reward them? You see, promotions don't only bring in new business. They're also important for rewarding customer loyalty. Your community members like to know you appreciate them, and actions speak louder than words.

Pitching without pushing

I'll come right out and say it: What we're told and what's expected are two different things. We're told that it's all about engagement and that conversation shouldn't be about sales and pitching, and this is true. The bottom line, however, is that community managers do have to sell and do have to pitch to get members to react without looking like they're selling at all. This isn't easy.

Guess what? If your members join your brand's community, they expect to hear about said brand now and then. If you work for a certain brand, your members are okay with hearing about it — just not every day. They know what they joined, so it's fine to talk about your product in a way that isn't pushy or pitchy.

Here's an example for you, taking a bagel company. You'll turn off all your fans and followers if you're on Twitter saying "Buy this bagel!" all the time. Rather than sell, discuss. Share interesting facts about bagels or link to cream cheese recipes. Look for news relating to bagels, cream cheese, or jams. Also, comment on your community's discussions, even if they're not related to bagels. Then, when you have something you need to put out there — perhaps a brand promotion — you can announce it without annoying your community. See how that works? Most of the time, you're talking about bagels and getting people to think about them without actually pushing your product on them.

Unless they're savvy online socializers, many community members don't have a clue that a good portion of the people with whom they're talking online are there because they have something to sell or promote — not necessarily because they appreciate the other members' sparkling wit.

Selling isn't always obvious. Here are few subtle ways that you can get people to respond to an online promotion:

✔ **Signature lines:** To keep members from spamming forums, blogs, and other online communities, a signature line (see Figure 3-1) may be available in members' account settings. Members can use this signature line to provide promotional information, such as links to a sales page or website, in a place where others can visit without being annoyed with constant pitches and spiels. The best part is, a signature line appears underneath each post so that everyone can see your links or promotion information every time you post.

✔ **Links:** Sharing links to a website, sales page, blog post, or other target is kind of tricky because most online communities have strict rules about spam. Most people who use communities for marketing purposes know and follow the rules; they share links only when they're invited to do so or when it's appropriate to the conversation. If a member shares links too often, other members of the community or community management call him on it. The best salespeople know how to contribute information without being pushy.

✔ **Participation:** When a person spends a lot of time in a particular online community, the other members get to know a lot about her. If a freelance writer mentions her job in a conversation, for example, members may remember that conversation. The next time they hear that someone needs a freelance writer, they may refer the potential client to her.

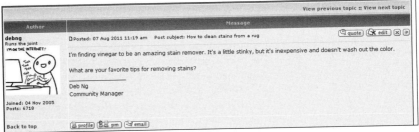

Figure 3-1: Use a signature line to tell a little about who you are and what you do.

Rewarding customers

You can't grow a one-sided community, and the benefits can't be only on your end. It's up to you, the community manager, to put promotions and incentives in place that reward customers and bring in new members.

Here are a few ways you can reward your customers:

- ✔ **Contests and giveaways:** Freebie and bargain hunters love contests, especially those enabling them to get something for nothing — not that customer loyalty is nothing. Rewarding loyalty by letting your community try new products for free will create some buzz while encouraging newbies to sign up and see what all the talk is about.

- ✔ **Member spotlights:** If your members are talking about you, share the love by talking about them. Go on a talent hunt to find interesting members to spotlight in your newsletters and blogs. Learn the stories behind the people who support your brand and give a little something back.

- ✔ **Discounts, coupon codes, and rebates:** Again, it's all about the rewards. You want to offer something to new and old members alike. Even if it's not cost-efficient to give products away to everyone, you might still offer discounts to everyone in the community.

- ✔ **Affiliate and incentive programs:** People will sign up for a newsletter or community group if there's something in it for them. Most won't sign up for a brand's regular mailings just to receive spam and advertisements in their mailboxes. If you offer some incentive or gift for every signup, however, plus regular discounts for subscribers only, folks are more likely to sign up. Offering them points or cash in exchange for every referral or product sale will also yield plenty of takers.

- ✔ **Referral rewards:** How do you reward the community members who refer friends? You don't have to award a big, expensive prize for every referral, but a discount coupon or points saved for a bigger purchase are nice ways to say thank you.

Pushy promotion

You're not the only person looking to promote something on online communities. Some members join solely for that reason. Obvious sales tactics are frowned upon or banned in most communities, and members who get smarmy with the sales don't last long.

Fortunately, pushy promotional practices are easy to identify. Spammers try to profit from nearly every conversation. Also, many spammers don't even use real human screen names. Instead, they use such screen names as Free iPad, Cheap Viagra, and Online Hosting. Alert community managers know that even if the people behind these screen names appear to be participating in the conversation, they're really there to sell, and they deal with these accounts accordingly.

You can't recognize all spammy types just from clever nicknames. Many of them use what seem to be real names, either their own or something made up.

Be on the lookout for people who always seem to have something to sell. They're easy enough to figure out because their advice to other community members usually directs those members to a sales page.

Creating brand loyalty

You know how some people buy whatever product is cheapest or the one they have the coupon for that week? Brands aren't fans of this practice because it means customers are using a variety of products rather than showing loyalty each and every time. Most people strongly consider price when making purchasing decisions, but they also know that they usually get what they pay for. They're more than happy to buy something a little more expensive every time they shop if they know without a doubt it's a superior product.

Enter brand loyalty.

People are loyal to brands that are loyal to them. They don't like products to change too much, and they want them to deliver what's promised. They take issue when they change flavors. They complain when social networks or websites change design or functionality or when a favorite magazine changes layout. Sometimes, they feel betrayed by change. Though most people know change is going to happen, they don't want that change to be disruptive. Changing too often and too abruptly doesn't inspire customer loyalty.

Creating buzz around changes, for example, announcing teasers in the weeks before said changes, prepares the community.

When brands tend to their customers' needs, they feel better about using them. If they answer customer questions and handle complaints without making those people feel at fault (even when they are), there's a better chance they'll use them again.

Brands need to be intuitive about their customers' needs. By monitoring conversations, reading comments and complaints, asking questions and providing surveys, you can learn more about what your customers are looking for.

Brand loyalty happens when customers feel they're being taking care of. If they know a company is listening and attending to their needs, they feel confident and good about using the brand on a regular basis. This is where the community manager shines. You can use your excellent relationship within the community and all the tools at your disposal to build trust and confidence.

Creating special programs

If being a spokesperson is tricky, creating special programs is fun. This responsibility is where you really get to dig in to your community's personality, theme, and sense of adventure. It's also where members in return can help to spread a message and get a great word-of-mouth marketing campaign going.

You'd love to think members join communities because they dig your sparkling personality or have a passion for the brand. The truth is, most people join a community because there's something in it for them. As community manager, it's up to you to provide an answer to "What's in it for me?" A warm and fuzzy vibe doesn't always fly. When you show the community they're appreciated in other ways, the love is reciprocal.

Here are a few examples of some special programs you can create:

- ✔ **Sponsorships:** Many brands now offer a variety of sponsorships, especially to bloggers. They advertise on blogs and help fund trips to conferences. Sponsorships can also mean sending someone on a junket or helping fund a project, such as a book.

- ✔ **Scholarships:** Very few things are more important than a good education, but not everyone can afford higher learning. By offering scholarships to community members, you're giving a chance to someone who might not have otherwise been able to do something, whether it's travel on a mission or donate books for children. Scholarships don't have to be all-expenses-paid Ivy League college stays. They can also be funding for an educational conference or a one- or two-day course. Determine a program that best fits your community and budget.

- ✔ **Mentoring:** Some career-oriented communities offer mentoring for newer or inexperienced members. Mentors might be fellow employees, volunteers from within the community, or professionals who don't mind sharing a little of their time and wisdom.

- ✔ **Charitable giving:** There's nothing more beautiful than a community coming together for a cause. Choose a charity that everyone has an interest in, and see if you can get a campaign going within your community. Match funds to give more incentive.

- ✔ **Webinars:** Online conferences and seminars are called *webinars*. Catchy, right? If your brand has something to teach or provides a service that can be tied into learning, try putting together a webinar. It doesn't have to be sales-y. Most people use webinars as online courses and classes. Besides leading to good feelings among your community, webinars lead to growth in sales and community.

- ✔ **Conferences:** Your brand might be in a position to host a conference. If you're niche-y and want to have a meeting of the minds and collaboration of community, conferences truly bring people together.

- ✔ **Meetups and tweetups:** Meetups are community gatherings held in restaurants or pubs, and tweetups are the same but put together via Twitter for communities gathered on Twitter. See Chapter 15 to find out more about hosting offline events.

Serving as a brand spokesperson

As the most public representation of your brand, you're the one whom everyone will be reaching out to with comments, questions, suggestions and even business propositions.

I can tell you that forwarding all these requests to other people won't endear you to them. You'll have to handle as many of these questions that are within your jurisdiction as possible while seeking out the answers to the rest.

You're also tasked with adding a human element to the brand and talking to the community so that you can bring ideas back to the product and business development teams. If written or video content is being handled by an editorial team, you're the one who has to monitor the reaction of the community, participate in the discussion, and report both positive and negative response to the creative team.

You're also keeping in touch with marketing and promotions, reporting back with feedback regarding those campaigns.

Be careful, though. Wearing too many hats can lead to confusion by both you and other teams in your company. The last thing you want is for the community management gig to be seen as doing the dirty work no one else wants to do or working as some sort of fancy administrative assistant. Make sure that both the community and the people you work with know your value; it's the people who have undefined roles who are the most expendable.

Here's the tricky part: Although you're expected to speak on behalf of the brand, you can't just say anything you want. You have to be polite, not hurt any feelings, and make sure that everything you say publicly is befitting the brand. You may even need approval for many of the public statements you make beyond casual tweets and Facebook updates.

Representing the brand

When acting as a brand spokesperson, you have many items to consider:

- ✔ **Policies on disclosure, transparency, and what to release to the public:** Sometimes the most innocent comments cause a stir. These comments may not even cause a stir for you or your community, but your company may feel they're inappropriate. Before getting started, lay some ground rules. Talk with your team about the kinds of things you like to talk about with the community and how you handle public complaints or discourse. Discuss what kinds of responses are appropriate, what you can handle on your own, and when you should check before making a statement.

- ✔ **Legalities:** Before releasing any public statement, you may have to check with the legal team. Sometimes everything has to be worded just so. If you have to run everything through legal, it will be one of the most frustrating parts of the job, especially because they may not understand the benefits of transparency or writing in a casual voice.

✔ **Going through the proper channels:** Because the community manager is wearing so many hats, you can easily step on toes if you're not careful. Always make sure to check with the proper departments before speaking of anything having to do with them. Always try to get the blessing of all parties involved.

✔ **Not addressing everything:** Not everything warrants a response. Gauge the situation and discuss it with your team. I'm not saying that you should sweep issues under the rug, but not everything needs to be a major production. If you have to issue a press release for every single company burp or make a public statement every time a misstep occurs or a coupon code is issued, folks are going to start rolling their eyes. Not everything needs to turn into a public issue.

✔ **Having someone else address an issue:** Now and then, you need to give someone else a chance to talk. Online communities love to hear from executives, corporate VIPs, and company celebrities. Even having them stop by community haunts to say hello goes a long way toward brand loyalty.

Because you're the voice of your brand, you're on your honor to behave in the best interests of the brand, especially on company time or while using the company social-media accounts. Speak in a conversational tone, but keep the salty talk to a minimum — or, better yet, no salty talk at all. Be careful about dropping too much information (TMI). Your dates and sex life don't concern the community. As brand and community spokesperson, it's up to you to represent both in the most professional light possible.

Community managers are public representations of their brand. They need to act in a matter befitting the brand and not be afraid to respond to public outcry. Keep in mind that most community situations aren't negative, and 99 percent of the job is in creating fun promotions and campaigns your community is sure to love. Just be sure to be prepared for that 1 percent when you have to battle negativity.

Being a brand evangelist

Brands hire community managers for two main reasons: to learn as much about the community as possible and to promote the brand in a positive way and get folks talking about their product.

Though they're very interested in gauging the needs of the community, the brand is more interested in promoting whatever it is they're looking to promote. Though the community manager isn't a salesperson, he's expected to drive sales, create buzz, and create overall interest in the product without really selling. Mostly, though, he's to show the brand in the best light possible and present a human element that may have been missing before.

Here are some ways that you can successfully promote your brand:

✔ **Provide news.** Community management tools such as blogs, the company forum, Facebook, and even Twitter help spread the word about the inner workings of the community, new product information, changes in personnel, and other company-related business.

✔ **Promote products.** Use your channels to introduce products to the community without being spammy or pitchy. Create contests, offer discounts, and use the many social-media tools available to make promotions fun events rather than boring business promotions. When you involve the community, they also act as brand evangelists and get some good buzz going.

✔ **Deter negativity.** On your daily patrols of the social networks, take note of what people are saying about the company and do what you can to handle both positive and negative situations. Any time anyone portrays your brand in a negative light, ask to take it private. Then get to the bottom of the matter and see to it that this person's situation is rectified either by you or the person on the team who is best equipped to help.

✔ **Drink the Kool-Aid.** You know what's kind of lame? Community managers who tout a brand but don't use it or believe in it. So they go on and on spouting prewritten niceties about something they don't even use, and it sounds canned and false. To advocate for a brand, community managers have to believe in what they do. They have to use the product, take part in the service, read the blog, and enjoy it all. People detect insincerity, and most know when they're being misled. If you want folks to trust you and the brand, you have to show them you're one of them, which means you have to believe in what your company does before you can begin to promote it.

✔ **Respond positively.** Even in negative situations, community managers are to answer honestly and positively. You may have to check with your team before responding to comments that might shed an unfavorable light on your company. It's always best to respond, however, especially if a situation has gone public. For more in-depth information on defusing negativity, see Chapter 8.

✔ **Provide blogger outreach.** Bloggers are your friends. They can make or break a brand, but they're also important community advocates. Taking the time to research the blogs that fit best with your brand is essential because nothing turns a brand campaign into a laughingstock like a community manager who didn't take the time to research the blogger. Avoid canned form letters and make sure that something is in it for the blogger. Reaching out to bloggers and asking them to write about you, without providing any benefit to the blogger, will put you in the bad graces of the entire blogging community, as word travels very fast. See Chapter 5 for more about blogger outreach.

Understanding a Community Manager's Value

Here's the thing about community managers: Sometimes they get a bum rap. They're seen as glorified customer service people or office assistants, and that's not the case at all. Though the aforementioned positions have hard workers handling their respective tasks, what the community manager does goes far beyond assisting. A community manager can make or break a company.

In 2009, a community manager named Tom Humbarger created a bit of a stir when he posted an image on his blog (see Figure 3-2) showing that traffic to his former brand's online community took a significant dive after he was asked to stop engaging with his community.

Figure 3-2:
This figure depicts what happened when Tom Humbarger was asked to stop engaging with his brand's community.

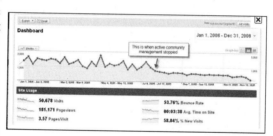

Tom used newsletters, blog posts, webinars, and social networking to reach out to community members. With no one to keep the community apprised of company news, the community lost interest. By capturing the analytics showing the decline in traffic after he stopped using these tools to communicate, he was able to prove that he, as a community manager, added value to his brand.

A community manager's role is more than a few tweets and answering some e-mails. You're tasked with making sure that a large, online community shows continued interest, even if the brand isn't actively promoting a product or service at the time.

Inspiring customer confidence

What gives you confidence in a brand? Is it a picture on a cereal box? Nutritional information? A fun marketing campaign? I'd like to argue that people are more confident in a community that is honest, transparent, and human.

But what does that mean?

Your customers have certain expectations, and they want a brand to deliver as promised. If Brand X says it can remove heavy grass stains from dungarees with nary a trace left behind, customers expect these results.

Now, as a community manager, you're not handling the product-development aspect, so you won't have much of a say in what goes into a detergent's formula and how it reacts to grass stains. You can play a large role in how information is presented, however.

If Brand X really can get those stains out, you can offer proof in the form of images, video, and other promotional campaigns. If Brand X is only talking the talk, it's up to you to discuss this with the editorial, advertising, and marketing teams to find the types of promotional materials that tell the truth about the brand while still making the customer feel good about buying it. This might mean the grass-stain campaign is out, but it also means you can find something more appropriate and enjoyable.

Customers also feel confident in brands that are up-front and honest. When they see a community manager on Twitter talking up members and discussing products with them, they see a brand as having nothing to hide. Customer confidence really isn't a difficult thing to achieve. It involves delivering what you promise, being an active presence in the virtual world, answering questions honestly, and not sweeping anything under the rug.

No one likes to feel as if they've been duped, and you don't want to risk your reputation working for someone who is looked at as a rip-off. Be truthful with your campaigns, be open and honest about what your brand can do, and don't promote a product you wouldn't use yourself.

Promoting community engagement

The brand or a new product promotion is what inspires members to join online communities, but it's not what keeps them coming back every day to participate. People don't follow a brand on Twitter, like it on Facebook, or even join a forum unless something appeals to them. A brand logo isn't what invites them to participate in community discussions; it's the discussion topics, the pleasant atmosphere, and the invitation and subsequent engagement from the community manager.

Most community managers are there only to guide the discussion. What they really want is for their communities to carry on productive conversations whether they're there or not. Indeed, the healthiest communities can run in a manager's absence while still following the rules and engaging.

So how does this happen? How does a brand representative get people talking and keep them talking? By giving them something to talk about.

Not only is it important to visit your community each day to make sure that it's not taken over by spammers and that your members are all having a positive conversation, but when you're building a community from scratch, you'll want to guide the conversation at first.

Choose topics that are appropriate to your brand that won't offend anyone. Light topics, such as the weather, are okay once in a while, but they can also be boring. Book and movie recommendations get people talking, as do the following:

- **"Caption this" contests**: Post an image (one you have permission to use) and invite your community to post a caption underneath. Brand-related photos are fine, but make them fun.

- **Fill in the blanks:** Post a sentence with a word or phrase missing and invite your community to fill in the blanks.

- **Limericks and haikus:** Pick a topic and invite your community to post a fun little ditty around it.

- **"What would you do?":** Post a news item that won't cause a debate or heated discussion and ask your community what they would do in the article's subject's situation.

- **Questions about the brand:** Ask your community a question along the lines of "What's your favorite way to use_____"

Some of these items may seem trivial and off-topic, but you're establishing a pattern early. Topics are upbeat, positive, and stuff everyone can relate to. Members come by often when they expect fun, not only for their own amusement, but to see how others are responding as well.

Something else is happening, though. Participants will want to do the same thing. They're going to post their own fun topics and conversation-starters. After seeing your example every day, a tentative few will start doing the same. Soon, many members are engaging with each other, and you don't even have to hang around. As long as you establish positivity and discourage negativity from the very start, your members are more likely to follow your example.

Also, just because the community can run in your absence doesn't mean you should make a habit of being absent. Make sure that your community knows you're there even if you're not a dominant part of the conversation. This will discourage trolls, spam, and other abuse.

Providing feedback to the customer

Customers have a vested interested in their favorite brands. They spend money on products or services and even provide word-of-mouth marketing. They don't like to be left in the dark. Community managers keep them apprised of news and updates through a variety of channels:

- ✔ Blogs
- ✔ Social networks
- ✔ Newsletters
- ✔ Webinars
- ✔ Commercials
- ✔ Marketing campaigns
- ✔ Meetups, tweetups, and conferences
- ✔ Responses to customer inquiries
- ✔ Surveys and questionnaires

Most customers and community members don't require a whole lot. If you want them to join your community and show loyalty to your brand, you have to bring them news first. They'll feel betrayed if they read about product launches in the newspaper or see you on TV talking about what's coming next. They want to be the first to know, so offer tidbits now and then to make them feel special and valuable.

Providing feedback to the brand

A community manager is a brand's most important tool — not because you tweet product information and distribute coupon codes, but because you can provide your team valuable feedback. The brand has to recognize that the community manager knows more about their customers than anyone else. It can be argued that the community manager is the most important person on the team because you know so much about your community's habits and needs.

Part of advocating for customers is to make sure that the brand is listening. It's up to the community manager to make sure that they take notice by hosting regular team meetings, distributing weekly or monthly reports, and sharing analysis of traffic stats and data.

The community manager's responsibility to both the brand and customer also means he has to monitor all his channels closely to make sure campaigns are working and the community is happy. If campaigns aren't going as planned or if negativity is in the atmosphere, the community manager has a duty to report this right away, in writing to ensure that there's no mistake, so things don't escalate out of control.

Maintaining a positive environment

No one goes to a party to have a bad time, so why would you invite anyone to join a lackluster community? You, as community manager, are tasked with making sure that everyone is happy. This is no easy feat, given the different types of online personalities. Still, it's important that a good time is had by all.

You're going to have to deal with customer issues; there's no getting around it. Some people are going to be less than cooperative, too. For a few, it's more about making noise and making you look bad than rectifying the situation in a positive, productive matter. Still, community managers have an obligation to keep things positive, no matter how difficult the other person is trying to be.

Here's what you can do when you have to deal with negative customers:

1. **Listen.**

   Is a community member making a complaint? What is being said? If left, even for a little while, the situation can escalate, especially if the member has a clique of friends backing him up. Follow the entire conversation to see where it began and what led to the complaint or public outburst.

2. **Reach out.**

   Offer to discuss privately via phone, instant message, or Skype. Listen to the other person's story without being judgmental or confrontational.

3. **Take action.**

   Do what you need to do to rectify the issue. You may need to handle it yourself or get another person involved, but do what it takes to get this customer satisfied and confident again.

4. **Follow up.**

   Don't rest on your laurels. Follow up and make sure that the situation was handled to the other person's satisfaction. If it has been, wish her a happy day and move on. If it hasn't, do what it takes again. And follow up. Again. Lather, rinse, repeat as often as necessary until there's nothing more to be done.

This four-step process accomplishes a couple of things. By taking the conversation private, you're keeping animosity or negativity out of the airwaves. This keeps bad issues out of the public eye, but also makes the customer feel as if she's receiving personal care. Also, negativity has a way of spawning more negativity. If you take an issue private, you're discouraging trolls and "me too-ers" from joining the party.

Also, by handling the issue immediately, you're not sweeping it under the rug. You're giving your customer faith and loyalty in the brand. By following up, you're showing the customer and other customers that person may talk to that you're seeing the issue through until it's resolved.

The more people who view you and the company you work for in a positive light, the more positive and productive your community will become. Both you and the brand will be seen as caring, and your community numbers will only go up.

Dealing with Resistance from Your Superiors

Many community managers speak of clashing with upper management who isn't sure that there's a need for their role or even for the brand to be so active on the social web. Having superiors who don't "get it" or don't want to put much energy into their online campaigns is frustrating and can lead to a stressful situation.

Don't worry. All isn't lost. If you're dealing with resistance from your superiors, it doesn't mean that you can't put suggested practices into place or start some new programs. It simply means that they're yet not convinced your ideas are good ones. It's up to you to change their minds.

Say, for example, that you have a great idea for an online campaign based on community feedback, but upper management isn't feeling it. How are you going to convince the people you work with your ideas are good ones?

✔ **Dazzle them with facts or case studies.** Don't enter the conference room unprepared. Upper management may not know online community or the social web, but they're sure to understand numbers, facts, and figures. Arm yourself with the data required to show your campaign will be successful. Create a presentation with all the bells and whistles if you believe it will help your case. Discuss your idea and why you feel it will succeed. If you can predict profit, that's even better. Research notable online communities and how their campaigns and community building efforts led to more sales, buzz, and signups.

✔ **Provide links and screen shots.** If community feedback gave you the idea for the campaign, link or show images of their discussions. If your superiors don't feel an online campaign or social media presence is necessary, show them why you know they are and especially show them it's what your customers are clamoring for.

✔ **Show other communities who have had success with similar ideas.** Research other communities who have successfully implemented the same or similar ideas in the past. Discuss how they presented their own ideas and the results. If you can get a case study from the other community to show the positive effects of the campaign, it will help your case.

✔ **Remain cool as you plead your case.** No matter how frustrated you come by the lack of cooperation, don't lose your cool. Staying calm will help you present your ideas without getting flustered.

✔ **Provide several examples.** If you're showing case studies, screen shots, or facts, bring more than one item to the table. The more data you have to back up your way of thinking, the better chance you have of bringing it to fruition.

✔ **Keep cost as low as possible.** When presenting an idea to upper management, especially if it's an idea they're not feeling, it's best to keep cost as low as possible. The less likely your bosses are to open their wallets, the more likely they are to go with your idea. Plus, if this idea is successful, they'll be more likely to spend money on special programs in the future.

✔ **Seek support from someone with seniority.** It always helps to have an ally. If you can, seek backup from a well-respected coworker to see whether she can help you get your point across.

✔ **Implement deadlines and timelines.** Give a timeline showing how your idea will take place and when you expect the different aspects to fall into place. What goals do you hope to achieve by what date? Be as specific as possible since vague ideas with no game plan are rarely accepted.

✔ **Be confident.** The conference room isn't the place to have doubts about your idea or ability. Practice what you're going to say and have a couple of private run-throughs so that you're self-assured when it's time to present.

✔ **Ask for a trial run.** If you're sure your idea is a winner, ask for a 30-day trial. Discuss what you hope to achieve in that time and what will happen if the results aren't as you intended.

✔ **Compromise.** Your superiors may not like all aspects of your idea, but they might see potential in parts of your idea. Be willing to compromise. You can't have your way every time. If things work out, they'll be more likely to run with more of your ideas later.

✔ **Give worst-case scenarios and their solutions.** Your bosses may ask what will happen if your ideas won't work. Be prepared to answer with the worst-case situation, but also figure out how you would rectify each of those scenarios. Turn negatives into positives.

If your idea isn't accepted, say thank you and move on . . . but don't give up. Just because this idea wasn't accepted doesn't mean that your next brain-storm won't be a winner. The important thing is that you stood up for what you think is important. Always remember that most bosses appreciate team members who are creative and thinking in the best interest of the brand. Though they may not want to run with your idea this time, they're sure to admire how you take the initiative.

If your idea is accepted, do your best to see that it has a successful result. The better it comes off, the more likely your team is likely to run with them in the future.

Community management is a hard sell for the people who aren't really sure this type of online presence is necessary. They have marketing teams to deal with special programs and customer service people to make sure that users and buyers are happy. If they're not convinced yet of the power of community, you'll have to show them why they're wrong.

Discuss the benefits of online communities and prove to your superiors how an active online presence is working for your brand. Show

- ✔ How community leads to sales
- ✔ The buzz on the social networks
- ✔ Blog posts saying nice things
- ✔ Community discussion and participation

If you're receiving resistance from upper management it's because they're simply not convinced of the power of an online community. It doesn't mean they'll never be open to it, only that they're skeptical. Do what you can to sway them in the right direction so that you don't have to deal with push back every time you share an idea.

Chapter 4

Establishing Community Policies and Guidelines

*I*n the book *The Lord of the Flies,* an island filled with shipwrecked, unsupervised children led to disaster. With no established rules or guidelines for survival, they turned against each other. I don't necessarily want to compare an island full of unruly children to a community of adults, but it's a good comparison of what happens if you don't establish a clear set of policies and guidelines. Perhaps the results won't be so negative — most people know how to behave after all — but there are always those who test the limits.

Guidelines ensure that members interact in a respectful and orderly fashion. Though the majority of your community's members have no intention of acting up, to host a governless society is to truly tempt fate. As its name indicates, guidelines "guide" members in the right direction so that they're aware of appropriate behavior. They're not meant to be smackdowns or angry rants about proper ways to act.

Creating a Positive Environment for Community Members

Have you ever joined a club or group, but the cliquey-ness of the members or constant bashing of others caused you to have to second thoughts? Online communities can be the same way. Members join them for a number of reasons, but mostly because they like to talk to and learn from like-minded people.

Positivity goes a long way in providing a valuable community experience. No one's going to hang around if it's not an enjoyable experience or they're not learning or benefitting as they should.

Impressing outside parties

Community members aren't the only ones who make decisions and assumptions after a quick look. A good first impression is also extremely important for other important parties:

- **Advertisers and sponsors:** The way that an online community is run reflects on the brand. If a community provides an enjoyable experience and has an abundance of well-mannered participants, it's also attractive to advertisers and sponsors, who see it as being a pleasant place to get their message across. Advertisers don't want their names or money associated with communities that have a reputation for being poorly moderated— especially if the members argue all the time and thrive on drama and negativity.

- **Bloggers who may write about your community:** Today, everything is worthy of a review, rant, or recommendation. Bloggers sound off about poor online experiences and put in a good word for the Internet spots that impress them. Even small communities warrant a tweet or status update if members aren't getting what they should out of them. All this commentary eventually gets associated with the brand. If the brand is popular, news about a good or bad experience can go viral.

- **The people you work for:** The people who hired you to run their community may not be monitoring your efforts every day because they trust you and feel that you're capable enough without micromanagement. Be assured that they'll visit now and then,

though. Not maintaining a positive image or letting the inmates run the asylum won't bode favorably for you. Never relax rules or let the community run itself because you figure that no one is watching; you never know who will come by.

If word gets out that your community is poorly run or provides a negative experience, you'll be viewed as someone who isn't effective, and this impression can put a damper on your career aspirations.

- **Competitors:** It would be cool if similar communities stopped seeing competitors as competitors, but rather as an extension of their own communities. That's because community managers should be encouraged to look at other communities and community managers as collaborators or colleagues rather than competitors (see next bullet). Though you can all work and cross-promote together, you can also be assured that they are viewing you as competition. They're watching your community to see what you do right so that they can try the same things. They're also watching to see what you do wrong so that they can avoid those issues.

- **Collaborators:** You may be interested in working with outside sources on special projects. If they see your community in a positive light, they're happy to have their names associated with it. A community that's in the spotlight for the wrong reasons will only scare them away.

There's an old expression, "You never get a second chance to make a first impression," and it holds true for online communities. If you don't like what you see in the first few minutes, it's not very likely you're going to stick around to learn more. If you see a positive experience, such as a community filled with members who are sharing ideas, having a respectful conversation and enjoying the company, you're more likely to stay.

Benefiting from a good impression

A positive community experience leads to more positive actions. For example, members who are having a good time invite others to join the party. They'll reach out to other online friends as well as family and neighbors with recommendations to join. Satisfied members also share your content whether it's a blog post, a fun comment on your Facebook page, or a promotion or sales opportunity. Happy campers provide the best word-of-mouth promotion.

A true sign of a positive community is watching members return each and every day and interact and participate. If you have a large group of return members who are welcoming and encouraging to newbies, congratulate yourself on a job well done.

Setting the right tone for your community

Many online arguments are caused by misunderstandings, which in turn are usually caused by unfortunate wording or a misunderstood tone. When you read and put words together in your heads, you hear the words the way you talk unless you have an idea of the other person's tone and inflection. Someone who isn't angry may be thought to be simply because of a few unfortunately placed words. Someone who doesn't know any better, for example, may type in all caps because she's new to online socializing and doesn't realize that it's perceived as yelling. It's easy to mistake tone, not only in a single post but also in the general community.

To help set a positive tone for your community:

✔ **Enjoy the company.** When you enjoy your members and have fun managing your community, it shows. The atmosphere is pleasant and congenial. If you're funny and encourage humor in others, your community is happy and lively. Treat your community as you would your real-life friends and neighbors, and your infectious attitude will be inspiring to your members.

✔ **Welcome everyone.** Everyone in your community is important. You know it, but you have to make sure that they know it. Let everyone know how happy you are they joined your community. Say "hello" and "welcome" to your newbies and encourage them to join in the festivities. Give them a reason to come back again.

✔ **Establish a regular presence.** When your members know you're monitoring a community and available for questions and comments, they're more confident about participating every day. When they know you're there, they're comfortable contributing to the community because they know members are going to behave according to the rules. Plus, if your presence is funny and pleasant and you're a joy to be around, your members look forward to interacting each day.

Keeping it positive from day 1

One popular online writing community allows members to explore and discuss all writing genres and careers. If newbies ask the wrong questions, however, they're not led to a FAQ page or helpful thread by a moderator. Instead, all the community members pile up and make the newbie feel small and unwelcome. They dissect each of the newbie's posts and point out misspellings or grammar missteps. The community moderator even joins in on the pile-on.

The members of the community may think they're setting a newbie "straight," but to lurkers and other newbies, this treatment is akin to bullying. The community moderator is setting the wrong tone for this community by allowing it.

In many online communities, a popular line of thinking (especially among their more outspoken members) is that if other community members don't like negativity or swearing or daily rants, they should find another discussion thread or, better yet, find another community.

If the community manager allows this line of thinking, his community is now an elitist clique that isn't welcoming to people who don't appreciate strong language or negativity.

Plenty of people of feel that they have carte blanche to talk down to others because they're being "brutally honest." They use "honesty" as an excuse to insult and belittle.

Good community managers know honesty is never an excuse for rudeness. If they allow rudeness to happen, they'll have a community of honest bullies and not much else.

Although these examples are extreme examples, they happen in online communities every day, and they happen for one reason: It's allowed by community management. Being nice or effective doesn't mean not being tough or strong. It means setting the right tone from the very beginning.

Using positive words

Setting the right tone for your community means choosing the right words and not leaving any room for misinterpretation. You'll find that you're dealing with a variety of personalities and that some members are more sensitive than others. You want to choose topics and a tone that isn't offensive and that folks aren't going to take the wrong way.

Here are a few tips:

- ✔ **Watch your "you" language.** How does this sound?: "You need to . . . you have to . . . you didn't. . . ." Many times, using the word *you* sounds like you're pointing a finger or accusing someone of something. If you're going to use the word *you*, reread your text before clicking the Send button. Would you want to have that comment directed at you? Would you take it the right way?

- ✔ **Give directions, not orders.** When you're teaching or sharing information, the last thing you want to do is lecture or give orders. No one wants to stay in a bossy forum. When you make requests, always remember manners. Saying "Please" and "Thank you" goes a long way toward setting the right tone.

- ✔ **Cool down before you post.** The biggest social-networking mistake is posting a comment in anger. Though a message can be deleted, you may not get to it before other people see it. Moreover, some people like to save screen shots and send them to your team or throw in your face later. Sending out an angry post can cost you your community . . . and your job.

- ✔ **Be sincere.** Just as you don't want to be too negative, you don't want to be so positive that you seem fake. Being sincere is more important than being chipper.

- ✔ **Accentuate the positive.** Try using positive words in negative discussions. Instead of saying "Don't post your links in the forum," say "Hey, I really like your blog. Thanks for your links. Moving forward, please use the promotion folder to share links." Now your comment doesn't seem like such a smackdown.

You don't have to be Polly Perky all the time because that gets old with the community as well. Just think about way you say things and how your words will impact your community. If you have to stop and wonder whether someone will feel angry or hurt, chances are that's exactly what will happen. Use words and phrases that leave no room for mistake.

Leading by example

Your community takes its cue from you. If you swear and nitpick, members will know that this behavior is okay. If you greet everyone cheerfully each morning, however, they'll follow your example. Even people who are turned on by drama and negativity will either join in on the good cheer, or they'll get so tired of having their comments moderated that they'll move along.

There's an expression that unruly children crave discipline. This is kind of the case with online communities. Online community members are not unruly children by a long shot, but they do need to be molded and guided. Members can't be expected to act a certain way if they don't know what's considered unacceptable.

Being a positive example for your community isn't difficult and can be put into play by following a few best practices:

- **Treat everyone like a friend.** Greet everyone with good cheer.

- **Give helpful advice, not smackdowns.** Don't ever make anyone feel small or silly for asking questions — even questions that have already been asked.

- **Congratulate.** Offer good wishes for achievements.

- **Encourage members to achieve their goals.** Provide motivation and support.

- **Keep topics on topic.** Don't let discussions stray too far from the original point.

- **Include everyone.** Cliques lead to exclusivity. Everyone should feel welcome to participate.

- **Avoid getting sucked into the negativity trap.** Count to 10 or walk away before firing back in a heated exchange.

When you care about your community and each individual member, it shows. Your members feel good about visiting and are comfortable returning each day. If they see you using unfortunate language, berating members or griping and nitpicking, they're likely to do the same.

Nipping negativity in the bud

Negativity keeps people away. If your brand or business wants to foster a positive community — one that reflects well on the brand and perhaps drives some sales and creates good buzz around its products or services — you don't need the kind of negativity that an unmoderated community provides.

Knowing what's really negative

It's important to understand what a negative comment actually is. Some people consider disagreement to be negativity, though that's not the case at all; if debate is respectful, it's absolutely allowed. What you need to look out for is behavior that makes people feel bad and brings down the overall mood of the community, such as the following:

- ✔ **Swearing:** Whether or not you allow swearing or vulgarity is up to you. However, it's important to consider the context and usage. It's one thing to use a choice word to illustrate a point, but it's a whole other ballgame to direct profanity at other members or the brand. Consider how allowing these words would reflect on your place of business. What would advertisers and clients think, for example?

- ✔ **Typing in all caps:** Writing in all caps is considered to be yelling online. When a member uses all caps, even if his motives are completely innocent, others take the bait, and arguments ensue. Prevent confrontations and misunderstandings by asking all-caps typists to refrain.

- ✔ **Launching personal attacks:** Debating points, policies, ideas, and discussion topics leads to lively conversation. Name-calling, finger-pointing, and character assassinations don't add anything to the discussion and cause bad feelings.

- ✔ **Posting another member's personal information:** The amount or type of information that community members want to share is entirely up to them. Most people know better than to post personal details, such as phone numbers, addresses, and places of employment, for all to see, because revealing these details can lead to bad situations. Bad situations can get even worse when members post other members' personal information. They do this for a variety of unsavory reasons, and it's always best to moderate this type of activity, especially out of respect for the victims of this type of abuse.

- ✔ **Constant baiting:** There are always community members who live for drama. You don't hear from them much during productive discussions, but when the claws come out, they're there. It's not enough for them to stay in the background, either. They drop leading comments for the sole purpose of sucking others into an argument. Half the time this sort of behavior isn't noticed by management, but it frustrates the heck out of community members. Take care to notice who your problem children are and take whatever necessary steps possible to keep them in line. If the same people are front and center during community arguments, it's a good bet they're there for the drama.

- ✔ **Sniping and snark:** Not everyone in your community is going to get along. It doesn't take long to realize the personality clashes. Many times, people who don't usually agree have to get their barbs in. They snipe and snark at each other hoping to insult or provoke an argument. Sometimes it's good to remind people who don't get along of the comment policies.

✔ **Pile-ons:** Twenty against one isn't a fair fight. This goes way beyond disagreement. A *pile-on* is what happens when a clique stands together against one person to shoot down an argument or idea. It's rarely ever done in a respectful manner.

Suffering the consequences of negativity

Plenty of online communities have very few moderators, if any, and those who own or manage the communities really don't care if members use obscenities or fight all the time. Want to know what happens?

First, it's hard to have a decent conversation. In an unmoderated or poorly moderated community, the members are more interested in picking a fight than in having an actual discussion. Serious members become frustrated by their inability to have a conversation without trolling or attacks.

Further, some members go a little too far. When you don't set limits, some members like to see how far they can go before you finally say "Enough!" Sometimes, abuse is so rampant that the community's host pulls the plug.

Finally, participating in the community isn't enjoyable. Community management ensures a pleasant experience for everyone involved.

Many people who spout negativity are testing the limits: Sometimes it's not what's said but how much one can get away with. If you don't set clear guidelines and draw the line at profanity, abuse, and personal attacks, you can lose members and gain a reputation for letting your community run amok. This reputation reflects poorly on your brand, and your community becomes a haven for trolls and spammers.

The bottom line is that negativity keeps people away. If your brand or business wants to foster a positive community, one that will reflect better on the brand and perhaps drive some sales and create good buzz around your products or services, you don't need the kind of negativity an unmoderated community provides.

Make no mistake — if you allow a single negative comment, more will follow. Negativity is enticing. It attracts copycats and me too-ers. It sucks some people in and makes them want to try it, too, until it escalates out of control. Folks are going to snark back, and soon you have anarchy. Keeping the peace is hard once it's out of control because members won't take you seriously anymore. They'll wonder why you're trying to change the rules now, after letting it go on for so long.

Preventing negativity

Fortunately for you and your community, having a positive community from the start is a lot easier than trying to moderate a community that's gone out of control. Most community members don't want to party in a cesspool. Most of them are respectful and positive and do what they can to keep the peace. Here are some ways you can make it clear from the beginning what will and won't be tolerated:

- ✔ Set clear guidelines.

- ✔ Post your community guidelines and comment policy in a prominent location and refer members to those documents as often as necessary. (I cover guidelines and comment policies later in this chapter.)

- ✔ Contact uncooperative members via private message, phone, or e-mail to discuss the effect of their negativity on the community.

- ✔ Simply don't allow negative or abusive behavior. Stand firm about what is and what isn't allowed in your community.

Encouraging community participation

Your community is only as good as its members, and most of your members aren't participating at all. According to a study by Internet usability expert Jakob Nielsen, community participation follows the 90-9-1 rule:

- ✔ 90 percent of an online community is made up of lurkers.

- ✔ 9 percent of an online community drops by to chat now and then.

- ✔ 1 percent of the overall community are the truly productive members.

Nielsen refers to this situation as *participation inequality*. His research challenges community managers to get more of that 99 percent of members into the conversation. High participation is especially important in communities that relay on sales or donations.

Members don't care to take part in discussions for a variety of reasons. The conversations may not be interesting to them, for one thing. Also, if a comment thread is nothing but "I agree" comments, members either feel that those comments are too boring to add to or are afraid to disagree when everyone else is so supportive.

Though I often mention that the healthiest communities are the ones that can run themselves without incident, a community manager needs to be a regular presence, at least to make sure that conversation is flowing. You also want to find other ways to bring the lurkers out of hiding, such as the following:

- **Award prizes for the best comments.** Have community members go beyond "I agree" comments.

- **Award badges and status upgrades for levels of participation.** Issue a fun status level or prize after members make certain numbers of comments. A member can graduate from Newbie to Regular to Superstar for every 50 to 100 comments, for example.

- **Specifically ask for lurkers' opinions.** Don't call them out by name, but try inviting them. Say something like "I'm especially interested in hearing from those of you who aren't regular commenters."

- **Be sure that discussions invite comments.** Topics should be open-ended and inviting.

- **Keep away negativity.** Lurkers are reluctant to participate if they feel that they'll be attacked. Make them feel equal and welcome.

- **Make everyone feel welcome:** Don't just hang with the cool kids, everyone is equal.

- **Invite new or lurking members to introduce themselves.** Asking for introductions may give longtime lurkers their "in."

- **Make participation fun.** Games, polls, puzzles, and contests always bring in fresh faces.

- **Make participation easy.** If members have to jump through a lot of hoops simply to make a comment, it's not going to be worth their effort. Avoid having them register or fill out *CAPTCHA,* that alphanumeric code many forms require you to fill out before submitting to prove you're not spam for every single comment. Make it as easy as possible for them to engage with others.

Keep in mind that some members are still going to lurk, but the more encouragement and enticement they have, the more likely they are to come out of hiding.

Exploring More Established Communities

Have you ever seen a community with thousands of members interacting and enjoying one another's company? These types of communities are good role models, and they're worth your time to explore them so that you can see what makes them so successful.

It's always a good idea to check out the competition. It's especially interesting to observe competitors at both the top and bottom of the ladder to see what defines success . . . and failure.

For an online community, success depends a lot on your on the brand's goals for that community, in addition to how the community responds and interacts. For example, if community discussions are met with enthusiasm with plenty of responses, that's a sign of success. If a brand is using community to drive sales, a good reaction to promotions and sales events is also a sign of a successful community.

You should also look out for these signs as well:

- ✔ Good response to promotions, sales, and events
- ✔ New members signing up each day
- ✔ Positive reviews and write-ups
- ✔ Requests for interviews with the community manager, especially if a brand is a model of success
- ✔ Inclusion and harmony among members
- ✔ Many active users (versus lurkers)
- ✔ Positive buzz on the social networks
- ✔ Word-of-mouth marketing by community members
- ✔ Members achieve their goals (learning about ongoing promotions, receiving professional tips, or sharing ideas as hobbyists) for joining the community
- ✔ Mutual respect between members and management

I use the word *positive* often in this section and throughout this book because positivity is the sign of a healthy, successful community. Positive results, such as lots of comments or high response to a promotion, are true signs of success.

Searching for thriving communities

How do you find successful communities to use as a gauge? It's not like you can Google *"the best online communities on the web."* Or can you?

Using search terms can yield a mixed bag of results, but you can still find examples of successful online communities via online searching. You have to weed through a whole bunch of other stuff, too. Using terms such as *"best online communities"*, *"popular online communities"*, and *"top online communities"* will yield lists of favorite places to visit. However, the key word here is *favorite*. Online lists can be subjective and include the authors' favorite online haunts. Unless the choices are backed up with facts and figures, it's difficult to determine whether these communities are truly the best or most popular.

Still, if several people are writing positively about the same communities, it stands to reason that those communities are worth looking into. Sit in at a few of these places and see what makes them so special.

Search engines aren't the best or only ways to find successful online communities. Work your channels to see where everyone hangs out online. Ask friends, family members, colleagues and social-networking contacts. Find out where they're spending their time online, and pay a visit.

Also, monitor the online buzz to find out which brands are getting the most play and which communities folks are raving about. Here are a few things to look for when monitoring community buzz online:

- ✔ **How are they managed?** The best communities have managers who are hands-on and interactive. They do their best to get everyone involved and keep up a regular flow of topics.

- ✔ **Who is commenting?** Successful communities have regulars, but they also have brand-new members and people who pop in from time to time. If the same few people are the only ones who are participating, see whether you can figure out why.

- ✔ **What is the reaction to campaigns**? If you see a good response to campaigns and promotional opportunities, it's a good indication of a positive, healthy community. When a product, sale, or other campaign is introduced and hardly anyone comments or shares the news, it's a good indication the community isn't very psyched about the brand or the product.

Using Facebook communities as a guide

Blogs, brands, businesses, and individuals all use Facebook fan or "like" pages to grow a community. Facebook's Share and Like buttons, as well as the ability to upload videos, drop links, and comment on content, allow members to interact, too. Even lurkers can click a button to show approval without having to commit to making a full-fledged comment.

What these successful Facebook communities demonstrate is that people will come out on behalf of a brand, if the brand is engaging, and members can share in fun and interesting ways.

Notice the ways other brands are using Facebook pages and use them as an example in shaping your own Facebook content:

- ✔ By creating a fan page, you're telling customers or followers that you appreciate their feedback.

- ✔ By allowing feedback, you're making your customers feel that they have a say in product or business decisions.

✔ By allowing members to share stories, tips, links, videos, cartoons, and anything else that's relevant or interesting to the community, you're telling them that it's their community, too.

✔ By allowing likes and shares, you're not only giving members an opportunity to bring nonmembers into the conversation, but you're also letting them take partial credit for discovering and sharing something that's clever or funny, even if they're not the ones who created that content in the first place.

Members invest major chunks of time in their favorite online groups and causes. How boring would it be if a community wasn't so interactive and all you (as members) did was read someone's opinion or story without the ability to remark or share that content?

The appeal of Facebook groups is that they do more than allow members to be part of a conversation. They allow them to create content and even share their approval, even if it's only to give a thumbs up.

When you see Facebook communities positively engaging, think about your own community's engagement and interactivity. Some things to note are how one-sided content rarely gets a response. By leaving open-ended, engaging content, readers can't help but respond.

Finding successful forums

Online discussion forums have been around since the Internet's early days, and though they've evolved over time, they're still a gathering place for like-minded community discussion. Plenty of forums on the web have thousands of active participants, and some have been around for many years. Their success is no accident.

Forums don't grow and maintain longevity out of sheer luck. They're successful because they have the right management and the right community. In fact, most successful forums boast the right mix of participation, plus authority.

Successful online communities also have

✔ Mutual respect

✔ Appropriate, on-topic conversation

✔ A high number of participants

✔ A positive environment

Though not all forums are created alike (some have different themes or require a paying subscription to participate), usually the same general rules and guidelines apply.

Many people land on forums during a web search or receive recommendations from other members of a community. As the average person stays on a web page for only a few seconds, you want him to see at first glance that your community is the right place for him. By the same token, if you're researching forums, you can tell almost immediately which forums are appealing and engaging, and which aren't very welcoming.

The following are signs of a thriving community:

- ✔ **Fresh content served daily:** If the posts on the front page are months or years old, with very little current content, move on. The most engaging forums have daily discussions geared toward all members.

- ✔ **Respectful disagreement:** When each comment is met by pile-ons, personal attacks, and rude disagreements, it's a sign that the community is poorly managed community. No one should be afraid to voice a respectful opinion. In a thriving community, the members respond to comments with pleasantly worded responses and points of view, even if they don't particularly agree with the original poster's point.

- ✔ **Clearly posted comment policy:** Most forums have a clearly marked starting point that includes a welcome message, information about the community, and rules for commenting. Making the rules "sticky" so that they stay on the top page forever ensures that everyone is aware of the rules. (I discuss creating a comment policy for your community in the section "Understanding the Importance of a Comment Policy," later in this chapter.)

- ✔ **Welcome page:** The best online communities are welcoming to all new members. Most have a folder where all members are invited to tell a little about themselves and read about the other participants (see Figure 4-1). See Chapter 8 for more on welcoming news members to your community.

- ✔ **FAQ page:** A community's FAQ page allows the community manager to answer the same questions one time, rather than over and over through the course of time. Also, members can learn everything they need to know at a glance, and at their convenience, rather than asking the same question many others have already asked. Read several different communities' FAQ pages and note how they cover all the bases. The best FAQs cover everything you need to know about a community and a brand, in one fell swoop.

- ✔ **Positive tone:** If a community is a hotbed of negativity and tension, it's immediately apparent after reading only a few posts. Chances are, unless a forum is popular because it's a haven for trolls and insult hurlers, you'll find very few instances of purposeful negativity. Good discussions are good natured, productive, and respectful. Members are helpful with their comments, positive with their criticism, and know how to disagree without getting angry.

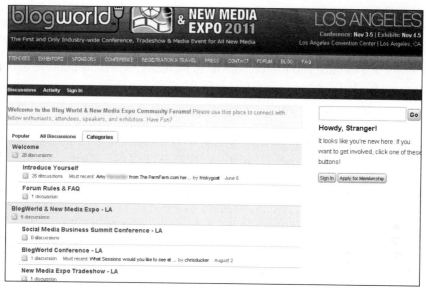

Figure 4-1:
Make sure
that your
forums wel-
come area
is posted
at eye level
where it
can't be
missed by
new mem-
bers of your
community.

✔ **Very few technical issues:** Online forums require a technically savvy person to make sure that everything is running smoothly. If it's slow to load, has frequent "board burps" where posts magically fall off the forum, or if it's often down for hours at a time, participating in the community isn't going to be an enjoyable experience for members. The forum is quick to load, intuitive to use, and posts or comments don't disappear.

✔ **Positive buzz:** A true sign of success is when a community's members sing its praises, even when they're offline or at another online haunt. If they mention the community to their neighbors or on social networks and recommend that others join them, it's a good indication that things are going very well.

✔ **A visible community manager:** You may not see a community manager, but there's no mistake she's there. Most managers are not an "in your face" presence in their communities, but they're participating enough to interact with the community and enforce their rules. A successful online community can run itself in the community manager's absence, but most managers and moderators don't stay away for too long.

✔ **An element of fun:** If participants aren't enjoying themselves, there's no need for them to stick around. Making sure that there's a good mix of serious topics and light-hearted fare keeps a forum from being a downer. (Negativity doesn't only come from abusive members; dismal, depressing topics and heated discussions also drives people away.) Using contests, images, polls, and other fun elements keep things from getting too serious.

> ✓ **Loyalty:** Most online community members wouldn't take a bullet for their community managers, but they're loyal in that they choose their current community over others. They participate in discussion topics, share content, and invite others to join in. They may even defend their communities and community managers when there's negativity directed toward them. That's why so many community managers like to reward member loyalty with some cool perks.

When members are confident in and comfortable with their communities, they make it a regular stop in their regular routine. The most successful forums provide a positive place to carry on an intelligent discussion and to share tips and resources. Look for all these traits when you're researching online forums and note what they all have in common.

Discovering blogging communities

There used to be a difference between a blog post and a more newsy article, but now those lines are blurred. Each allow for comments and discussion around a topic. What's interesting about many of the more prestigious news sites allowing comments is how many are inappropriate or spammy and having nothing to do with the discussion topic at all. Many online news services don't have a community manager to handle comments and guide conversation, and that's one of the key differences.

Blogs are conversational. The comfortable tone bloggers use endears them to their readers. For the most part, people can relate to blogs. The blogger is one of them. They don't use intellectual language, and the information provided is brief and easy to digest.

Whether bloggers blog for themselves or on behalf of a brand or client, it's up to them to patrol the lot and clean up any nasty bits. And that's where the community management part comes in.

Blogs are discussions geared around a specific daily (or regular) topic. The blogger writes up the topic *du jour,* and his community responds in kind.

It's not a "set and forget" kind of arrangement, though. Content has to be open ended in order to invite a response. The blogger has to ask the right types of questions rather than post "my way, and that's all there is to it" points of view.

When comments or traffic aren't coming easy, bloggers sometimes rely on controversy or *linkbait* — that is, content written specifically to attract so much attention that bloggers and readers will link to it on other blogs and social networks. The problem is that this kind of traffic is short lived, and controversy always brings out the trolls and negativity. That's why it's best to create *evergreen,* or timeless, content that appeals to everyone even years later.

Blogging communities are unique and incredibly loyal. Most members stand by and defend their favorite bloggers with a passion. In return, the bloggers ensure positive conversations centered on thought-provoking topics. They do so by making participation simple and inviting.

The best blogs have these features:

- ✔ **It's easy to comment.** Blogs that make commenting difficult eventually discourage that very thing. It's understandable that commenters have to use a name and e-mail address to offer thoughts, but a rigorous registration process, complete with unreadable CAPTCHA and long waits for approval, may keep out trolls and spammers, but it will also keep a community from growing.

  You might notice other community blogs using commenting plug-ins such as Disqus (pronounced "discuss") or Livefyre. These plugins allow commenters to register once. Thereafter, their information is remembered on every blog they visit. Watch how community managers are using the different plug-ins and consider using them for your own community.

- ✔ **The conversation is instant.** Many bloggers hold comments in moderation to ensure that no spam comes through. If the blogger is away from his desk, however, it can take days for comments to be moderated, so a conversation isn't happening. Commenters are reluctant to come back again and wait another three days for the conversation to take place. To remedy this issue, many bloggers will use a comment plug-in, or they'll hold only a new member's first comment in moderation to ensure that he's not spammy. A blog's comment moderation tools make removing abusive or spammy comments simple, so you don't need to hold comments in moderation for more than a few minutes.

- ✔ **It uses questions and phrases to invite discussion.** Bloggers and community managers take a different approach at stimulating conversation with blog content than, say, Facebook pages, forums and social networks. With these other types of communities, brevity is key. Blogs are more expansive, and discussions are centered around a particular topic or niche. On Facebook, you might ask questions of your community to elicit a response, and on blogs, you write much longer discussions geared also toward eliciting a response. To do this, bloggers ask questions throughout their posts and make sure that there is room for all to respond. Take note of how the blogger is communicating with his community and inviting a response.

- ✔ **It discourages negativity.** Too many commenters see disagreement as a negative, which couldn't be farther from the truth. Bloggers love lively discussions and especially enjoy another perspective. However, there's a difference between respectful disagreement and abusive or negative comments. Responding by calling someone names or making personal attacks isn't disagreement. Many blogs prominently display a comment policy helps to keep this type of negativity at bay. Use these policies as a model for your own.

> ✔ **Respect is mutual.** The most successful blogs are those blogging with community in mind. They don't talk down to or belittle their readers, and they keep angry rants to a minimum. They also don't make anyone feel as if they're "doing it wrong." When bloggers treat community members as equals in the discussion, the blog and subsequent community will flourish. Note the exchange between bloggers and community members and see how they encourage mutual respect.

Bloggers are fiercely protective of their communities and communities are fiercely protective of their bloggers. By creating discussions that make it easy to participate, members feel as if they helped to create the content too.

Looking at e-mail groups

E-mail groups are more private types of online communities, and the reasons people like them are also the reasons many people avoid them. You have to be truly committed to the community because some e-mail groups send hundreds of comments to your inbox each day. Yet e-mail groups are so convenient because you don't have to commit to a forum or try to figure out which posts are new. You can even set it up so that you receive all of the day's e-mails at once in a "digest" format so that your inbox isn't cluttered.

Be aware that e-mail groups, such as those provided by Yahoo! and Google, are also spam magnets. These types of communities have different rules than many of the social networking communities you see online.

For example, on a blog, if you hold all comments in moderation and approve one by one, you'll scare people away from commenting altogether. It's sort of different in e-mail groups. Not only is approval required for all members before they can take part in the day's discussion, but many community managers or group moderators also approve each individual comment to ensure that it's not spam.

Some e-mail groups, such as the groups created by Freecycle.org, require moderators to be extremely hands on, and for many volunteers, it's almost a full-time effort. The more rules a group has, the harder job a community manager has to moderate. Freecycle, which has regional Yahoo! groups all around the world, has very specific rules about posting. For example, members have to use "Offer," "Taken" and "Wanted" in their subject titles along with the name of the item being offered (or taken or wanted) and the location of said item, in each individual subject line. Any title missing any of this information is automatically rejected, even if the member is someone who contributes every single day and everyone knows who he is and where he's located.

Many of the freecycle groups receive hundreds of messages each day requiring dedicated managers to be close by. Now, this isn't the way every e-mail group works, but most have heavy moderation in order to provide a positive user experience.

Still, for those who just want to participate at their own pace and don't want to have to create avatars, user names and bios, e-mail groups are simple to join and participation requires only return e-mail. They don't all require heavy moderation, such as the Freecycle, but they'll definitely need someone keeping an eye out to make sure that scammers and spammers aren't hanging out nearby.

Discovering positive e-mail groups is trickier than searching for blogs and forums. Because most e-mail groups are private, they're not picked up on the search engines. Some do have websites, but unless you know specifically what to look for — for example, a name of the e-mail community — it's still hit or miss.

To search for or browse for individual e-mail groups, visit the host's home page (see Figure 4-2). For example, Yahoo!, Google, and LinkedIn all host e-mail groups. By doing a web search for *"Google groups," "LinkedIn Groups,"* or *"Yahoo! Groups,"* your first result will be the host's home page with a browse-able data base of the various individual groups. They're broken up into subject matter, so find the groups that closely match your own community.

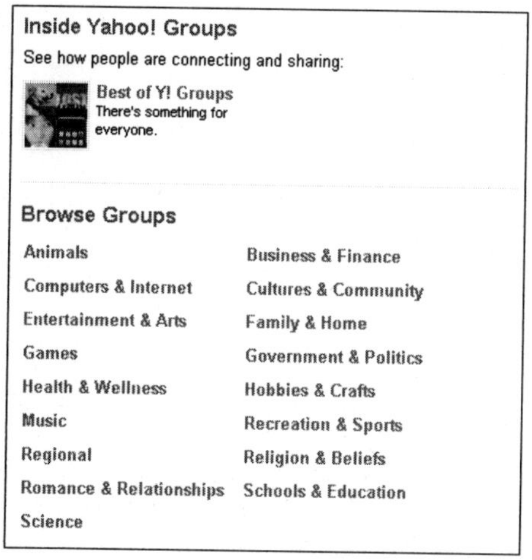

Figure 4-2:
Visit the host home page of the e-mail group to browse topics and choose groups you find interesting or relevant to your own topic.

> **Inside Yahoo! Groups**
> See how people are connecting and sharing:
>
> **Best of Y! Groups**
> There's something for everyone.
>
> **Browse Groups**
>
> | | |
> |---|---|
> | Animals | Business & Finance |
> | Computers & Internet | Cultures & Community |
> | Entertainment & Arts | Family & Home |
> | Games | Government & Politics |
> | Health & Wellness | Hobbies & Crafts |
> | Music | Recreation & Sports |
> | Regional | Religion & Beliefs |
> | Romance & Relationships | Schools & Education |
> | Science | |

Another tricky part comes in to play because so many communities are closed and require permission to participate or observe. If a community's topic intrigues you, you can request membership to observe how the members are interacting with each other and how the group is being used.

Establishing Respectful Rules and Regulations

Here's the thing about rules; no one likes being told how to behave, but after a while, community members realize it's good to have some guidelines. In the real world, there are reasons kids are asked to keep elbows off the table or not talk with their mouths full. While kids may not recognize the importance of these rules when they're young, they appreciate having good table etiquette later on in life.

It's a similar scenario within an online community. Perhaps new members may be intimidated upon reading a long list of guidelines, but after a while, they'll come to appreciate the reasons behind it and the positive atmosphere.

Averting anarchy with guidelines

Years ago, there were a website and forum called F***ed Company. At first, the forum catered to technical people who wanted to discuss tech issues and share tips. However, the forum had no rules, and the owner planned on keeping it that way. Soon, the trolls took over. Every post was met with a personal attack, and members sought out other members' personal information and posted it online. They even attacked other communities. Over time, the only members participating were the trolls. The people who continued to participate in this community enjoyed that type of atmosphere, but it was anarchy. Eventually, the owner got tired of all the abuse and negativity and closed the whole thing down. Even if he had added community managers, by that time it would have been too late. The inmates were already running the asylum.

A few similar communities exist online, and they attract only certain types of people. You were hired as a community manager because your brand wants to avoid this type of situation, so it's up to you to create a fair list of guidelines for your community to follow.

In the next section, I talk about creating a comment policy. Here, I focus on establishing guidelines and rules, which are necessary for several reasons:

✔ Members know right off the bat what is allowed.

✔ Members know what will happen if they don't adhere to the guidelines.

✔ After reading the guidelines, members can choose to participate or move on if they feel that the rules are too strict.

Though every community is different, many of the guidelines are along the same vein. Consider these common guidelines:

- ✔ **Follow the comment policy.** Your community comment policy is only a small part of your guidelines. It helps your members to be respectful in conversation, but there's much more to having a productive community than a comment policy.

- ✔ **Set rules regarding linking.** Many newbies have good intentions and don't realize that constantly posting links to their blogs, websites, and sales pages is considered spam. Establishing linking guideline helps keep spam, inadvertent or otherwise, at bay.

- ✔ **Search for previous posts on the topics before creating a new post.** To avoid done-to-death topics, some communities request their members search previous posts to make sure that members aren't posting previously addressed topics.

- ✔ **Do not sell.** Obvious selling by community members is usually forbidden. Members come to have a discussion, not receive sales pitches.

Though I often remark that the sign of a successful community is mutual respect between management and members, I also allow that not all members think rules apply and like to do what they can to stir up trouble. With guidelines in place, there are no surprises, and they can't say, "Well, no one told me I couldn't do that."

Issuing warnings

After you have your guidelines in place, you're ready to take appropriate action when necessary. Every broken rule must have a consequence, and the severity of that consequence depends on the severity of the broken rule. Sometimes, of course, consequences are subjective, and you can handle them on a case-by-case basis.

Most of the time, a warning is a sufficient reaction to a broken rule. If profanity is against your comment policy, for example, you can simply issue a warning: "Please note profanity isn't allowed in this forum. If you'd like to edit your post to include a more appropriate word, please feel free to do so. Otherwise, we'll have to delete the comment."

Of course, this type of warning can go either way. Inappropriate comments are often innocent because the member didn't read the commenting guidelines properly. In this case, he'll usually apologize and remove the offending word. On the other hand, sometimes members raise a fuss and complain about not being able to freely express themselves, in which case another nicely worded warning or explanation may be in order.

Public warnings do more than tell someone he has broken the rules. It also shows the entire community you're watching, and certain behaviors won't be tolerated. Also, you're issued a first and second warning, the offending party, and all who've witness the events, can't say that you're picking on the person you've banned.

There's a big difference between a gentle reminder, a nicely worded warning, and a message meant to embarrass the offending party. Warnings aren't meant to humiliate; they're meant to remind.

Taking it outside

The best communities show very little negativity, but that doesn't mean it's not there. Public chastising is embarrassing, and hurt feelings may ensue, even if you feel the member deserve it. Also, sometimes public warnings can backfire, and you have an entire community defending the person who caused the problem in the first place. Sometimes, you even have to request to step outside the community.

People don't always take warnings seriously. If they're not heeding warnings, it may be time to take it offline.

If you can send a personal or direct message to the offending party, that's your first step. Always be pleasant and polite and never fire off a note in anger. Let the other person know this type of behavior goes against your guidelines and if he doesn't want to follow the rules, you have no choice but to ask him to leave.

Sometimes it's also a good idea to explain why these rules exist. The other person may feel he's just having a little fun, but the reality is public negativity disrupts a community and makes other members feel uncomfortable. They no longer feel as if they have a safe place to discuss the issues.

In addition, some community members don't necessarily break rules but push the limits and test your authority. They may challenge everything you say or do to make you look silly or appear that you don't know what you're talking about. These types of people may also require a private conversation to find out what the problem is and why they're constantly challenging your authority. Again, you may want to explain that this behavior is bringing down the mood of the community. Expect a good argument as the type of people who like to bait management rarely ever see themselves in the wrong.

After explaining about how your members are uncomfortable with constant rule breaking, be prepared for the offending party to say something to the effect of "Well, they can go somewhere else if they don't like it." That type of statement creates cliques, not community. Explain that it's not in the community spirit to suggest folks ignore bad behavior if they don't like it. Instead, try explaining that asking people to not participate in negativity drives most them away and creates cliques and that you'd rather have a community with content that is welcoming to all.

Hopefully, having a private conversation will help the member see why you have guidelines and how this behavior is affecting the community. After explaining to the member about why your rules are important and what will happen if he continues the inappropriate behavior, take a wait-and-see attitude. Consider it a probation. If the community is important to the member, he will curb the rude or abusive behavior. If that member is only there to disrupt, that goal will become apparent as well, and you can take the appropriate actions (see next section).

Banning community members

Asking members to leave a community sort of goes against the grain when it comes to building a community. You want to add new members, not get rid of them. Still, on some occasions, you have to revoke memberships because members simply refuse to play by the rules:

- When you've warned them on more than one occasion, but they still test the limits
- When they continuously spam the community with links to their own blogs or sales pages
- When they make personal attacks against others in the community
- When they publicly question your decisions or authority on a regular basis, for the sole purpose of making you look bad and disrupting the community
- When they create different names and personalities in order to troll other members

The decision to ban someone is usually made on a case-by-case basis, and there are different levels of banning. For example, if a repeat offense is sort of minor, perhaps a ban of only a week or two is in order. For more serious offenses, six months sends a good message. For repeat offenders, a lifetime ban shows the offending member and the rest of the community that you mean business.

You should have already warned the offending member what would happen if he continued his behavior so that the decision to ban doesn't come out of left field. Always use banning as a last resort, after you've exhausted all other avenues to get certain members to "play nice." (You can find out more about banning in Chapter 9.)

Recognizing respectful disagreement versus personal attacks

A common mistake made by community managers, especially bloggers, and people who are commenting in a community, is to take comments that aren't in agreement as a personal affront. Not all content has to be rainbows and puppy dogs, and it's not a sign of discourse if everyone in attendance isn't in agreement. The healthiest communities are those that allow all members to present their points of view in a civilized and respectful manner.

Respectful disagreement is when a community member doesn't agree with a comment or post and states his case without belittling, name-calling, or finger-pointing. Respectful disagreement adds to the value of the conversation and allows an accurate portrayal as members are given all sides of a discussion to consider.

Even discussions turning to debates are fine as long as each member respects other opinions. Without disagreement, you're fostering a one-sided, always-in-agreement, cliquey type of community that makes folks with differing opinions feel as if they don't belong — not to mention it's boring.

Now, trolls and people who aren't skilled in the fine art of debate may choose to disagree without having a valid point. Instead of adding to the discussion, they stir up a hornet's nest and create drama and arguments. If this type of behavior is allowed to happen every time a discussion occurs, you'll lose your community. If you're able to guide members back on track to a productive positive conversation, your members will feel comfortable about providing a wide range of opinions, even if they don't all agree.

Responding to a discussion by questioning someone's intelligence is not a proper response or rebuttal, and the commenter should receive a warning. Ditto name-calling, cursing, and any remark meant to be a personal attack. You might also give the commenter the opportunity to remove or rephrase his comment before you delete it for good.

It's up to you to decide whether or not to have your conversation publically or in private, but your members will appreciate having a spirited discussion without fear of attack.

Some members also take it personally when others disagree, even if there's no instance of attack. Their comments get more heated and defensive and sometimes border on attack on their own. You may also be needed to diffuse this type of situation as well.

The bottom line is that a community allows all voices to be heard. Mud-slinging, character attacks, and rude behavior just lead to everyone being afraid to speak their mind or speak truthfully. Knowing the difference between discussion and attack can help you keep the conversation flowing in a peaceful and positive manner.

Knowing when to let things slide

Just because you have the power to do so doesn't mean that all issues require warnings and bannings. Yes, you want to nip negativity in the bud, but no, you don't want to get petty about it either. Sometimes letting an issue slide is okay.

As community manager, it's your job to know your community. Sometimes regular, upstanding members have slip-ups. Sometimes newer members who don't do more than scan the rules may use one of your naughty words. Determine whether or not these occasions are innocent. Take it private, note the error, and move on without making it a big deal.

Sometimes a heated post or rant is important to get a point across. You don't need to remove the content if it's still within the guidelines, and it isn't hurting anyone. Not all negativity is disruptive, abusive, or cause to get out the big guns.

Community members want to respect and enjoy interacting with those who manage. They don't want to fear them or associate them with parents or bosses. In most cases, everyone is an equal, except the community manager is there to ensure a positive experience. You're there to guide, not punish.

Responding to cries of censorship

If someone is a visitor at your home and uses foul language in front of your children and you ask him to please not use those words, it's not censorship. You're asking someone to respect your rules and your home. Likewise, it's the same thing with online communities. The owners of each community have the right to create and enforce any rules they want. It's not censorship to remove a spammy link or comment that uses profanity or vulgarity; it's being respectful of the entire community as well as those who host the community. You're not stifling an idea or even the thought behind a comment. You're simply asking them to remove inappropriate words.

Still, many people who are asked not to sell, spam, use profanity, or personally attack other community members cry censorship after being asked to play by the rules. Many of these people know it's not censorship really, but enjoy publicly denouncing you as a censor anyway. Don't lose your cool.

If you're accused of censorship because you remove a post, you have several recourses:

- ✔ **Ignore it.** Your community knows the rules. Allowing one malcontent to make his accusation and move on might be the most peaceful way out.

- ✔ **Respond and then move on.** If other members of the community get involved and begin protesting, you'll have a melee on your hands. A better course of action than ignoring may be to respond, hear the other person out, and put it all behind you.

- ✔ **Respond privately.** Contact the member and offer to discuss the situation. Explain where you're coming from, why you have rules, why you removed the offending word or post, and why it's not censorship. There may be some back and forth between you, but at least it's a private conversation, and you're allowing the other person to have a voice. Be careful not to let it escalate into a spitting contest and don't fire back in anger. Have a calm, reasonable discussion. You still may not be able to convince the other person to see your side, but he might appreciate your allowing him the opportunity to voice his opinion. Plus, you're keeping the negativity away from the community.

- ✔ **Respond publicly.** You don't need permission from your community to handle matters as you see fit. If you feel the need to remove a comment, do it without fanfare. Just know that sometimes the commenter because upset and offended by this action and takes it public by telling others you're censoring his comments. Sometimes these types of public announcements, made in the community itself or on the social networks, are ignored. Other times, accusations get so out of control, you have no choice but to address it. (See the upcoming section "Recognizing the Importance of Being Transparent.") You can do so with a single tweet, comment among the community, or blog post. Again, it's up to you how and when to respond and if to respond at all.

You'll never be able to please everyone in your community. You won't be able to convince someone who refuses to listen that you're not censoring, so your goal should be to keep the peace in your community. Just know that the more back and forth that occurs over a particular issue, the less likely it is to die down right away.

Using policy and guidelines pages

Online communities are only as good as their rules. Seriously. If you don't put a comment policy and community guidelines into place, everyone will run amok. Some members like to see how much they get away with, and many of them behave quite differently under the cloak of computer anonymity. With policies in place, your rules regarding comments and expected community behavior aren't a surprise.

Every active community needs a *comment policy,* a list of guidelines specifically for comments and discussion topics. The best comment policies list the type of behavior you're not willing to tolerate and what happens if you don't abide by the guidelines. It's extremely important to set the standard from the very beginning. It's much easier to have fair rules in place from the get-go, than to go around and change how things are done after things are out of control.

Posting a comment policy everyone can see shows them yours is a community respectful of its members and a place where they can interact without fear of being trolled, spammed, and attacked.

You'll find most members don't have any problems using comment policy or terms of service pages. Most approve because it means they can interact with others and not have to worry about trolls or abuse.

Most online communities should have established guidelines in place before opening for business. Prominently displaying them in a Welcome folder, About page, blog sidebar, or any other area immediately visible to the eye to ensure that they're the first stop for new members.

Creating your comment policy

Comment policies should be fair and balanced. If you have too many rules, participants may feel stifled and get a little turned off. If you don't have enough rules, anarchy ensues. Create guidelines that everyone can follow so that you're not asking too much from your community.

Most comment policies have similar elements:

- ✔ **Overview:** Talk about your community goals and why you feel the guidelines are necessary. This section needs to be a paragraph, at most. If your guidelines are too long, no one will want to read them. They have to appeal to the short attention span of the people who read and surf on the web.

- ✔ **Rules or guidelines:** Talk about acceptable behavior and what will and won't be tolerated, such as spam, profanity, personal attacks, and respectful disagreement.

- ✔ **Consequences:** Discuss what happens to members who don't adhere to the guidelines. For example, they may receive a series of warnings before they're banned outright.

- ✔ **Agreement:** Many forums, e-mail groups, and other social networks require members to check a box stating that they agree to the terms of use. This way, they can't be surprised if you have to call them out on an infraction.

Showing examples of community behavior

You may want to avoid confusion by posting examples of what is and what isn't acceptable community behavior. This is an excellent idea, perhaps in the form of a list of do's and don'ts or a series of screenshots.

When showing examples, the last thing you want to do is single someone out or choose a scapegoat. Be fair.

Keep these guidelines in mind when preparing your examples:

✔ **Don't name names.** Pointing fingers or making someone the poster child for bad behavior is mean-spirited. Use screen shots only if they don't identify the offending party in any way. Try to use a made-up example when at all possible.

✔ **When listing examples, also list consequences.** For example, say, "In this instance, we'll issue a warning. . . ."

✔ **Avoid comments under your guidelines.** Most comment policies and user guidelines are closed for comments so as to avoid trolls. Your community FAQs can list questions that arise with their respective answers.

By showing examples of unacceptable behaviors, you're making sure that everyone understands what's allowed. Like your comment policy, this section shouldn't be long and detailed, but it should show enough examples that no one can tell you they didn't know a certain behavior isn't allowed.

Avoid lengthy diatribes and pontification about manners and proper behavior. No one wants a lecture, especially if they haven't done anything wrong. A brief rundown of the types of comments and behaviors you will and won't allow will suffice.

Displaying your comment policy

How your members learn about your community guidelines has a lot to do with the type of online community your managing. For example, many forums require brand new members to agree to guidelines before they can sign up for membership. Once the "I agree" box is checked off, members can participate as they like but their first stop should be the Welcome folder where they can introduce themselves and read comment policies, FAQs, and other important information.

Many e-mail newsgroups and communities send guidelines to members via e-mail and have members agree to guidelines before participating.

For other communities such as Twitter chats and Facebook groups, it's not as easy to post comments and guidelines, but directing members to a specific policy or guidelines page on a blog or website will help them to understand which behaviors won't be tolerated and what words and actions are acceptable to conversation.

The key to all policies and guidelines is to put them in a place where everyone can see them immediately upon landing on the community. If possible, guidelines or links to guidelines should be placed "above the fold" or at immediate eye level and not in a place where members have to look around or scroll down to read.

Creating a comment policy and posting it somewhere no one sees it doesn't make sense. Always place your terms of use or community guidelines where they're immediately visible, as Table 4-1 describes.

Table 4-1	Where to Post Your Comment Policy
Community Type	*Placement*
Forum	Your forum's Welcome folder or wherever you host the first stop for newbies
Blog	A static page with visible tab, hopefully above the fold, or at eye level
E-mail group	Send to new members immediately upon signing up, but also posted in a folder on the group's home page or website

Your community guidelines, FAQs, terms of service, and comment policy are all-important documents, deserving of a prominent place of honor in your community. Make sure that they're placed where they easily catch the eye so that users don't have to hunt to find them.

Appreciating commenting etiquette

Commenting also has its own list of unwritten rules. Most regular online community members discover these universal do's and don'ts after a few months of participation. Some of them are common sense, while others aren't so easily apparent, especially to newbies:

- ✔ All caps means that you're yelling.

- ✔ Only post links to your own stuff in signature lines or posts inviting you to do so.

- ✔ Practice respectful disagreement, not personal attacks.

- ✔ Try to post something that adds value to a conversation ("me, too" doesn't add value).

- Stay on topic.
- Ignore trolls.
- Be brief and don't turn every comment into your own personal blog post.
- To avoid redundancy, read previous comments before posting your own.
- It's not all about you so avoid making every comment a testimony as to how awesome you are.
- You're a guest, so keep this in mind when commenting.

The beautiful thing about commenting etiquette is that it keeps most people in check, which makes your job a lot easier. In the real world, most rules of etiquette are embedded in memories, and people follow them simply because they're the right thing to do. The same holds true of commenting etiquette. You don't often drill these unwritten rules into participants' heads, but it's stuff they know and follow anyway. It's when commenters don't care to follow the proper etiquette that the community manager steps in.

Recognizing the Importance of Being Transparent

Transparency is a big word in the social-media space right now. It's a fun, fancy term for honesty. It means gaining a community's trust by not having anything to hide. By being transparent, you give the public a look into your brand's inner workings. You don't sweep bad press or discontent under the rug.

Being transparent with your community means you're trusting them enough to reveal certain bits of information, without offering too much information. For example, your community doesn't need to know about your love life or other private details. It also means that you answer their inquiries with as much information as possible and without tap dancing around the issues.

Being transparent doesn't mean sharing details that aren't meant for public consumption. A brand is still allowed to have some privacy.

Knowing what you should keep to yourself

You don't have to air the details of every single discussion or step-by-step developments of new products and services. Transparency, while meaning there's nothing to hide, doesn't mean you have to disclose every burp and giggle from every team meeting.

Being honest with your community **_does not_** mean they have to know every single step every employee for your brand is making. Make good choices about the information you reveal.

Here's what you should keep to yourself:

- ✔ **Private correspondence:** If you're going to release e-mails, memos, and other correspondence, first make sure to get permission from everyone involved in said correspondence. Then make sure that this information is relevant.

- ✔ **Private conversations:** No one needs to know about arguments among team members or corporate gossip. Releasing this type of information may damage the brand and cause trust issues between you and your coworkers. Also, transparency doesn't mean that you should disclose off-the-record discussions.

Knowing what you can share

On the other hand, your community members enjoy feeling as though they're part of the brand. Knowing about product launches before anyone else, for example, makes them feel special and rewarded for their loyalty. Responding to questions without hesitating or beating around the bush ensures their trust. It's okay to disclose information and be honest with your community.

What follows are some of the ways you should be transparent with your community.

- ✔ Teases and leaks regarding new products, services, content, or members of the team are fun and create buzz around your community and brand.

- ✔ Always disclose when earning money on an affiliate link, or if free product has been sent to you for review or promotion.

- ✔ Disclose community goals and purpose behind the community.

- ✔ Disclose the name behind the brand — that is, the person who posts on the Facebook page, Twitter account, and other channels.

- ✔ Take disclosure on a case-by-case basis, depending on customer inquiries and comments.

Transparency doesn't mean the general public needs to be privy to every internal discussion held by your organization. It simply means being honest about who you are and what you do.

Being honest with your community

Transparency doesn't mean a blog post each day giving away company secrets. However, honesty does mean answering questions and responding to negativity truthfully and without anger. When you're asked why some members were banned or why profanity isn't allowed, for example, you don't respond, "Because I said so." You say honestly and respectfully that the community reflects the brand and that you have to maintain a positive image.

Also, if you're asked whether if it's true that a particular product is being recalled or that someone within your organization made a very public gaffe, you respond truthfully, even if you can't give out certain bits of confidential information. Say something like this: "Yes, that happened. I wish I could tell you more at this time, but I'm not at liberty to do so. However, I'm learning as much as I can about the situation, and I hope to have some answers for you soon."

Here's the thing: Your community members invest a lot of time in your brand. You owe it to them to treat them as equals and to be honest with them. Backpedaling, tap-dancing around issues, or pretending that you didn't read or hear something are insults to their intelligence.

Also consider these best practices regarding being transparent with your community:

- ✔ If you're not sure how to respond to something or don't know whether you're even allowed to address it, discuss it with your team and your superiors first.
- ✔ Address criticism and rumor head on without sweeping it under the rug.
- ✔ Respond to questions and inquiries honestly. At times, you may have to reveal information that hasn't been released to the rest of the world in order to rectify a situation. For example, if a customer tells you that she doesn't like a particular aspect of your product and you're planning to discontinue it, you may want to reveal that information to make the customer happy and continue the trust.

Looking at the TMI factor

Do you know the difference between honesty and too much information? Honesty means that you're being true to your community by giving responses that answer the questions, not avoiding the issues. Too much information (TMI) means that you're sharing private information that doesn't need to go beyond family members or your offline inner circle of friends.

Avoid providing too much information by following these guidelines:

- ✔ Your community doesn't need to know about your sex life or your relationship status.

- ✔ Telling anecdotes related to the day's topic is fine, but no one needs a play-by-play account of what you do in your offline life unless it's relevant to the topic at hand.

- ✔ No one needs to see you in sexy clothes or a sexy pose.

- ✔ Religion and politics have no place in your forum unless it's a religious or political forum.

Admitting mistakes with grace

At times, you or someone involved with your brand missteps or makes a public mistake. It wouldn't be the first time, and it won't be the last. Everyone makes mistakes. From the CEO to the mailroom, someone is going to screw up sometime because it's human nature. Not every mistake needs to be outed to the community, but every now and then, an apology or explanation is needed.

Say what you have to say, answer questions, and move on. Don't put it off and don't minimize the issue.

Take the following steps to address the situation and move on.

1. **Check with your brand before you say anything.**

   You're going to have to check with your brand before making public statements that admit to mistakes. The company may want to check with its legal department to make sure that your mistake — and the subsequent admission of it — aren't lawsuit-worthy. The company may even want to approve the wording of the public disclosure. In this case, you won't be speaking in your own voice or using your own words, which can lead to an awkward situation, but it may be absolutely necessary.

2. **Own up to your mistake.**

3. **Don't make excuses.**

4. **Make apologies as necessary.**

5. **Move on.**

   Dwelling on things only prolongs the agony.

Appointing peer moderators

Sometimes negative situations arise because the community manager can't be everywhere at once. Bigger communities need someone on hand at all times, especially if it has a history of members sniping at each other. When Demand Media Studios, a popular writing community with thousands of members, experienced regular fighting and pettiness among community members, they appointed several moderators from within the community. These volunteers were recruited from positive, productive members of the community and used to help keep the peace while the community manager was handling other things. By appointing community peers as moderators, DMS showed their community the following:

✔ Its members are all equals.

✔ DMS cares about having a community that gets along.

✔ Even though the community manager is off planning an offline promotion or community charity project, someone is still there to make sure that they all get along. People, especially grownups, groan when they learn they're going to have to abide by rules and regulations. The truth is there are rules of etiquette and proper behavior everywhere we go. An online community is no different.

Even if you don't need permission and don't have to go through the legal department to admit a mistake, as the voice of the community, you're still the person to whom people will come to with both anger and good wishes. You may be worried about how making a public disclosure or responding to negativity will make you look to your community and the public. Know that these things always blow over, usually in a matter of days. Brands that are transparent are more easily forgiven than brands that sweep things under the rug. Also, your community will appreciate your honesty.

A little humor goes a long way. Don't make a mockery of the situation, but don't take yourself too seriously all the time.

Rectifying a negative situation within the community

Not all negativity is worthy of a public address. Many times, situations arise from misunderstandings during discussions or community events. The situation may not even have anything to do with you or your brand, but because it happened within your community, it's up to you to iron things out. Here's what you need to do:

1. **Assess the situation.**

   Don't jump to conclusions and don't dive in blind. Follow the trail of events. Find out who all the players are and read all the comments, feedback, and discussions relating to the event.

2. **Determine whether the situation should be handled publicly or taken private.**

   If the negativity involves only one or two people, it may be easiest to settle matters during a conference call or Skype chat. If the issue has become a community free-for-all, a public discussion may be necessary.

3. **Never take sides.**

   Although you may be able to identify a clear instigator or scapegoat, taking sides only escalates the situation.

4. **Listen.**

   Hear all sides of the story, from the major players to eyewitnesses. Try to assess who is being truthful and who is simply backing up a friend.

5. **Ask questions.**

   You may know all the answers from watching the situation unfold, but ask questions anyway. Your community wants to know that you care.

6. **Take action.**

   The action may be an apology on your part; an apology on someone else's part; a new rule; or a perk such as a discount, freebie, or free membership offered to an offended member. Determine how to make things right and take the appropriate action.

7. **Move on.**

   When the situation has been handled and everyone is satisfied, move on. Don't dwell on it or discuss it inappropriately with other members of the community.

Part III

Building a Productive Online Community

The 5th Wave   By Rich Tennant

"Just how accurately should my online community reflect my place of business?"

In this part . . .

Online communities are vital to any brand. Members share feedback and help to create a word-of-mouth marketing campaign. Part III touches on what happens when the members of an online community work together and with the brand.

Chapter 5

Getting Started with Your Online Community

. . . .

In This Chapter

▶ Working with other communities

▶ Pinpointing your membership

▶ Picking up operating tips

. . . .

*Y*ou can't take any action within your community without knowing something about them. It's important to learn who you're readers are, who you're selling to, who makes up an audience, and exactly why the people in your community are joining up. If you have no desire to learn anything about the people who gather in your networks, you may as well close shop right now.

Learning about people goes way beyond knowing how they like to drink their coffee. Knowing demographics, such as age, sex, income range, location, education and career experience, can also help you pinpoint the majority of your community members' wants and needs. For example, you wouldn't run the same promotional campaign for 20-year-olds that you would for the over-50 crowd. You also wouldn't market to a high-end community the same way you would a working class crowd.

In this chapter, I tell you what you need to know to get your community off the ground and running.

Finding Your Target Audience Online

Though your community may be diverse, you can't target them without finding some sort of common ground for the majority.

✔ If 75 percent of your community eats cereal for breakfast, that's common ground.

✔ If 80 percent of your community is over the age of 36, that's common ground.

✔ If most of your community prefers coffee over tea, that's common ground.

✔ If 90 percent of your community is made up of parents of elementary school children, that's common ground.

✔ If 95 percent of your community is male, that's common ground.

✔ If 75 percent of your community enjoys country music, that's common ground.

Part of your job as community manager is to capture this information and run with it. Your marketing team can't properly target your community with campaigns without even this basic information. Knowing the predominant gender, marital status, and age of your community members already gives you a starting point.

People notice poor targeting and they take issue when you appear not to know who they are. Take the time to learn who you're catering to, and once you do it will become much easier to create campaigns bringing results.

Finding the right people for your community

So how do you find your target community? Do you stand on top of a building with a megaphone and tell everyone to visit your website? Do you drop spammy links in other communities or networks? Do you send mass e-mails to everyone on the web?

Of course not. None of the above.

The key to finding the right people for your community is to learn where they hang out, their wants, needs and things they do for entertainment, and common ground. People don't like it when they're targeted for something they don't have any business being a part of so it's important to take your research seriously.

The key to community recruitment is in building relationships. Nothing is more of a turnoff than an obvious pitch.

Have a conversation and see where that takes you.

Reaching out to bloggers

Bloggers as community evangelists are a wonderful match. Not only do they have the potential to join your community, but they have their own established communities as well. If they like what they see and like what you do, they'll recommend your community to their community which has the potential to add many new members.

You can reach out to bloggers in a variety of ways, but the best way is to build a relationship. Comment on the blogs, but don't make it about your business. The nice thing about participating at blogs is that if the members there like what you have to say, they'll follow your link and perhaps join your community.

You can also offer to guest post on another blog and even invite that blogger to create guest content on your own site. Again, your post shouldn't necessarily about your community but relevant to the blog's focus. At the end of your post you can leave a brief bio about who you are, what you do, and include a link back.

If you have a nice list of bloggers who you feel are a good fit for your community, you can also reach out to them by mail, and here's where it gets a bit tricky. Obvious form letters and spam. as well as sales pitches and campaigns that aren't a proper fit, are a sore spot for bloggers.

First and foremost, make sure that your community and the blogger's community are somehow related to each other. If you reach out to a book blogger to invite her to your fried chicken community, not only will you get an angry response, you may find yourself ridiculed on the social networks.

Once you find an appropriate match:

1. **Introduce yourself.**

2. **Talk a little about your brand and community:**

3. **Note the connections between you're the blogger's community and yours.**

4. **Discuss why you think it would be a good idea to work together.**

5. **Make it less about you than the blogger.**

   Let her know how the campaign will benefit her and her brand.

6. **Leave contact information so that you can discuss.**

7. **Follow up in a week or two.**

Using the social networks

You're going to find that when it comes to bringing in new members for your community you'll have to rely on the fine art of conversation. "Hey y'all come join my awesome community" is never going to fly. Like blogging, social networking is about building relationships and seeing where they take you:

✓ Follow or friend the people and brands you feel will benefit to your community.

✓ See what they're saying and respond in kind.

✓ As folks begin to follow you ask questions and interact.

✓ Share some links — not only to your content, but other interesting topics relating to your niche.

✓ Make sure that your content (tweets, status updates, and so on) is more conversation than links.

✓ Take part in hashtag chats on Twitter where you may even be encouraged to talk about your community.

✓ Join Facebook fan pages and discussion groups to take part in the conversation and hopefully drive traffic to your community.

✓ Every now and then, invite folks from your community and the social networks to participate in a comment thread, contest, promotion, or debate that's taking place in your community.

Notice how there's no real pitching going on? Working the social networks and building relationships is one of the favorite community management tasks because you're spending time chatting up some truly terrific people.

Most of the people who join your community aren't going to join your community because you asked them, but they may follow you there from somewhere else. Be sure your bio or profile says a bit about you or the brand and links to your community. New members like to think they discovered a great new spot, even if they don't want to admit you guided them there in the first place.

Visiting other online communities

Like the social networks, it's okay to join other online communities and participate in the conversations as long as you're not being spammy or stepping on another community manager's toes. Simply take part in the discussion.

I can tell you that if join up and say to everyone that you're interested in the community in order to drive traffic to your own community, you'll get called out on it. However, if you're there to take part in the discussion and enjoy the company, you have a better chance of having other follow you back to your community.

Here's the thing: Though you're actively recruiting new members, you're not there on some covert operation to take over someone else's community and steal their members. Your purpose is to build relationships with people who may also be interested in your brand. You're not there to steal, snark, spam, or make waves with the other community's manager. You're there to have a conversation and see what comes of it.

The trust factor comes in when you've participated for a little while and folks see that you have good advice, or that you're witty or making other productive contributions to the conversation.

Promoting without spamming

Did you know that a lot of the people who spam online have no idea they're spamming? They either think they're sharing something very cool or that it's okay because they're being paid to do it by someone else who knows all the rules. Of course, some unsavory people spam, know they spam, and don't care that they do so, but some people are a little green and not sure how this whole online promotion thing works.

Here's a good rule: If you're jumping from network to network, community to community, blog to blog and dropping links and not doing much else, you're spamming, not promoting.

It's spamming when

- ✔ You set up a Twitter search to ping you when certain words or keywords are mentioned so that you can immediately send a link to a sales page.
- ✔ You send out mass e-mails that sell, without getting permission from each and every one on your mailing list.
- ✔ You comment on a blog with a sales pitch and a link.
- ✔ You stop in to a forum and say, "Hey! Check out my stuff!" with a link.
- ✔ Your Twitter stream or Facebook status page is nothing but links.
- ✔ You give a sales pitch to people without their permission.

On the other hand, it's promoting when

- ✔ You send your customers or community members a newsletter they have opted in to receive.

- ✔ You have an active Twitter stream filled with conversations with friends and community members, and every now and then you share a link to a promotion or blog post — either yours or someone else's.

- ✔ You offer a discount code on your Facebook page.

- ✔ You comment on blogs or forums without selling and use a link in the appropriate signature line.

- ✔ You take the time to have a conversation with people, build up relationships, and every now and then invite those people to take part in a conversation or promotion within your community.

- ✔ You give a public address and talk about what you do in a very brief bio synopsis or during the last PowerPoint slide.

Can you see the difference now? Spamming is when you're pitching or selling to people without their permission. It's when you make a pest of yourself and drop links at other communities without asking the host if it's ok.

Promotion is when you have something to sell or share with others but you do so in a way that's non-invasive or annoying

Borrowing Ideas the Right Way

Have you ever seen a product or idea and wish you had thought of it? In the online world, people borrow from one another all the time. I'm not talking about outright stealing, but taking inspiration from other people.

Beyond the rules of manners and etiquette, though, there are legal implications when it comes to other people's stuff. Plagiarism and copyright infringement are two things you need to think about before you borrow anything online.

Giving credit where credit is due

Have you ever used Google Images to find a picture to illustrate a blog post or community newsletter? Before downloading the picture, did you ask the photographer for permission, and after receiving permission, did you give him or her credit? You'd be surprised how many people think "online" means "help yourself."

Crowdsourcing for creative ideas

Have you ever gotten on Twitter to ask for answers to a question or used a forum to help brainstorm ideas? If so, you were *crowdsourcing* — taking advantage of collaborative brainstorming.

There are different types of crowdsourcing. For example, sometimes businesses will ask a community for design ideas or help creating a catchphrase. Sometimes it's actually for a high-profile job, and the crowdsourcing is more like an audition. In this case, you're likely going to be crowdsourcing for feedback, ideas, and content.

Crowdsourcing can be another way to solicit feedback for your brand, but it can also be a way to gather some creative ideas that your team can run with:

✔ Get your community's opinion on logo designs and have them vote on their favorites.

✔ Invite members to taste test new ideas and vote on which ones will launch.

✔ Have a tagline contest.

✔ Ask your community what new products and services they'd most like to see.

✔ Find out issues facing your community regarding your specific topic or niche.

✔ Ask for productivity tips, synonyms or other types of advice.

✔ Ask what your community most wants to learn from your content.

✔ Ask what sort of discussion topics they enjoy least and what you've done to death.

✔ Use your community to help choose new designs for product packaging and websites.

You can also encourage crowdsourcing among community members so they can brainstorm ideas and collaborate on projects. Harness the power of your community and you may be very pleasantly surprised.

Ditto goes for any content online, whether it's a blog post, news article, or forum entry. When you're looking for content from online sources, it's illegal to cut and paste someone else's stuff and use it on your own website. It's even worse to let everyone assume that you're the source of the aforementioned content. If you don't have permission, don't use it. Passing someone else's content off as your own is illegal and unethical.

What about borrowing other types of ideas? The idea may not be copyrighted, and the borrowing may not even be obvious, but if you want to use someone else's idea for something you want to do, give a shout out to the person who gave you the inspiration in the first place.

Suppose that another community had a scavenger hunt. Members had to find various items posted throughout the content, and everyone who found an item was entered into a drawing. Maybe you have a content-heavy community, and you'd like to do the same thing. It's not unethical to do something similar, but it's good juju and unwritten etiquette to give props to the place where you saw the idea. You don't have to make a billboard or shout from the rooftops, but the first time you announce or discuss your contest, you can say something like "We saw a similar type of contest over at Joe's Community and thought it might appeal to you as well." Link to Joe to let him know you're giving him the credit, too.

If the idea was unique, and it's very apparent that you're borrowing, contact the person who dreamed up the idea and mention that you'd like to try something similar. Usually, you'll get that person's blessing, but it's a nice thing to do to ask. The other person may even help you promote your contest.

If you blatantly rip off someone else's idea, someone will recognize it and call you out on the social networks. Give credit where it's due and don't use anyone else's content without permission.

Doing the same thing differently

Rather than take someone else's ideas outright, try to riff on the same idea, but not so much that it's obvious you're not the brain behind the brainstorm. Ideas are there for the taking, but wouldn't you much rather be seen as someone who's innovative, not someone who scours the web for ideas to steal?

Consider an idea from an online community I used to own to see how many different slants you can take on the same contest. A few years ago, I wanted to change the look of my community's home page, so I had a photo contest. The winner of the contest received a cash prize, and the photo (with credit) appeared as part of the logo on the home page for all to see. For many people, the prize was the money, but for the photographer, who was looking to make a name for herself and build her portfolio, the prize was her photograph displayed on the number one community in its niche. This contest was very well received and brought the community members together because they voted for the image.

Now brainstorm some ways to do the same contest differently:

- ✔ Instead of having a photo contest, have a logo contest, an essay contest, a web-design contest, or even a contest that has nothing to do with changing the look of your community at all, such as a limerick or haiku contest.

- ✔ Instead of a cash prize, the winner can receive a case of your product, a desirable item such as an iPad or laptop, or gift cards.

- ✔ Instead of having the community members vote on the winner, you can appoint a panel of judges.

Now no one can accuse you of doing the same thing. You took inspiration from an idea but ran with it, making it more appropriate for your community and your budget.

Collaborating with Other Online Communities

The fun doesn't have to stay on your forum, blog, or Facebook page. In the online world, the possibilities are endless. You can even team up with other communities for a little cross-promotional fun. It's a way to bring in new members and create awareness around both your brands.

Too many people see similar communities as competitors, and though there's some element of truth to this, it's important to know that *competitor* doesn't have to mean something bad. Your competitors also have the ability to become collaborators and colleagues.

Members shouldn't have to choose one community or the other; when you and another combine your efforts, you have the ability to reach more people.

The best communities take a "more the merrier" approach to both the number of people in one community and the number of communities gathering together for a cause or promotion.

Don't be afraid to approach so-called competitors. You may walk away pleasantly surprised and ready to produce a kickin' joint campaign.

Meeting other community managers

Thanks to a variety of communities for community managers, as well as blogs and social networks, it's easy to hook up with other community managers for a little conversation and commiseration. The best part is that other community managers want to meet you, too. They want to talk about issues facing community managers and discuss methods for bringing in new members or launching promotions.

Many terrific resources are available to enable you to meet up with others who manage online communities. Most community managers join these groups and chats or attend conferences for the same reason as you, so collaboration with them won't be a hard sell.

Here are a few ideas for collaborating with other community managers:

- Follow the `#cmgrchat` hashtag on Twitter for weekly discussions among community managers.

- The Community Roundtable is a prestigious community for community managers. Visit `http://community-roundtable.com` or follow @TheCR on Twitter.

- e-mint is a community-manager Yahoo! Group based in the United Kingdom but accepting members globally. Sign up at `http://tech.groups.yahoo.com/group/e-mint`.

- Community Manager, Advocate, and Evangelist is a popular Facebook discussion group for community managers. Join at `www.facebook.com/home.php?sk=group_3553055120&ap=1`.

- The Community Manager (`http://thecommunitymanager.com`) is a resource and community for community managers.

- Conferences — especially those geared to social media, blogging, technology, and online communities — are terrific ways to meet other community managers. Some conferences to attend are South by Southwest (SXSW) Interactive, BlogWorld & New Media Expo, the Online Community Unconference, and the Community Leadership Summit. As the dates of these conferences change each year, do an online search to find out when they'll be coming around next.

Holding contests for cross-promotion

Have you noticed that the most creative campaigns also get the best responses? When you think outside the box and embrace new people or communities, you're bound to come up with some epic ideas that get epic results.

Consider the other online communities that will benefit most from cross-promotion. Also consider whether you should work with a community that has a similar theme and content, or whether if it's more beneficial to both communities to seek partners elsewhere.

Reach out to a community manager you'd like to work with. Understand that it may take a few days or even longer for him to gain approval from his superiors. You'll also need approval before embarking on a campaign with another business or brand to make sure that no political or legal issues are involved. After everyone has signed off on whatever needs to be signed, you can get down to business:

✔ Determine what your communities have in common.

✔ Look into the demographics of each community so that promotional campaigns are a good fit for both.

✔ Spend time visiting with the other community to get a good idea of how its members interact and the sorts of things they enjoy.

✔ List the types of content and promotion that will benefit both communities.

✔ Research other communities that have run joint campaigns.

✔ Have regular brainstorming sessions with the manager of the other community.

✔ Set a launch date for contests and discuss ways you can both promote them.

✔ Consider creating a case study to present to team to discuss whether or not this type of campaign is worth it to do again.

A big contest between two communities should have a big prize. It seems anti-climactic to give away a free box of spaghetti or a discount coupon after all the fanfare. Make sure that it lives up to the hype.

Chapter 6

Communicating with Your Community

*F*or a community to truly be successful, the community manager has to be accessible. Being accessible means more than showing a regular presence in the various online networks. It also means being responsive on the many different communication channels. Your members enjoy finding out news about your brand. They especially appreciate knowing that if they have any questions about your brand, products, or services, their inquiries won't go unanswered.

In this chapter, I discuss the various ways community managers communicate with their communities and why that communication is so important.

Making Yourself Accessible

Nothing is more frustrating than wanting to reach out to someone at a brand or business and not being able to find any kind of contact details. Because you're considered to be a spokesperson for your business, you're the person your community will want to reach out to. Thus, you need to post contact information where your members can easily locate it.

Here are a few ways to share contact information with your community:

✔ **Blogs:** Post contact details on About or Contact pages, which should be listed in tabs at the top or in the sidebar of each blog page.

✔ **Forums:** Create a *sticky,* which is a geeky term for a forum folder that doesn't move from the top of the page. Most forums have main Welcome folders that contain any rules and regulations, as well as a place for new members to introduce themselves. Place your sticky contact-information subfolder in the Welcome folder so that new members can find you easily and older members remember how to find you.

✔ **Facebook pages:** Use the profile function to list contact details in the information area on your page. Contact details will appear on your company Facebook page's sidebar. To add your information to your sidebar, click Edit Pages and look for the "Basic Information" function. Click Basic Information and add your contact details to the appropriate spot (see Figure 6-2).

✔ **Twitter:** Twitter profiles don't have much room for contact details, though you can squeeze them in if you're so inclined. You can also create and upload a Twitter background page that lists all your contact details so that people know how to get in touch with you. Several free and paid Twitter background services are available on the web if you're not sure how to do add this information on your own. A few good places to find Twitter backgrounds are Twitbacks.com, Twitrbackgrounds.com, and TwitRounds.com.

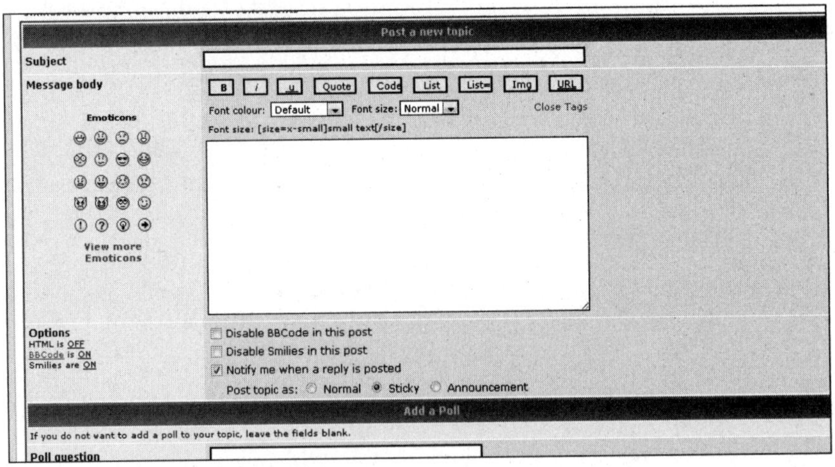

Figure 6-1:
Using your forum's administration tools, create a static or sticky folder for important information.

Most social networks have profile or bio areas where you can add as much or as little information about your company as you like. Be careful not to list too many personal details, as you don't want people contacting you at home (trust me, if they can, they will) or via improper channels.

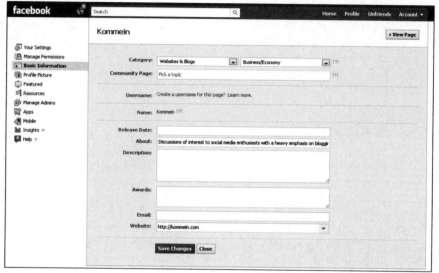

Figure 6-2:
By using Facebook's Edit Pages function, you can list your contact information, and it will appear in the right sidebar of your Facebook page.

Post contact information at eye level so that members don't have to scroll up or down to read it and they can see it at a glance.

Deciding on a Communication Method

You can communicate with community members via various means. You can also publicly post contact details for some or all of these methods.

E-mail

Of all the methods of communication that you'll use as a community manager, e-mail is most important because most customers still prefer to use e-mail as their primary communication method after the phone.

If you're worried about community comments, questions, and complaints mixing in with other business e-mail, you can create a separate e-mail address for feedback only.

Phone

You may not want to list your phone number in your contact information, because if you do, your phone might ring off the hook. Still, some situations can be resolved only with a phone call. In such a case, make an appointment to call the other party or parties.

Snail mail

Some people prefer physical mail (aka *snail mail)*, and it's only right to accommodate them. Also, listing a mailing address on your website makes your company seem more real. You probably won't receive much snail mail, but it's always a good idea to post your business location somewhere on your website. Many businesses and individuals still send thank-you notes, catalogs, coupons, product samples, and important correspondence via snail mail.

Regular community chat sessions

Live chats are extremely valuable for growing community and creating trust between you, the company you work for, and the people who make up your community. Keep in mind that these sessions require a bit of a commitment as you have to promote the event, invite the community, and moderate the chat.

Many community managers choose to have regular chats once a month or every quarter because they take up so much time, but all agree they're worth it to keep up the community morale.

Live community chats are terrific ways to reach more than one person at a time. Consider these events to be town-hall meetings in which you provide updates and answer your community members' questions.

Chats can be weekly or monthly events, but if you plan to hold them regularly, be sure to schedule them at the same time and day of the week so that community members consider them to be part of their routines.

Many forums host regular chats with team leaders or prominent members of the community. Simply create a host folder for the live chat and use the forum's announcement folder to alert the community to the day and time. On the day of the chat, create a thread where community members can ask questions and you or your guest of honor can respond. The beautiful thing about forums is that the transcripts remain in the folder for members to view on demand.

Skype

A live Skype conversation is easy to follow, and you can even save the transcripts and post for community members to access later. What sets Skype apart from other chat methods is that members have to commit in advance so you can individually invite them to the chat. If you have a regularly scheduled chat, most members can save the account so that they don't have to receive invites every time. Choose a different topic for each chat so that they're not a free for all and bring in special guests to make them more interesting.

Skype (download at Skype.com) is a popular form of instant messaging. If a community member has a question that needs an instant response, you can arrange a Skype chat with him via voice, video, or text. Most community managers don't list their Skype names as they don't want to be pinged throughout the day. However, it's not unheard of to make Skype appointment only or list certain Skypeable hours. Skype does come with Invisible and Do Not Disturb settings so you can make it clear that you're not available, if you're too busy. You can also use Skype for community chats.

You may not want to publicly list your Skype name, on your contact page as you may not want to be pinged throughout the day. Alternatively, you can make Skype appointment-only or list certain hours when you can be reached via Skype. The service has "invisible" and "do not disturb" settings that you can activate when you're too busy to chat.

Twitter

You may have noticed your friends and followers using *hashtags* (#) to follow particular topics on Twitter. Hashtags work especially well for live chats because they allow anyone to search for and isolate the tags in their Twitter applications.

For a popular example of a hashtag chat, check out #blogchat every Sunday at 9 p.m. Eastern time. Use Tweetchat.com or Tweetgrid.com as an easy way to participate in Twitter chats.

Facebook

Many Facebook communities host chats for their members or those who "like" their pages. In fact, participants can keep track of the chat from their own Facebook status pages. Because Facebook updates tend to fall off status pages after a while, it's best to announce upcoming chats every day for a week in advance. At the time of the chat, start a post to receive questions and comments from the community and respond in kind.

Be mindful of posting too many posts on your community Facebook page. Members will unlike the page if they see to many status updates from a brand. For a Facebook chat, try and use the same post or thread for a Q&A so members statuses aren't cluttered with posts from your brand.

Online groups

Both Yahoo! and Google allow you to create groups. Groups allow you to keep conversations going without having to worry about members' schedules. They're simple to use; community members can sign up just by clicking a link. For a moderated group, you have to approve each new member. But moderating a group is recommended over letting people in without approval, because unmoderated groups are spam magnets.

The downside of groups is that you receive an e-mail every time someone posts a question or response.

Answering Common Questions

You may notice that as your community grows, you're asked the same questions over again. Though you may roll your eyes and think "Not again," you can't fault new members for not knowing the same things that established members do. Thus, you want to be as gracious as possible with your responses.

Many community managers create questions-and-answers (Q&A) or frequently-asked-questions (FAQ) areas to avoid repeating responses several times over. The areas allow members to browse questions and answers at their convenience. Both types of areas have benefits:

✔ **Q&A:** A Q&A area allows members to ask questions as they come to mind. They don't have to hunt around for your contact info, and you know to check the area each day and respond to all questions. A prominent Q&A area also helps keep e-mail inquiries to a minimum. New members can read past questions and answers so that they don't have to ask the same things.

✔ **FAQ:** An FAQ area doesn't require as much effort as a Q&A area does. You post all questions and answers in a read-only document for members to read and digest at their convenience. Having an FAQ area doesn't mean that you shouldn't be open to questions from community members, but you can recommend that they read the FAQs before asking questions. As new questions come in, you can add them to the document.

Post your FAQ or Q&A area in a prominent location where members can't help but find it:

✔ **Forums:** Post FAQs in your Welcome folder. This folder gives new members a starting point and ensures that they read the questions before getting started. It's also an easy place for older members to remember. Make sure that the FAQs are sticky so that they remain at the top of the page.

✔ **Blogs and websites:** Pages on blogs and websites are excellent venues for FAQs. Make sure that FAQs are on static pages instead of blog post pages. Posts aren't sticky and tend to fall off the front page, but pages stay where they are. Set your FAQ page so that it's an easy-to-find tab or link at the top of each page or in a sidebar.

✔ **Groups:** Many Yahoo! and Google groups have areas for storing files and photos to share with members. These areas are the perfect locations for storing community FAQs. A good example is Freecycle.org's Yahoo group, which has several documents that people must read and agree to before becoming active members.

✔ **Social networks:** It's difficult to post static FAQs on the social networks, as they're not live chats, and most social networks don't lend well to static pages. You can link to a static question page in your information area, however, or refer members to that area from time to time.

✔ **E-mail:** Some community managers e-mail welcome packages to new members. These packages contain a welcome message, FAQs, and links to various places of interest in the community.

Responding to E-Mail from Community Members

It's frustrating to reach out to a business or brand representative and never receive a response. As community manager, it's your job to respond to or field questions and comments from the community. To not respond can be damaging to the brand, especially in today's social media world where disgruntled users and community members frequently call out brands for not meeting their needs. The last thing you want is to have a reputation for being unresponsive or inaccessible. Thus, it's important to respond to all e-mail in a timely manner.

Creating a members-only address

If you run a small community or receive very little e-mail each day, you'll probably be okay using your regular business e-mail account. If you receive large volumes of community e-mail, however, and it gets in the way of other business, you may want to create a separate address to separate internal or client e-mails from customer complaints and queries. Examples of e-mail accounts you can use are

✔ info@youraccount.com

✔ complaints@youraccount.com

✔ abuse@youraccount.com

✔ questions@youraccount.com

✔ admin@youraccount.com

The drawback of these types of e-mail addresses is that they're cold and impersonal. Community members and customers like to know who they're sending their inquiries to. When you list an e-mail address like the ones in the preceding list, it's best to personalize it with a message ("For questions, comments, or complaints, please contact Deb Ng at info@youraccount.com"). Now customers have a name to associate with the address.

WARNING!

If someone is taking the time to write to you, the reason is important to her, even if it doesn't seem so important to you. Thus, it's essential to treat all e-mailers with respect and not minimize their thoughts and concerns, no matter how petty you feel them to be. If you discard an e-mail or make someone feel silly for asking what you feel is a dumb question, your action can only lead to negative feelings. Treating each e-mail inquiry as though it's your most important piece of business for the day will help ensure trust and make the other party feel special and significant, which will reflect positively on your brand.

When you follow these e-mail best practices, they will soon become routine:

✔ **Set aside a specific hour each day for tackling e-mail.** When e-mail is on the schedule, it won't get overlooked.

✔ **Respond to all e-mail in a timely manner.** If you put e-mail aside to answer at a later date, it could fall through the cracks.

✔ **If you don't have an answer, find the person who does.** Don't leave the party at the other end hanging. Update him with the status of his inquiry. Say something like "I'm forwarding your question to a sales associate, but please let me know if you require further assistance" or "I'm sorry; I have to research the answer for that and should have an answer for you within the next day or so."

✔ **Follow up.** For simple questions and comments, a simple, one-time answer will do. For more complicated questions or complaints or if the customer is disgruntled, you may want to follow up. Wait a few days; then reach out to the person again and ask whether the problem has been resolved to her satisfaction. If not, see what you can do to make things right and reestablish the customer's faith in your brand.

When you respond to e-mail, your voice is everything. Keeping your tone positive and light will help provide a positive outcome. An accusatory, short, impatient, or condescending tone might make the recipient angry, which won't reflect well on you or your brand and may lead to backlash.

Creating Community Newsletters

There's no better method for providing updates, discounts, coupon codes, and community and brand information than the community newsletter. Customers often want to receive updates without participating in regular chats or social networking; newsletters keep them informed without their having to participate if they're not inclined to do so.

Using newsletters can lead to more sales as well as to community growth and trust. If your newsletter is sales-oriented, it encourages members to share deals with friends and family members who aren't on the mailing list. To encourage this sharing, simply say, "Share with a friend." Nonmembers not only may buy what you're selling, but also may be intrigued to find out more about the community and even participate in it.

Community newsletters are generally opt-in affairs, which means that no one is on the mailing list unless she signed up for it after following a link in the Welcome folder of a forum or a form on a blog or website.

One thing you don't want to do is put members on a newsletter mailing list without their permission, because you'll be crossing the line from community manager to spammer.

You can create several types of community newsletters, from simple text documents to PDF files. Alternatively, you can use a popular online newsletter service such as ConstantContact.com or AWeber.com. These services require paid subscriptions, but they're worth it for the tools and customer support that they provide. Newsletters contain

- ✔ **News:** Product launches or updates, awards and accolades, press mentions, and news about community members and internal employees.

- ✔ **Promotional items:** Coupons, contests, coupon codes, discounts for community members only, and sales announcements.

- ✔ **Information of interest to your community and niche:** Tips, how-to articles, and informational articles.

- ✔ **Letters from the community:** Questions comments and testimonials from community members, used with permission.

- ✔ **Letters from the author or editor:** A greeting from the community manager, CEO, newsletter editor or someone in authority.

Successful newsletters are informational and engaging. If they don't offer much more than advertising, members will mark them as spam.

Using Blogs to Provide Updates

Businesses takes advantage of the different social media tools in order to provide updates to their customers. In addition to taking to the social networks to cultivate and keep in touch with community, businesses and brands are embracing blogs.

People often think of blogs as personal journals or hobby sites for writers to share their passion, but businesses have a lot to talk about as well. Because blogs have a conversational tone, aren't as antiseptic as press releases and news articles, and allow for comments and conversation, they're attractive to community members, who are happy to subscribe.

Plus, as the manager of a commercial blog, you never have a shortage of stuff to blog about:

- ✔ **Product news and updates:** Share news about product launches, beta launches, upgrades, and more with the members of your community. Unlike social-networking sites and even forums to some extent, blogs allow a higher word count so that you can get into specific details. (For more information on sharing news about new product, see the section "Introducing Products to Your Community.")

- ✔ **Brand-related news:** Even if you have no news to report about your company, you always have brand-related news to share. If your company makes chocolate bars, for example, and a new species of cocoa bean has been discovered on a remote mountain in South America, this topic certainly is blogworthy. It also interests members who don't care to read only product information.

✔ **Inside information:** Give readers a glance at the inner working of your company. Let them know what a typical day is like in each department. Show videos featuring brainstorming sessions or product manufacturing. Transparency is a good thing, and your readers will appreciate knowing that the folks behind the scene are human.

✔ **Contests and promotions:** Alert your community members to sales, giveaways, contests, and other product promotions by blogging about them.

✔ **Photo essays:** Post images of coworkers, the company picnic, or points of interest within your company headquarters. Host photo contests for your community members and get them involved as well.

✔ **Issues regarding products, services, or bad press:** Use the company blog to address any bad press or issues that have come up regarding your business. This practice will create dialogue between you and your community members and ensure members' trust.

Introducing Products to Your Community

If you're a product-oriented brand, one reason to gather a community together is so they can find out about new products. The problem is, if socializing online isn't fun and everyone feels every interaction is going to be a sale pitch, they're going to stop feeling the love after a while. Mind you, most people are pretty smart and can figure out the community's purpose. They know it's all about the sale; they just don't want it to be so obvious, especially if they're giving up their spare time.

Introducing a new product without being overly pitchy about it is hard, but if you're creative about it, your community will be receptive to the launch and not have to wash off a dirty feeling afterwards. Have some fun with your community. You'll find that they're up for anything that's in good taste.

You can also try teasing them. Each day, drop a hint about what might be coming along with the launch date so that they know it's something big. Some members may guess, and some may not, but setting them up a week or two in advance will create some buzz and anticipation.

You might also give them some sort of discount or free product coupon and invite them come back to a specific spot to offer feedback about the community. They'll appreciate being able to tell you exactly what they think of your new product.

To get more people buying and create an even bigger buzz, find out how people are using your product. Ask for pictures, videos, recipes, and testimonials.

Product launches don't have to be boring or spammy. When you involve a community of people who trust you and your brand, you already have a network of people eager to try what you're selling. Give them the first shot at it at no charge, as this insider offer will make them feel special and important. Let them know feedback is essential and follow up to make sure that you hear from everyone.

If all goes well, your members will be talking about the product on all the networks and channels, and other people are going to want to see what the fuss is about.

With the right social media campaign, your launch can be huge.

Offering Deals, Discounts, and Promotions to Your Community

If you're bringing together a community around your brand, in order to drive sales, build buzz, and create awareness, it would be a total downer for them to receive nothing out of the arrangement at all. For product-oriented brands, your members are there because they hope to receive some sort of perk, such a product samples or discounts, for being a participant in the community. For others, it's to discover more about the brand or share tips for hobbies and careers. Your community is hoping to receive something of value from your community, so you need to consider how you'll provide that for them.

One way brands reward community members is to offer them stuff the general public won't receive — things like special coupons or coupon codes, free products, and giveaway items. You also might offer them swag, such as branded keychains, t-shirts, hats, and other promotional products. Even if everyone doesn't like what you're offering, they will appreciate the gesture because they feel like they're getting something in return for their participation.

Most products and perks offered to the community don't break the bank. You can use coupon codes and sales for community members frequently and entice others into joining your community as well.

Your community has no obligation to talk about or promote their coupons or swag. Their participation in the community should be enough. Therefore, unless specified, they shouldn't be expected to blog about, tweet about, link to, or otherwise promote a product after it has been offered to them out of the goodness of your heart. Generally, word-of-mouth marketing takes care of itself. If you've given your members a bargain, they'll talk about it on their own anyway. These perks and discounts are a way to give back to the people who are so supportive of your brand.

Creating Brand Awareness

Though your brand may be a recognizable name, you don't want to stop at name recognition. Brand awareness is more than having people recognize your logo. You want them to immediately know what it is you do and what sets you apart from the rest. Anyone can have a big name. It's what you do with that name that makes you special.

Often times, brand awareness is created not by the brand but rather the people who use the brand. They share and recommend products, they promote viral videos, they retweet fun phrases, and they post news to their Facebook statuses. Keep your tribe posted and make it newsworthy and shareworthy. You'll find most of the branding isn't done by you.

To create brand awareness:

- **Get people talking.** Do you recommend products and services to your friends and family when you feel you're getting a good deal or you walked away with a good experience? If so, you're helping spread the brand's message, just the same as you hope your community hopes to share your own brand's message. The best way to create brand awareness is to have a product, service, website, blog, or community worth talking about. If customers are receiving something of value, whether that's money savings or top-notch customer service (or maybe they just dig the way your product tastes or works), they'll talk about you.

- **Receive feedback gracefully.** Don't sweep your feedback under the rug or roll your eyes if you don't like something someone said about your brand. That's valuable information right there. Every bit of negative feedback is a chance for improvement. When someone tells you something isn't working, you're now armed with the information to make it right. If you're open to feedback and willing to act on that feedback, your brand receives recognition as a trustworthy product backed by people who care.

- **Make sure that your customers receive more than they give.** If you offer a $10 product worth $10 or less, that's not a bargain. There's absolutely no value in an equal exchange. However, if you offer a $20 product for $10, now your discount has value. When you add a supportive community, caring community managers, and a product people like, you're adding more value to the pile. You don't want your customers to receive an equal exchange; you want them to receive something of value, and you want them to know you value their patronage and input.

- **Be honest.** Don't promise what you can't deliver and own up to your mistakes. Even if you make a mistake, your community and the people who believe in your brand will appreciate your truthfulness.

> ✔ **Update often.** The more people know, the more they share. Send them updates in the form of opt-in newsletters, tweets, blog posts, Facebook updates, forum updates, and more. If your news is interesting or fun, your community will share.

Sharing Hobbies and Interests through Online Communities

In the early days, online communities had very little to do with brands or profiting. They were places to share online. Before brands jumped onto the community bandwagon, it was more about gathering to discuss favorite hobbies, interests, and even career choices.

Though online community management is now more about brands and selling, plenty of communities aren't interested in either. They just want to talk about their favorite things, their jobs, or ways to do certain things better. In fact, one of the more popular online communities is the FlyLady Yahoo!, which offers household productivity tips to over 500,000 members.

The hobbyist or special-interest communities are a good lesson in why people really join online communities. When it's about the brand, folks want their discounts. When it's about a pastime, people want to talk as much as they can about the things they enjoy.

The benefits of these types of special-interest communities abound. They offer a place to

✔ Share tips and advice.

✔ Discover where to find rare or difficult to locate products.

✔ Find jobs.

✔ Discuss issues.

✔ Share news articles, videos, and more.

✔ Read or watch tutorials.

✔ Share a passion.

Through these types of communities, friendships and collaborations emerge. These groups are more like a family or group of old friends than a forum of people who don't even know each other. Members get to know each other individually and share and interact on an individual basis. These relationships flourish and expand throughout the various social networks and even offline. Almost every member will tell you these communities are a valuable experience.

Online communities go way beyond a conversation on a Facebook page. Harness the power of your own community, and you'll come up with some brilliant ideas.

Communicating Successfully

The most successful online communities are those that are active and with regular updates. They have a community manager that's front and center who is a positive, daily presence. The communities that receive the most criticism and the highest turnover rates are those without moderation where the most negative members are also the most vocal.

Keeping your communication regular

No one has to join an online community. They do so because they're interested in participating in discussions and learning more about what you have to offer. When you consider how many people are busy with work, family and household projects, online community participation isn't a priority. Thus, you have to create an environment worthy of their precious downtime.

The key to community success is to keep up a steady flow of activity:

- **Create daily discussion topics.** Whether you're on Twitter, Facebook, or an online forum, if you're not doing anything to encourage community participation, everyone will stop paying attention. Try throwing out a daily discussion topic. This topic doesn't have to be anything deep or controversial. Find some fun, lively questions to ask your group. Encourage members to respond to each other. The best communities are those where members interact even when the community manager is absent.

- **Hold regular contests and promotions.** Reward loyal members with prizes and giveaways. This competition will attract new members who come for the perks but stay for the conversation.

✔ **Respond to comments.** Community managers who take time to participate in discussion topics among community members and respond to comments, even conversations they didn't start, are held in high esteem. Participants enjoy knowing that someone in authority cares enough to take part.

✔ **Don't play favorites.** Online communities can seem a lot like the high school cafeteria in that there are different cliques and popularity levels among the members. Though cliques are discouraged and a community should participate together, they're unfortunately a fact of life. The worst thing a community manager can do is play favorites or be a prominent member of a clique. You're there as an advocate for the entire community, not just a select few.

✔ **Have a backup plan.** An absentee community manager can lead to some interesting situations. Perhaps some of the more colorful community members will try to get away with stuff that doesn't fly when you're an active presence, or members might drop by and see nothing happening and assume that the conversation is drying up. If you're busy or going to be away from the community for a long period of time, have a backup plan. Designate another moderator to come in and enjoy the community in your absence.

✔ **Host interviews and guest appearances.** Mix things up by bringing in guest speakers for webinars, interviews, and community chats.

✔ **Encourage community members to talk about themselves.** When it's all about the brand, things get a little boring. Ask community members about their interests and remember details about them for later conversation. They'll appreciate your taking the time to get to know them better.

The best communities are the ones where the members all know each other well but welcome new members, too. There's a steady flow of conversation and positivity. They're places where members come to relax and enjoy the company of others.

Promoting without spamming

Outreach to new members is possibly one of the less attractive community management tasks. You're expected to grow your community numbers, but we can't always do so organically. As a result, you have to reach out to others to bring them in. If you're not careful, you can cross the line into spam territory.

The key to successful outreach and community building is to not be annoying. If your Twitter stream is only links and you bombard the same people over and over again with e-mail, you're not going to get their buy-in.

Here's how to build your community without annoying potential members:

- **Link intelligently.** It's fine to link to online conversations, news, and events from within your company when using the social networks, but if your only social networking activity is to link to your own stuff, it's problematic. Most people unfollow anyone who spreads only links. Sharing links is okay, but make them interesting and relevant to the community and make sure that they're from a variety of related sources.

- **Find out what community members think.** For example, if you work for a company that manufactures beauty products, link to articles that offer beauty tips or ask what community members think about the use of particular ingredient. Link to images of celebrities and models using makeup the right way and wrong way and ask for thoughts or tips. Make your links fun and interesting, but don't always make it about you.

- **After the first e-mail, everything else is opt in.** Don't make a nuisance of yourself if you're running an e-mail campaign. A one-time invitation to participate in community events is fine as long as you're sure it's something the other person will enjoy. However, sending weekly letters urging attendance is more than spam; it's annoying.

  Invite people to participate but make sure that you offer a box to check off to receive future updates. Also, make sure that you include a box for the people who don't want updates or e-mail.

- **Always offer something in return.** If you're doing blogger outreach, for example, to get bloggers to join and talk about your community in order to bring in other members, you need to offer them something. Bloggers are weary about promoting stuff and putting their reputation on the line. Plus, why would they want to promote someone for no reason or no money? Offer a perk like a link on your website, forum, or newsletter. Or you can offer to do a Q&A with them to help them build their own brands.

When you're promoting your community, ask yourself, "Would I want to receive" all this e-mail or "Would I consider all these links or announcement annoying?" If it's not something you'd want to receive yourself, chances are no one else wants it either.

Using incentive programs

Customer or membership incentive programs bring in new members and reward existing members for their loyalty, especially in a product- or service-based community. For example, some Facebook communities offer discounts and coupons only to members of their page. These member-only offers make customers feel special and exclusive.

Here's how you can use word-of-mouth from incentive programs bring in new members:

- **Offer rewards for online customers only.** If you receive e-mail newsletters and online updates from your favorite catalog companies or retail shops, you may notice coupons and discount codes for online customers only. Because so many people are online, these rewards are not only a good way to drive sales to both online and offline stores, but it also helps with community growth as more folks join up and opt in to receive perks and socialize with other customers.

- **Utilize location-based rewards.** Location-based smart phone apps, such as foursquare and Gowalla, are ideal for rewarding customers who visit offline businesses. Once a member checks in by finding the business on the location-based app and clicking the button, he will then be able to unlock hidden rewards.

- **Hold online scavenger hunts.** Have a scavenger hunt and hide prizes among your various online haunts. Invite the community to find specific items hidden in blog posts, forum posts, tweets, and Facebook updates, or a mixture of each. Award prizes to the winners who find them all.

- **Award loyalty discount points.** Award points to community members for longevity and participation. They can then trade points for discounts, merchandise and prizes.

For most members of your community, the camaraderie of like-minded people is enough. Still, it's always a good idea to offer incentives to new members and reward the veterans for their loyalty.

Communicating with others in your niche

A community isn't only made up of people who are part of a particular forum, social network or blog. It can also be expanded to reach out to others in the same niche, even though they may socialize through different channels. For example, if you belong to a freelance writing forum, that forum is just a small aspect of the much larger freelance writing community which includes blogs, forums, and social networks within that niche. Rather than eyeballing other similar communities as competition, consider them colleagues or collaborators and do what you can to encourage cross-participation and promotion.

Suppose that you are the community manager for a large freelance writing social network featuring useful articles, a Facebook page where you post updates and communicate with your readers, and a forum where members discuss issues relating to other freelancer writers. You can grow relationships with others in the much larger freelance writing community by

✔ Inviting guest blog posts and articles from writers and bloggers from other freelance writing communities.

✔ Following freelance writers and community managers from other freelance writing communities on Twitter and participating in their discussions.

✔ Liking other freelance writing Facebook pages and participate in the festivities there.

✔ Attend outside offline events for freelance writers, including conferences, meetings, and seminars.

Here's something no one tells you about online communities: They don't happen on their own. You can't just set up a website or put up a social networking page and hope the world will show up. If people aren't invited, how will they know you're having a party? It's up to you to bring people in and keep them engaged and interested enough to continue to come back.

Chapter 7

Listening to Your Community

· ·

· ·

*Y*our community is your most important asset, as it's made up of customers or people who use your product or service on a regular basis. The opportunities here go far beyond selling because now you can receive in-depth information about their habits, including why they like your brand, where you need a little work, and where you're falling short.

Customer feedback takes on many different forms. It's not all gathered in letters to the customer service department or calls to your 800 hotline. People are talking about your brand online; sometimes they reach out to you directly, and sometimes it's in the form of a rant on a blog post or a tweet sharing how happy they are with a user experience.

Gathering and receiving feedback is one of your top tasks. You're expected to respond to each individual complaint or compliment (even if it's not your department) — and even fight for your community if you feel they're being slighted — while still remembering your number one loyalty is to your brand.

Gauging the Wants and Needs of Your Community

You may assume that your community's members are there to find out more about the product or service, interact with others, or receive discounts, but how can you know for sure?

You can discover what your community wants by being vigilant.

It's not enough to set up a community and have a nice chit-chat every day. Your community wants more, and it's up to you to find out what this "more" is. The most successful communities evolve and grow as their numbers grow. They do well because management is open to new ideas and takes all feedback into consideration.

Listening to Your Community

Learning about your community requires more than some survey questions or a poll. Sometimes, the best way to know what your community is thinking is to not seem so obvious about your intentions. Here's how to determine what your community really wants:

- ✔ **Observe.** Having an ear to the ground enables you to pick up on things you wouldn't otherwise catch. Members talk among themselves on your forum or community pages or on the other social networks. In a forum comment, for example, a member might mention how nice it would be to have a Thumbs Up button so that he can show his approval for other comments or links. Soon, other members add their thoughts about a Thumbs Up button in the same discussion thread. You wouldn't have known that so many people wanted this feature until it was mentioned as part of a community discussion.

- ✔ **Listen.** It's one thing to watch and a whole other thing to listen. During your rounds on the social networks, blogs, and community pages, pay attention to what people are saying. How many members are saying the same things? Members won't come to you with every concern or request, but they may share ideas with one another. Pay attention to what they're saying and take notes. When you hear that you're doing something well, think about how to do it better. When you hear less than stellar remarks, think about how you can make things right.

- ✔ **Check the stats.** Stats and analytics may look like a bunch of numbers, but they're also a valuable glimpse into your community's habits. These stats, or web analytics, help you find out where new members are coming from, who is linking to you and why, and how long people are sticking around. I discuss stats in Chapters 12 and 13.

 Observing your community unearths valuable feedback about its needs, even if it's not originally directed at you. However, that doesn't mean you should rush and take action for every comment or critique you receive. Carefully weigh the merit of every compliment and criticism. (For more on this topic, see the section "Reacting to Member Feedback," later in this chapter.)

Finding Out What Others Are Saying Outside Your Community

Paying attention to your community also means discovering who is talking about you outside of your immediate online community. When people have constructive criticism, they don't always bring it to you. They like to post it to their own blogs or networks to receive the traffic or create their own discussion. Sometimes they'll add criticism or controversy directed toward you or your brand because these kinds of updates yield lots of comments. If you don't know where or how to look for online mentions, you won't know what anyone is saying about you.

To find out what people outside your community are saying, try these tips:

✔ **Set up Google Alerts:** If someone's mentioning or searching for you, you'll receive an e-mailed Google alert that includes a link so you can read the mention and comment, if necessary.

✔ **Twitter searches:** Use a Twitter application, such as Seesmic, Hootsuite or Tweetdeck, or the Twitter search engine at `search.twitter.com` to set up a keyword search.

✔ **Google Blog Search:** A search engine for blogs, Google Blog Search lets you do a keyword search that can help determine who is blogging about you or your brand.

Receiving feedback

Don't be afraid to ask for feedback because you don't want to hear bad news. The reality is that there's no such thing as bad feedback. Still, when the negative feedback comes, sometimes you can't help but take it personally. You spend so much time cultivating your community and promoting the brand that when someone doesn't like something, you almost feel it's a reflection of you.

The thing is, you shouldn't avoid feedback; you should embrace it. All feedback, even if it's negative, is a positive opportunity to reflect and change. The other side of the coin shows that members are likely to offer praise when they have a positive experience, so don't assume that feedback is always going to be bad news.

Always be gracious in accepting feedback, whether it's good or bad. Your members come to you with compliments or criticism because they care. When you're approached with feedback, always respond in a professional manner.

When you receive feedback:

- **Have a plan in place.** Your brand should have a plan for receiving feedback from customers and members. This plan should discuss proper responses and determine which departments should react to different types of feedback. (See "Sharing feedback with your team and superiors," later in this chapter.) If no policy is available, talk to your team about setting one up.

- **Realize that not all feedback requires immediate action.** Sometimes, a member or customer tells you he doesn't like a particular aspect of the community or brand, or he wants to compliment you on something you've done well. This type of feedback isn't something you need to act on right away, but you do need to thank the person and let him know that you'll share the feedback with your team.

- **Keep a record of all feedback.** Due diligence is very important. Sometimes the most minor issues have a way of coming back to haunt you. Customers may say one thing to you and another to your superiors. Sometimes members even deny contacting you at all. Note all feedback and save all correspondence until you're sure t the case is closed.

- **Make sure members that know you're grateful they took the time to contact you.** Members may be taking a brave step by contacting a brand or a person whom they see as being in a position of authority. Do your best to make them feel comfortable.

- **Do good research.** Make sure you have all the facts. Community members who relate news, especially in the case of a bad customer experience or spat with other members, tend to tell only one side of the story. Always dig a little deeper. If the feedback involves criticism of a person or situation in the community, or a technical error, ask for links or screen shots that show specific examples.

- **Respond professionally, not personally.** How can a member trust you and the brand if you get your back up every time someone says something negative? Always remember that feedback isn't personal. Be pleasant and polite and don't forget to say thank you.

- **Respond promptly.** Respond promptly to all queries, complaints, concerns, and comments, even if some require an answer that you don't have yet. Thank the member for caring enough to leave feedback and let her know that you're doing everything you can to look into the matter. If the feedback doesn't require a response, simply say "Thank you so much for taking the time to comment."

When you receive feedback, the most important thing is to let the other party know how much you value his time and comments, but don't let it stop there. Listening to your members is more than just saying thank you and moving on to the next person. You have to determine whether this type of feedback requires action and then take care of it in a timely manner.

Sharing feedback with your team and superiors

In short, your brand can't function properly without feedback. Feedback tells you

- ✔ What you're doing right
- ✔ What you're doing wrong
- ✔ When an advertising campaign is offensive or inappropriate
- ✔ When you release a product or service that works
- ✔ Whether customer-service issues were resolved to a member's satisfaction
- ✔ Why your customers buy your product

How you present feedback to your team varies from job to job. Much feedback is just that — feedback. It may be a compliment or criticism that doesn't require action. Still, it's important for your team, and all the people you work with for that matter, to know what's being said.

Much of the feedback you receive will be about issues that aren't your responsibility to handle, especially technical or customer-service issues. You're there to field the feedback and direct it to the proper channels. Also, though customers or members might reach out to you online, the majority of the folks offering feedback for your brand will probably do so via e-mail to the proper departments or via phone call. So there's a good possibility the individual departments in your brand are discovering when issues arise long before you do. If so, they'll handle it accordingly, and you won't need to do anything unless you're asked for help.

 When feedback does come directly to you, be careful not to step on any toes. Instead, pass it on to the proper department, and follow up, but not do much more unless it falls within your job description. With so many departments and policies in place, doing someone else's job can lead to resentment.

When you begin working as a community manager, it's important to define the roles and tasks of everyone on your team so that you don't run into animosity-causing situations. It's also a good idea to delegate to the right people because they have different experience and expertise and are trained to handle the different situations. That's not to say you won't be handling customer service issues. It all depends on your place of business and their policies and procedures.

If feedback doesn't require immediate action — it's not an emergency, and you need to only pass on a compliment or a nitpick — it can wait until your regular team meeting to share it. If you don't have team meetings and your company's policy isn't to share feedback in that manner, save feedback to share at a proper time, such as when you have to turn in your regular report.

If the same issue is brought repeatedly, it deserves more attention. One or two mentions means an issue is something to think about. More than that, and you'll have to take action one way or another:

- ✔ **Determine the nature of the feedback and the level of severity.** Is it something needing to be reported immediately? Can you add it to a team's "to do" list? Is it only a matter of forwarding an e-mail to the proper department or coworker?

- ✔ **Determine whether an explanation is necessary when reporting feedback.** Is it simply a matter of saying, "one of our members said she loved the new design," or is the feedback deserving of a longer report featuring links, quotes, and diagrams? If feedback requires backup, be sure to provide it.

- ✔ **Determine who gets the feedback and whether anyone should be copied.** As different departments have different duties, it's important to determine the proper channels. Normally, customer complaints go to a customer-service team, for example, but sometimes the advertising, marketing, and tech teams need to be made aware of issues. Also, public feedback, especially if it's extremely positive or negative, needs to be reported to upper management.

Negative feedback isn't the only type of constructive criticism requiring action. Positive feedback also requires discussion. If you or your brand is doing something your community loves, use that as a guide to create similar programs or see how you can make the original program even better.

Reacting to member feedback

If you have an issue that affects everyone in a negative way, you want to avoid taking too long to act. There's the potential here to make one of two mistakes; either rushing into a situation without giving it enough thought, or taking too long to mull things over.

When you do react to member feedback:

- ✔ **Avoid being all things to everyone.** Don't fall into the trap of changing the way things are done every time someone complains or remarks. This makes you look a little wishy-washy and as if you really don't know what direction to take. Just because someone complained on a blog doesn't mean you have to tear things down and start all over again. Also, not every complaint is valid. Sometimes people complain just to complain or nitpick because they're disgruntled. Carefully weigh the merit of each remark.

- ✔ **Know that you can't please everyone.** The sad truth is that everyone won't be happy with you or what you're trying to do, and it's not always your fault. Do consider constructive criticism but also know that certain things aren't doable or in the budget. It's also important to remember that some people complain no matter what direction you take. You can't make everyone happy, but you can make most people happy.

- ✔ **Don't dismiss small issues**: It's a funny thing about nitpicks. They seem really small and not worrisome, but then you discover that they bother a lot more people than you think. Don't wave something off as being minor. Every comment at least deserves the benefit of consideration.

- ✔ **More than one person escalates a concern into an issue.** If one person complains or offers a suggestion, it's noteworthy and worthy of investigation. When more than one person complains about the same thing, it's an issue having to be dealt with in one form or another.

Avoid the "if it ain't broke, don't fix it" mentality. There's a reason people upgrade technology on a regular basis. It may not be broke, but it can always be better.

Responding to both positive and negative feedback

All feedback is valuable even if it hurts to read it. Most of the time, it's from people who care about your brand and want to be sure that it's not going in a bad direction. Even negative comments are worthy of consideration, and it's the steps you take upon receiving that feedback that decide how you and your brand are viewed in the future.

The first step is understanding the importance of feedback and why it's necessary to succeed. Sure, you can plod along, blissfully ignorant about what's being said to you, but how will you ever grow? The dark ages are over, and if you want to stay competitive, you need to have your finger on the pulse of your people and take their concerns seriously.

Though you respond to both positive and negative feedback differently, it's important to respond to both types of feedback in a timely manner. To sweep it under the rug or put it off is to show the person who took the time to send you his thoughts that you don't care.

If someone is writing to compliment you on a job well done or to compliment the brand, always respond with a thank you. Make sure that you mention the person by name and make the letter as personal as possible. In short, form letters suck. While they're necessary on certain occasions, everyone thinks they're cheesy. So if you can, send a brief thank you to anyone who sends compliments and good wishes. If you can, include coupon codes, freebies, or other perks so that they know how much you value their time.

Negative feedback is different because it involves investigation. The most important thing is to never minimize the complaint or make the sender feel silly or dumb. You're important to him or he wouldn't be writing to you, so make sure he knows how much you value his input.

There are different levels of negativity, and they're all handled differently. The first step is in responding to the other party, even if you have no response. After that, how you handle it depends on the complaint. Also, you might be a person who only fields complaints rather than "handle" them. If something is not your department it's up to you to hand it off to the right person, but follow up in a reasonable amount of time to be sure it's done.

Here's what you need to do in common scenarios:

- **If a product or service didn't live up to expectations:** You'll find that even though you have a good relationship with a community member, he may not like your product, service, or whatever it is your promoting. If someone reaches out to tell you he didn't like something, you want to determine what kind of action is needed. Is it a case of refund, or is he just venting? Is it one particular item or everything you do in general? Talk to your customer service team and see what it recommends. Send a return note apologizing and offering to make things right.

- **If the person wants a refund:** Community managers don't always issue refunds, but they can recommend it happen. However, not every issue requires a refund. Some people even make a hobby of writing to brands with complaints so that they can get their money back. Never treat a customer as if he isn't telling the truth, but always weigh the situation. If you believe this person deserves a refund, make your recommendation and follow up to make sure that it's been done. If you don't feel a refund is in order, send a nice note to the other party explaining your reasons.

- **If someone complains about someone who works with you:** If someone who works with you was rude to a customer or used inappropriate language in your community gathering place, an apology is in order. First say you're sorry and you're looking into the matter and then have the offending party come in and also apologize. No one, no matter where they rank on the corporate ladder, should make your community feel uncomfortable.

✔ **Complaints about other community members:** Some community managers feel as if they're back in school. You'd be surprised at how many members write to tell they're being picked on or that someone is calling names or being mean. Don't take these complaints lightly. Many times it's someone trolling, and that person is easily banned. Always nip this kind of negativity in the bud before it turns into something worse, like cyber-bullying. However, not every situation is serious. Some community members just enjoy drama. After a while, you'll be able to realize who has a serious issue and who is trying to get someone in trouble. Always respond and let the person know that you'll look into all allegations. If you do have to talk to another community member about his behavior, do so in private, as it's no one else's business.

✔ **If a situation wasn't handled to the customer's satisfaction:** Sometimes customer service falls flat. If a member reaches out to you with this sort of complaint, the worst thing you can do is to pass him off to the person who didn't help in the first place. This might lead to a lack of cooperation or push back for both parties. Plus, it looks as if you weren't listening. Instead, let the other person know that you'll take care of it and take the complaint to the person who can fix it and stay with it until it's fixed. Usually, a community manager can let everyone do their jobs without micromanaging or getting in the way. Once the customer brings you into it, you have no choice but to get a little involved.

✔ **If the customer is complaining just to complain:** Every community has a chronic malcontent who complains because it's what she does best. The problem with chronic complainers is that you're not sure if their feedback has merit after a while. These types of complaints require case by case consideration. Still, it's always important to make the other person feel important and let her know you take her concerns seriously.

✔ **If you're being trolled:** Ignore it. Never feed the trolls.

Handling Criticism and Negativity about Your Brand

Your least favorite part of being a community manager may be reading negative comments or blog posts about your brand. As community manager, it may fall to you to deal with the negativity. At times, you may even be blamed for the negativity because a community manager is tasked with ensuring a positive online image.

The truth is, not everyone is going to love your brand. You or someone else in the company may do something that doesn't sit right with the community, or someone in the blogosphere may have a negative experience and decide to write about it. You may even encounter a disgruntled community member who has made it his mission to drag you or the brand through the mud.

Bad buzz seems mortifying at first, but the good news is that it won't stay that way for too long. You're probably going to worry about several questions right off the bat:

✔ How can you get the situation to die down as quickly as possible?

✔ Will you get into trouble or lose your job?

✔ Will your reputation take a hit?

✔ Should you address the situation or ignore it?

First, take a deep breath and understand that the uproar won't last. Online negativity generally lasts a couple of days and no more than a week. The longevity of the negativity depends on how you choose to handle the situation.

Also, remember that not every situation requires action. If a blogger writes about your strict comment policy, that's not necessarily a bad thing. It means you don't put up with a lot of trolling or nonsense at your community, and your members can interact knowing they don't have to put up with a lot of silliness. You don't need to do anything in this situation. If one person doesn't like a policy, you can certainly thank her for the comment and tell her that you'll keep it in mind, but you don't have to take other immediate action.

If, however, one person writes publicly about your strict comment policy and lists the reasons why it's unfair, and it's soon followed by dozens of comments in agreement, you have a more difficult situation on your hands. Consider taking the following actions:

1. **Determine whether the comments have merit.**

   Before reacting, be sure to read everything written about the situation, including comments on the social networks and your own community pages. Then decide whether the comments are valid. Be honest.

2. **Determine whether a response is in order.**

   Don't react when there's no need to react. Discuss the situation with your team, if necessary, and figure out whether the situation will die down on its own or whether you should make a comment or statement.

3. **Respond, if necessary.**

Responding with dignity

When you decide that a response is necessary (see preceding section), keep these pointers in mind:

- ✔ **Don't fire back in anger.** You're probably so vested in your community that you take criticism personally. You wouldn't be the first community manager to do so. Understand it isn't personal. It's community business. The worst thing you can do is go on the defensive and act as if the negative commentary holds no weight. If you're angry or hurt, let it go for a while. Do something else and come back to it with a clear head. When you fire back in anger, you tend to say things you regret. It's even worse in a public setting where everyone picks apart your words and finds unintended meanings in your words.

- ✔ **Be fair.** Though you may be angry or hurt by the negativity, you also have to consider the argument. You can't always be right, and sometimes others see things in a situation you don't. Listen to the other person's argument and consider whether or not it holds water. If you're wrong, admit it with grace. Your community would rather you were honest and human than go on the defensive or sweep something under the rug.

- ✔ **Say thank you.** Even if you don't agree with the criticism, be appreciative of the person who took the time to bring it to your attention. I liken these situations to broccoli in the teeth. You'd rather be momentarily embarrassed when a friend tells you that you have broccoli caught in between your front teeth than to have to go through the day with a big green smile, and no one bringing it to your attention at all. It's off putting, it's embarrassing, and it makes you feel very self conscious, but it's better to deal with it early and head on than to be ignorant of a situation.

- ✔ **Don't go tit for tat.** No matter how much you feel you have to respond to every single comment, the worst thing you can do is go back and forth on the comments. Arguments, fights, one-upmanship, and having the last word only shed more negativity on to your brand and your community. Say what you have to say and leave it. You don't have to reiterate every point or correct every single person. If you made a point once, you don't need to rehash it over and over again.

- ✔ **Be transparent.** Be honest and admit when you're wrong or things are out of your hand. If you lie, you'll eventually get caught, and the backlash over that will be even worse than the original negativity. Say, "Yes. That happened, and here are the steps we're taking to correct it." If you're not at liberty to discuss an issue or circumstance, say, "I'm sorry. I'm not at liberty to discuss that at this time. However, I can tell you we're handling the situation internally and hope to make an announcement or take action soon." For more on transparency, see Chapter 4.

You can use the preceding tips for many different types of situations and not only a negative blog posts. The important thing to keep in mind is not to lose your cool, be transparent, be gracious, and don't worry about publically responding if a public response isn't necessary.

Understand that people are criticizing your community because they care. Most people criticize because they want something to work and are disappointed it didn't. In short, they care. There's a difference between negativity from people who want to see the community succeed and negativity from people who only want to cause drama. Be grateful for the people who want to be productive members of your community but are having problems doing so because of difficult circumstances. Know that you must be doing something right if they care enough to talk about the community and how it needs fixing.

Participating in heated discussions

Sometimes, community discussions escalate from lively to heated. Topics that invoke passion, such as religion and politics, inevitably lead to spirited debate. Your community may have certain hot-button issues of its own as well. For example, in a freelance writing online community, free and cheap labor may be hot issues because writers disagree on whether or not writing for free is the right thing to do. In a child-rearing communities, whether to breastfeed and whether to let a child "cry it out" at night may lead to debate. As community manager, your job is to stay close to the discussion when a hot community topic emerges and to keep the conversation on track and positive, especially if members get a little passionate.

You can't leave a hotbed discussion for a few days and hope for the best. As you learn about your community, you'll also discover which topics cause the most controversy. Even if it's a new community and you're a new community manager, a few warning signs indicate that a conversation is about to spawn a heated debate:

- ✔ More people than usual comment.
- ✔ Members take issue with certain comments.
- ✔ The language members use to comment becomes less polite and more heated.
- ✔ Members take sides.
- ✔ The drama seekers, trolls, and people who only come out for a fight or argument appear.

You don't necessarily have to quash heated discussions, but you do have to stay close and monitor the conversation just in case. As long as members are being respectful, you don't need to step in beyond providing gentle guidance. If things get out of hand, however, you may need to close comments.

You may want to mention your comment policy and remind members that name-calling and disrespect are against your guidelines. (Refer to Chapter 4 for more on comment policies and guidelines.) Start asking the types of questions or making the types of comments that take the discussion back on track in a respectful, positive manner.

In certain situations, you're only recourse is to close comments:

- ✔ **If the discussion has gotten so negative and so far off track there's no saving it:** If members are going off track, and no manner of gentle guidance can save the discussion, it's time to close comments. If you leave them open, you risk the discussion's becoming a free-for-all.

- ✔ **If the discussion is nothing but insults and profanity:** Community members have to know they must adhere to your guidelines and comment policy (refer to Chapter 4). If they can't play nice, close the comments. Otherwise, this type of negativity will ensue in future discussions. Nip it in the bud immediately, and folks will get the message.

- ✔ **If the trolls and drama seekers are coming out to play:** Certain people come out only when there's drama — or to encourage or cause drama. When these types of members come out from under their respective bridges, it's time to close comments, because those comments are only going to make matters worse.

When moderating Facebook comments, you can't close a thread like you do with a forum or blog post. Though Facebook discussions don't stay on the front page for more than a day or so, if a discussion is too negative, you have to either keep it up for everyone to see or delete it altogether.

Being fair and impartial

It's not always easy to remain a neutral party. There are going to be times when you agree with a certain side in a heated discussion or argument, and your personal beliefs may cloud your impartiality. You can't let that happen. No matter how much you want to jump in and tell people they're wrong, you have to control the urge.

Dealing with personal scandal

Uh oh. Those pictures of you doing tequila body shots in your bikini somehow made their way off your private Facebook page and into the public eye. Of course, it's embarrassing and humiliating, but also, your personal life now going to reflect upon the brand.

Now, you may be thinking, "What I do in my personal life has nothing to do with my job," and you'd be right. As long as your personal life stays personal there won't be an issue. However, once your personal life crosses the border into public consumption, you have a problem. Now you're no longer "Jane Doe, private citizen," you're "Jane Doe community manager of Brand X who is doing bikini body shots." It's like a politician who gets caught cheating on his wife. Though it's personal, the public is now turning it into a character issue.

It's a funny thing about the online world and communities. Many times our difference communities collide. In your case, not only are you part of your brand's community, but you're also part of the community management community, maybe even the blogging or social media communities, too. Plus, your brand and personal communities might even have the ability to span several different niches. So the bigger your brand, and the bigger your online reach, the more scandalous the scandal. Some online community managers are well known on the web. If shots of you partying with very little clothing on are making their way around online, it may be an issue for both your personal and public brands.

I can't tell you how many community managers and other online professionals have lost their jobs and damaged their reputations due to poor choices. Keep this in mind any time you or a friend post anything to personal accounts.

The end result depends a lot on how you address the situation.

✔ **Let it go.** Your personal scandal will be the talk of your communities for days. If you continuously comment on it and go on the defensive, you run the risk of keeping it in the public eye for a longer period of time. If you let it go, the uproar will die down in a few days, and you can get on with your life. You and your brand are going to have to deal with some embarrassment, and you're going to come across those pictures now and then in the future, but people are forgiving.

✔ **Address it with humor.** You don't have to hide and pretend the scandal didn't happen. Instead you can joke about letting off steam or find another way to make light of the situation. By dealing with the scandal head on and using humor, you show your community you're human. People like human.

✔ **Apologize.** Even though you may not think you did something wrong, it might be a good idea to apologize to your brand and your community. You may not feel apologetic — after all, someone released personal pictures of you, and it's not your fault — but your brand has to deal with the fallout as well.

It's unfair — you did everything you could to keep your personal life personal — but the public is now viewing you in a different light. Hopefully, your brand has your back and understands how you never intended for an inappropriate situation to turn public.

Still, this is a good lesson. A community manager is a public person. It's always a good idea to not let too much of your private life out on the Internet, even if you think you're in a private community.

Not everyone you friend on the social networks is a true friend, and you never know who may betray you to the public. It's always a good idea to never post anything online you wouldn't want splashed across the headlines of a major newspaper, especially if you're a community manager with a large following.

Give yourself a Google now and then to see what search engine results reveal. You may find yourself on the receiving end of praise from your community members or find some nastiness you'll need to deal with right away.

In any conflict, you have to be the voice of reason. Your community is counting on you to keep the peace and prevent a tense situation from escalating out of control. If you agree with the person who's stirring up all the controversy, your community can no longer trust you as the person who's looking out for their best interests.

Sometimes, community members ask you for your personal views during a controversial exchange. Even though you were invited to give your opinion, you have to remain on the fence. You can tell your community you don't feel it's appropriate to add your response or give another polite, pleasant answer that doesn't ignore the request but still shows them you're a neutral party.

There's no place for any kind of bias in online community management. As soon as you take sides against another person or group of people, you may as well kiss your credibility goodbye. Becoming part of a community clique or being an obvious best friend of a community member will cause other members to mistrust your judgment. If you can't treat every member the same way, you're in the wrong job. You're employed by your brand to manage the community; to keep positive, productive discussions running smoothly; and to retain the trust of the community. When your personal views and preferences come into play, your job goes out the window.

It's important to practice what you preach. You can't ask your community members to play nice if you're not doing so yourself. The best way to have members follow comment policies and guidelines is to lead by example.

At times, adding your opinion is absolutely appropriate, such as in a technical discussion or a request for advice related to your community. The impartiality bit comes into play when a hot topic is taking place and arguments ensue. Don't take part in the types of discussions always leading to arguments.

Doing Damage Control

What should you do when a community argument gets out of hand or your brand receives bad press? Knowing how to prevent damage is great, but you also need to be capable of handling unfortunate experiences that have already occurred. When you can't deter damage, you can take steps to ensure it doesn't get any worse.

In this section, I explore some examples of damage and show you steps you can do to put things right.

Undoing community damage

If a community can't get along or has a bad reputation for being hostile or argumentative, it won't attract the right kind of attention. First and foremost, if your community has become a place where the members snipe at one another and don't respect you or your rules, you're going to be seen as an ineffective community manager. As your job is a very public one, you can't afford that hit to your reputation. Also, if you let a situation get out of hand once, it's likely to happen again. When the damage is already done, it's difficult to come in and keep the peace after the fact. It's sort of like a sheriff coming in to run a town of outlaws.

Still, you can take steps to prevent a bad situation from getting more out of hand, while enforcing the policies and guidelines needed prevent a similar situation from happening in the future.

Keep your damage control low-key. When you announce that you're cleaning up the community after the community has been running amok, you only open the door for hecklers and nay-sayers who may tell you that you're censoring their free speech. (You're not. For more on what censorship actually is, see Chapter 4.)

Also, determine whether to close comments to s discussion. If you do so, do it without fanfare. If community members complain and the complaints are not something you can handle privately, explain to all how the conversation violates your comment policy, and you closed it down in order to prevent it from escalating further out of control. Don't allow for arguments as there are certain times when you have to wear your authority hat. You may even need to close the comments on your any announcements (about closing comments) if you don't think it will go over well. Be honest but not so brutally honest that folks take offense.

It may also be time to reintroduce everyone to your comment policies and community guidelines. First, see whether your guidelines need an update and make any necessary changes. Second, invite your community to read over the guidelines. They don't need scoldings or smackdowns, as this is very insulting for adults. Simply point them in the right direction. (For more on establishing rules and guidelines, see Chapter 4.)

With the offending discussion topic closed for business and re-established community guidelines in place, you're now in a better position to keep the peace in the future.

Handling bad press

The days of avoiding bad headlines and news that's capable of hurting your reputation are over. Not only is today a time when everything is public, but it's also a time when you have to own up to your mistakes and confront problems head-on. The statement "All publicity is good publicity" is untrue. Bad publicity can do damage. However, the degree of damage depends on how you choose to handle the situation.

Unless you work for some huge, famous brand, most bad press is viewed only by the people in your immediate community and a few other people who have an interest in what your brand does. Also, unless the bad press is due to something wild and scandalous that's splashed across the front pages of all the major newspapers and websites, the crisis may not be as epic as you may originally think when the news first breaks. Determine first whether the situation is worthy of a public address. The biggest issue is in making sure that the news doesn't get bigger or more scandalous, especially online. News dies down, but it stays findable in the search engines forever.

If your community is clamoring for answers or the ensuing community discussion is causing a bit of turmoil, don't ignore it. Create an open dialogue and answer questions as honestly as possible without betraying your brand.

Answer all questions to the best of your ability. Don't ignore anyone or tap-dance around the discussion. If you can't give an answer, let the other person know that you'll look into the question and respond as soon as possible. Publicly confronting the bad publicity and responding honestly to community questions helps continue the trust and mutual respect you share with your online network.

Besides answering questions publicly, you may choose to respond to bad publicity in a blog post, press release, or other online statement. Again, don't gloss over facts or dance around what really happened. Admit mistakes, apologize if necessary, and put the situation behind you.

Delegating damage control when necessary

Though your job is to maintain a positive image for your brand, it's not necessarily your job to handle damage control. Your company may choose to let someone else deal with fallout after a negative situation. The public-relations department can issue a press release, for example; the president or chief executive officer can release a statement; the marketing team can create a campaign that features a more positive image.

Before you decide to address an inappropriate, unfortunate, or negative situation, discuss it with your team members. They may decide to hand the job to a different person or a different department.

You should also discuss whether the designated spokesperson should field all questions, press inquiries, and mentions on social networks.

Seeing the humor in difficult situations

Not every crisis has to be hush-hush or super serious. You'll find that people appreciate brands showing a human side. If you can treat negativity with humor and not insult the intelligence of your community, you'll not only control the damage, but also may attract a slew of new members.

Recently, the American Red Cross encountered a situation that could have been scandalous but instead turned into something positive. A member of its social-media team forgot to switch to his personal Twitter account and sent the following tweet from the Red Cross account:

> Ryan found two more 4 bottle packs of Dogfish Head's Midas Touch beer...when we drink, we do it right. #gettingslizzerd

The public tweet and its ensuing hashtag insinuated that the Red Cross team was imbibing on company time, which wouldn't go over well with the general public. Instead of deleting the tweet and pretending it didn't happen, a spokesperson released the following tweet:

> We've deleted the rogue tweet but rest assured the Red Cross is sober and we've confiscated the keys.

The Red Cross did the right thing. By not hiding the fact that someone mistakenly used the brand account to send out a personal and inappropriate tweet, it created some fun on Twitter as people retweeted the comment.

And the fun didn't stop there. Dogfish Head Craft Brewery got into the act as well, encouraging its community members to give blood and then buy a beer. Soon, the Twitterverse was filled with comments by Dogfish community members who were doing just that. The Red Cross/Dogfish tweets not only became a popular case study on handling a negative situation correctly, but also became one of Twitter's top trending topics for that day.

Dealing with Trolls

Ah, trolls. They make a community manager's job so interesting. In case you haven't walked over the bridge lately, trolls are the anonymous people who come out to cause arguments and drama. They crave attention like a dieter craves a pizza. Trolls use the web's anonymity to attack and belittle, and they think you're not intelligent enough to place them as trolls or even know who they are.

You should feel flattered, really. There must be something attractive about your community for the trolls to come out. Something you or someone else said elicited a response, even if it's not the response any of you were hoping for.

But you have to get rid of trolls if you want your community to thrive.

Identifying trolls

In case you're still not sure if the trolls are coming to feed at your community trough, they all share a few identifying characteristics and markings:

- ✔ **Trolls are anonymous.** Most trolls use a nondescript first name, one that could be anybody — that is, if they care to use a name at all. Some are kind of lazy and don't want to take the time to create a whole personae.

- ✔ **Trolls have throwaway e-mail addresses.** As most places that allow comments require an e-mail address, trolls get around this request by using made-up e-mails. Most are from free services, such as Yahoo!, gmail, or HotMail, while others even troll in their own e-mail addresses — for example, Sue@youarealoser.com.

- ✔ **Trolls are there to get a rise out of people.** They're not polite and not ashamed getting in a zinger. They call names and make accusations and rarely do they sound anything but angry.

✔ **Trolls use anonymous proxies.** Here's the thing about trolls: They're probably someone you know, maybe even a productive member of your community or a competitor. They don't want you to find that out, though, because if word gets out that they're trolls, it may lead to losing face among so many people. So trolls uses *anonymizers,* or proxies, that show a different IP address than that which you're used to.

✔ **All trolls make mistakes.** They slip up with their e-mail addresses or their words and phrases. They might even forget to use their proxy. Eventually, trolls are caught and figured out, which leads to an embarrassing situation.

✔ **Trolls rarely add anything of value to the conversation.** When trolls respond to a community discussion, they don't add anything meaningful to the discussion. Instead, they joke, berate, and insult.

There are also the trolls who do it under the guise of being a productive member of the community. Some are only there to troll you or other community moderators. Every decision or comment you make is called into question. Not only do they question your authority at every turn, they encourage other community members to do it, too, citing free speech and how it is "their" community. These types of trolls are off base. Truthfully, it's not their community, it's your brand's community, and they're invited to participate, just like someone who is a guest in your home. And just like a guest who is abusing other guests or treating you poorly at your own party, they should be asked to leave. You have your guidelines and anyone who can't play nice or follow the guidelines doesn't have to stick around.

Managing trolls

Trolls troll because they want attention. The more attention they receive, the healthier they are, and the bigger and fatter they grow. As community manager, it's your job to discourage this feeding thing:

1. **Identify your troll.**

   See the section "Identifying trolls," earlier in this chapter.

2. **Encourage your community to ignore the troll.**

   Explain to your members that the trolls are looking for a big honking fight and the last thing you want to do is give it to them. Make sure that they know that it's okay for trolls to feed in their own homes, but it's frowned upon to toss them breadcrumbs anywhere else.

3. **Don't engage.**

   Nothing fills a troll's tummy like having a battle of words with a community manager or flame war with other members of the community. Remember, the goal here is to eliminate the troll, not keep her around.

4. Ban the troll.

In addition to banning the troll, you can ban his IP address, too. Trolls like to sign in under a variety of monikers, so name and e-mail banning doesn't always work. Banning IPs doesn't always work the fast or second time as your troll finds new proxies, but eventually they run out or get tired of the game and their off to bug someone else.

If you find a troll under your bridge, your best recourse is to ignore it and go back in the house. It may try and get your attention for a while, as all trolls do, but the less attention you pay to it, the more likely it is to trip trap away to find another bridge to haunt.

Taking action when a situation gets out of hand

I have an anecdote to share. One of the communities I managed had a duo of troublemakers among its members. Most of the time, their bark was worse than their bite, but sometimes they took things too far. Their goal with the community forum wasn't to drive members to their sales page, as you'd expect. They were there to bad-mouth the brand and cause as much turmoil as possible because they weren't happy with the service they were receiving.

If I moderated a comment, they'd cry "censorship!" If I asked them not to post provocative images in the forum, they complained. If they felt they weren't getting as much attention as the other members, they raised a clamor and got their own negative attention. One day, all they did was bait me and the other moderators. They argued with everything we posted even if it was only a "good morning." Finally, they drove away most of the community. My superiors didn't like the idea of banning people, but I was finally able to get permission after they took it too far.

After I banned them, they came back under another name, and another, and another. Every single time they were banned, they came back again. I banned IPs, and they found new IPs.

They wouldn't go away. Finally, we cancelled their account with our brand, and the technical team fixed it so that they weren't allowed back in. It was drastic, and it took a whole big team effort to get rid of them, but it's a good lesson on what happens if you don't nip negativity in the bud right away. In this case, I wasn't allowed to do more than ask the duo to play nice, but they had no interest in that. When we finally took serious action, most of the community was gone, and it took some convincing to get them back . . . but we did.

I didn't share this story to show you my ineffectiveness as a community manager, although this duo certainly made it seem that way. Instead, I wanted to illustrate how situations can get out of hand and tear apart a community. When management is reluctant to issue warnings or moderate comments, things escalate out of control.

Keep in mind that banning is a last resort. The goal is to grow your community and make sure that all members play along. However, when you have no other recourse, you have to sacrifice the offending member for the sake of the community.

Chapter 8

Building Kids' Communities

Managing kids' communities isn't the same as managing grownup communities at all. Grownups can more or less fend for themselves online, but kids need a safe environment. You wouldn't use the same language, nor would you have the same guidelines. Even your member acceptance policies are vastly different.

In this chapter, I explore how kids' communities are different from grownup communities and ways for children to have an enjoyable online experience in a safe environment.

Knowing the Differences Between Grownup and Kidcentric Communities

Because kids aren't always aware of the dangers of interacting online and because adults aren't necessarily looking over kids' shoulders every second to guide them or protect them from inappropriate content, it's up to you to present them with a positive, safe haven for their online interaction.

Kids are kids; they're not miniature adults. Treat them respectfully, but treat them as though they're kids. Adults can pretty much be left to their own devices when they're using online communities. Kids need more guidance. They don't know the right online etiquette yet, and they're more trusting.

Kids' communities have to be more intuitive than adult communities. Buttons and links should be obvious, and games shouldn't require a telephone-book-size manual filled with instructions. In fact, most online activities for kids should require little or no instruction at all.

Kids' communities are more visually stimulating. They're more colorful and lively. What adults might consider to be a distraction, such as blinking virtual Christmas lights, is a fun aspect of an online community's design to kids. The websites use less text and more headlines and illustrations. It's not unheard-of to see hundreds of avatars doing hundreds of different things at the same time. Adults don't like cluttered communities; kids thrive in them.

Making Social Networking Safe

Though it's up to parents to teach online safety to their children, the onus is on the online community manager to provide an experience for children that's fun, educational, safe, and appropriate. Kids aren't thinking about ominous strangers lurking in the shadows to find a vulnerable child to manipulate, and they're certainly not thinking that the 8-year-old they think they're talking to online might be a 40-year-old predator. The burden of creating a place where unsavory types are unwelcome and can't gain entry is up to the creators and managers of the various online communities. Fortunately, most kids' communities are fun, educational, and safe because those in charge have strict measures in place.

Most elementary-school students are online more for playing games and participating in activities than for chatting. There are different types of interaction, and they shouldn't be discouraged, but make no mistake, they're not there to chat. Instead, they like to explore different games and experiment with *avatars* (pictures used to represent the members because using their own photographs is frowned upon).

Tweens (10- to 12-year olds), on the other hand, do have more opportunities to chat, and that interaction should be strictly monitored.

Children's social networks aren't as easy to sign up for as grownup communities are, and the interaction that occurs is different. As managers for these types of online communities, you're presented with a different set of challenges.

Obtaining parental permission

Most children's social networks require parental permission before a membership is activated. The safest networks require parents to jump through a variety of hoops before a child's account is approved. The children's social network whatswhat.com, for example, requires parents to submit a credit card, plus they require parents to submit three images. Unsavory types want to give out as few identifying details as possible, so the more a social network does to identity parents and get their approval, the less likely someone who's looking to harm children is to get in. What's What also includes a resource center for parents so that they can find out more about the network before signing up and read up on safety issues for kids. (They call them mug shots.)

When planning your own kids' community, consider taking these measures to deter the wrong people from signing up:

- ✔ Asking for credit cards may scare off anyone who doesn't want to leave a trail.

- ✔ Taking webcam shots of parents deters anyone who doesn't want to be identified.

- ✔ Asking questions of parents that require identifying answers, such as the last four digits of a driver's license number, may discourage anyone who doesn't want to give out information.

- ✔ Requiring parents to read and sign a terms-of-use agreement may deter some people, though most community members admit to not really reading terms of use.

With more grownup communities, you want to make signing up as easy as possible for new members. No one likes to answer a hundred questions or refresh a CAPTCHA code over and over again, and these are the sorts of things that discourage new memberships. For kids' communities, though, it's different. You almost want to make it difficult for just anyone to get in. So if you ask parents a dozen questions before allowing a signup, you may discourage someone who isn't serious about participating in that community or is up to no good.

You can also use parental permission and controls for different aspects of the social networks as well. Many children's communities allow parents to choose among varying levels of conversation. For example, kids can talk only to people they know, choose among prephrased messages, or not chat at all. You can even create an option so that parents can approve buddies so that they know who their children are talking to.

Parents can set other kinds of controls. They have the ability to allow their children in only certain areas of the networks and play certain games. In communities where kids can keep blogs and receive comments, parents are allowed to set controls allowing all members to view a blog or to allow no one but specific friends to view it. The controls also give parents the ability to decide what types of content their kids can read while visiting the community.

The level of parental permission grows as kids grow. A 14-year-old wouldn't have the same type of restricted access as a 9-year-old. However, it's still up to parents to determine how much access their kids should have to any community. For this reason, parents should have options to choose among and levels of control. For example, a 6-year-old using a social gaming community mostly to play games may have a strict level of security so that he's not allowed to chat or interact. A 13-year-old, on the other hand, may have a softer level of control, with chat allowed but parents having the ability to approve friends. All kids are different, and all parents know their kids better than you do. By providing them with varying levels of controls, you're allowing parents to make the right choices to keep their kids active in the community for several years.

Setting age limits

Most kids' social networks have age limits so that children can hang out in an age-appropriate atmosphere. Networks such as Facebook aren't for tweens or younger kids, but what do kids do before they're teenagers? Most join communities that allow them to interact with others, but in different ways from Facebook, Google+, or Twitter.

Most kids' communities don't accept children younger than 7 or 8 because before those ages, they're too young to grasp the importance of the rules and implications of sharing too much information with strangers, or because they're simply too immature to participate in the available activities.

Programs are available for kindergarteners and preschoolers, but they're basic learning games, not places where very young kids interact. When they're older — say, 7 or 8 — they might begin with the social-networking sites, but more for fun and games than serious networking. Kids play games using creative avatars and see other kids playing in the same community, but they're not having full-fledged conversations. Because children socialize differently, it's important for these networks to set limits so that that 7-year-olds and 14-year-olds aren't interacting in the same room.

Age limits do more than prevent kids from viewing inappropriate content. They also ensure that kids are interacting with other kids in their own age groups.

As children get older, their levels of membership and the types of content they view can also change. Allowing them to unlock new areas of the community on each birthday will give them a special gift, and they'll feel more like a grownup as they explore new experiences within the community.

Common spaces

Communities that allow a wide range of ages should denote the appropriate ages for all aspects of the community, whether they're games, chats, or articles. However, it's nice to have special *common areas,* too — places where the entire community can get together for a common cause. Perhaps older kids can offer advice or mentoring to younger kids.

If you'd like to have one of these areas for your community, it requires continual moderation.

Content

Communities have different types of content. In addition to community-sponsored content such as informative articles, newsletters, and community updates, they have user-generated content. If a community allows teens, and a member is writing about dating, that content isn't appropriate for an 8-year-old. If content isn't appropriate for everyone, age limits need to be imposed.

Chat rooms

Unless you want to have someone on call to moderate all day, every day, it's not a good idea to have chat rooms in younger children's communities unless they're occasional special events. Sometimes networks offer chats or interviews with celebrities or authors, and members can ask questions. Moderated chats for these special occasions are a fun way for the community to interact. Note the age level of the chat so that a teenager doesn't get bored in a very basic children's chat or a young child doesn't attend a chat that's way over his head.

Games

As many children's communities are made up of games, it's important to note the age levels of the games. You wouldn't want a 7-year-old to play violent shooting games, and a 12-year-old doesn't want to play first-grade-level matching games. This doesn't mean you have to check IDs before allowing others to play, but parents may want to set the controls so that younger kids can't play mature games.

Making the right kinds of friends

What's a social network without friends? If a community didn't allow for some sort of interaction, it wouldn't be a community at all. The problem comes when kids make friends with people they don't know. Young kids don't always make the best choices, which is why you need to join parents in helping kids make the right kinds of friends.

Think of a moderated community as a party with a chaperone. You're on the lookout for anything inappropriate. Fortunately, parental controls can help you keep inappropriate behavior in check. When you allow parents to decide whom their kids can interact with online, you're protecting both the children and the brand.

Let parents choose the kids they want their own kids to hang out with by setting limits. Offer them the opportunity to decide the ages and genders of the children their kids are socializing with. Also, allow them to receive alerts so that they know when their children make new friends.

Encourage parents to work with children on their profiles. For younger kids, it's best not to have them put pictures up of themselves. Instead, they can use an avatar to illustrate their personality. An avatar can be a cartoon character, a picture of an animal, or anything appropriate that the child feels best represents him.

It's also a good idea to offer parents the opportunity to limit the amount of friends their children have in the community. There's no reason a 9-year-old should have 10,000 friends in a community. She won't be able to interact with them all, and it's difficult for her parents to monitor the conversations among many friends.

Consider setting up your community to monitor kids' friendships to make sure that the matches are appropriate. If a 14-year-old boy wants to be friends with a 7-year-old girl, for example, all their parents should know. This type of friendship should be discouraged. As you're making your rounds, also note what's being said. Make sure that all interaction is appropriate and that conversations are positive, enlightening, and educational. Don't allow name-calling or bullying. Kids' communities should be fun, not stressful.

Getting strict with the rules

Even enforcing rules is different in kids' communities. You need to post guidelines and comment policies in such a way that both kids and parents can understand what's expected, as well as any repercussions.

The usual rules apply. Swearing and bullying have no place in a kids' community, of course, but words that may seem relatively harmless in a grownup community also may be off-limits in a children's community. For example, if a grownup called something "dumb," it might not raise a fuss.

If a kid said another kid was dumb or an idea was dumb, hurt feelings or even an argument can ensue. Write guidelines so that kids understand what isn't acceptable and what types of repercussions happen after unacceptable behavior. Also, kids aren't necessarily looking for welcome folders and guidelines. Having rules, guidelines, or terms of service available upon signup, requiring members to check a box to say that they read and agree to the guidelines, is probably best.

Here are some common rules in kids' communities:

- ✔ Be respectful of others.
- ✔ Don't call names or use insulting or swear words.
- ✔ Don't threaten or bully other kids.

Make sure that kids know where to find a link to contact the moderator in the event that someone is picking on them or using bad language in their presence. You'll find that most kids abide by the rules and play nice. As in any online community, however, there are still a few who like to test the limits or make waves. In that event, make sure that you're enforcing the rules:

- ✔ **Always issue warnings in the event of an infraction.** Many times, infractions are innocent because the rule breakers didn't read up on the rules. Issue a warning. Also tell the rule breaker that this kind of behavior won't be tolerated and that the next time she speaks to someone in that manner, her account will be suspended for a certain number of days.

- ✔ **Contact parents.** Make sure that parents know when their kids are breaking the rules. Send a polite note listing the infraction plus the repercussions so that they're aware of their children's online behavior.

- ✔ **Suspend or ban accounts, if necessary.** If a child repeats an infraction, you can get a little stricter with the rules. Suspending an account for 24 hours will certainly show the little rule breaker that you mean business. For repeat offenders, an outright ban may be in order. Make sure that parents are aware of developments.

It's very rare for younger children's communities to experience the negativity that teen or grownup communities can face. When a child steps out of line, usually a warning will suffice, and then it's back to business as usual.

Hosting a Fun, Productive Kids' Community

Kids' communities aren't necessarily discussion-focused. Most children younger than 13 would much rather play games, design virtual houses, and look at fun images. Still, a fun kids' community hosts a mix of favorite things: stories, videos, games, and good things to read, as well as town halls or other types of discussions.

You don't necessarily interact with kids in these communities, especially in activity- or game-focused communities. Instead, you observe, plan programs, respond to questions (mostly from parents), and stay on the alert in case a moderation situation does arise. Mostly, you're there to make sure that members are having an awesome time.

Leading discussions for children

Kids have online discussions in different ways. A community for kids younger than 12 or 13 may not have discussion forums, but you can still host certain chats and discussions with members. Bringing in an author, sports figure, or other kid role model and allowing kids to ask questions is a wonderful experience.

Another idea is to host a monthly town hall where you can discuss a topic of interest to kids. Discussions can be a mix of serious and fun topics, such as bullying and favorite television shows. Don't expect kids to participate the same ways that adults do. Some may ask questions; others may prefer posting funny icons or smileys (images with facial expressions on them).

Also, don't be frustrated if kids aren't exactly attentive to the subject matter. They may act silly or immature while the discussion is happening or talk about other things among themselves. It's fine for them to do this as long as they're being respectful of the rules, other members, and any special guests. You may have to steer the conversation back on track sometimes if it's too raucous, but for the most part, your young members are just learning how to interact with other people online.

Selling to kids

It's probably not a good idea to put kids in a position to buy stuff without permission. Otherwise, you'll have a crew of unhappy parents on your hands. If you have products or services of interest to kids, it's fine, but selling shouldn't be the entire focus of your community. Legos and Club Penguin (refer to "Keeping members busy with activities," earlier in this chapter) are two good examples of communities that sell to kids but aren't obvious about it.

Keep sales pages and game pages separate. In the Legos community, for example, the game and club areas are in different subdomains. Kids can play games, watch videos, and even subscribe to a free magazine without any obvious selling going on. Many of the games and videos incorporate Lego products, but no one is saying, "Buy this!"

If you do have something to sell, make sure that kids get parental permission to buy. Use parental passwords and credit cards so that it's not easy for kids to make a purchase on their own. Parents can receive community perks such as discount codes or clearance items in the community newsletter, so any obvious selling is on the parents' end and not the kids' end.

Make no mistake — many communities for kids have something to sell. But it shouldn't be easy for kids to buy or even know that they're being sold to.

Keeping members busy with activities

Most communities for kids are gaming communities, with dozens of games for each child to choose among. Club Penguin (clubpenguin.com), for example, an extremely popular online kids' community owned by Disney, features a variety of areas boasting dozens of games. Kids can become ninjas and earn black belts by playing virtual card games. They can also act as spies and undergo a series of missions by solving puzzles and finding clues. They can even get a job and work behind a virtual soda counter or in a pet shop. Though they do encounter other kids and each kid has a customized penguin avatar, the conversation is limited to a series of prephrased comments unless chat is enabled. Though kids can also create content and share in other ways, most of them are there for the games.

Games are perfect for kids, in that they stimulate and educate. Communities like Club Penguin are good starter communities that help kids learn online social skills.

It's not enough to throw up random games, though. Communities have to have a theme and a purpose, and games should fall in line with those themes. Also, games and activities should have some sort of result, such as a badge earned at the end of each level.

Here are some best practices to keep in mind when creating activities for kids:

- ✔ **Have a reward system.** Kids love prizes, even if they're virtual. At Club Penguin, for example, kids receive coins for every game or challenge they complete. They can exchange these coins for virtual pets (called piffles) or items to decorate their avatar penguins or igloos, which can also be purchased with coins. Kids can also donate coins to charity. Consider offering virtual badges, coins, or points that kids can exchange for something awesome.

- ✔ **Educate *and* entertain.** Having fun isn't the only goal of a kids' community. Activities should teach life lessons as well. Perhaps kids can work with other members on completing a task that teaches teamwork or play word-search games to help with spelling.

- ✔ **Mimic life.** Games should mimic reality. Though kids may have avatars representing animals or mythical creatures, the practices and lessons in the various games should have some basis in reality. Kids enjoy role-playing, and if they pretend to be firemen, police officers, doctors, astronauts, teachers, or singers, their play may fuel career aspirations.

- ✔ **Be careful of being too violent.** Be mindful of age groups. Shooting, crashing cars, punching or hitting, and other violent acts have no place in a kids' community. Games and activities should be kid- and family-friendly and should send a positive message.

Part IV
Growing Your Community

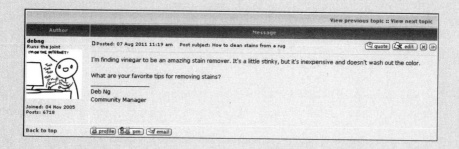

Author	Message
debng Runs the joint I'M ON THE INTERNET! Joined: 04 Nov 2005 Posts: 6718	⬜ Posted: 07 Aug 2011 11:19 am Post subject: How to clean stains from a rug 🔲 quote ✏️ edit ✖ ip I'm finding vinegar to be an amazing stain remover. It's a little stinky, but it's inexpensive and doesn't wash out the color. What are your favorite tips for removing stains? ――――――――― Deb Ng Community Manager
Back to top	🔲 profile 🔲 pm 🔲 email

View previous topic :: View next topic

In this part . . .

The online community is transient. Very few members stick around forever. That's why it's best to continue to find ways to grow your community, even if you feel you have enough members for now. Besides, new members always breathe new life into a community. In this part, you discover what you need to do to attract, welcome, and encourage new members.

Chapter 9

Welcoming New Members

In This Chapter

▶ Creating a welcoming presence for new members

▶ Allowing introductions within the community

▶ Sending welcome e-mails

*M*aking community members feel comfortable and welcome is similar to making house guests feel at home. If you invite them in, encourage them to have a seat, and introduce them to your other guests, they'll feel that you truly want them to be there. With an online community, if you hold the door open, offer some words of welcome, and invite members to interact, they'll appreciate your kindness and want to explore and find out more.

In this chapter, I discuss the various methods of welcoming new members. I also talk about how to make introductions and the perks members can expect to receive upon signup.

Creating a Welcome Plan for New Members

A lot rides on a new member's first impression of you and your community. If the atmosphere is friendly and helpful and information regarding the community is easy to find, there's a very good chance that a new member is going to pay another visit. If the community is a disorganized mess and there's no obvious management, he may think twice before coming back.

Having a plan in place to welcome new community members and to offer guidance to both new and existing members is essential for community growth.

Rolling out the virtual welcome mat

A virtual welcome mat isn't a screen shot of a fuzzy green rug proclaiming "Welcome!" It's giving new members the tools to navigate the community and become contributing participants.

As the host of your community, it's your job to see to it that all participants have everything they need to become positive, productive members. You're there to hold the virtual door wide open and greet everyone with a smile. You don't necessarily have to provide coffee and biscuits, but you should remain alert to make sure that no one is wandering aimlessly with no one to talk to and that everyone is comfortable enough with their new memberships to start or participate in conversations on their own.

Being a welcoming community manager means encouraging all members, including newbies and lurkers, to start conversations and participate in existing discussions. Being welcoming also means you have to see to the housekeeping to make sure that all your informational folders are up to date and all policies are still relevant.

A few best practices ensure that everyone is on equal footing, and no one feels left out:

- **Notice new members.** If you notice a new member taking part in a discussion, say hello. Welcome the new member to your community and encourage her to visit your Welcome folder (see the next section) and introduce herself. Also direct her to the comment policies and other guidelines, and make her aware of your contact details. Let her know that you're at her service if she has any questions.

  If this type of information doesn't fit in with the discussion topic, don't hijack the conversation thread. Instead, take it private via direct message or e-mail.

- **Make sure that all your brand information is up to date.** Review your About page or the page that provides information about your brand. Also review contact details, especially if you've undergone management or address changes. If your brand's mission statement has changed or you're refocusing or rebranding, you're going to want to make adjustments. It's also a good idea to check back every month or so to make sure that nothing is old and outdated.

- **Check guidelines and policies often.** Your comment policy and frequently asked questions (FAQs) page are the most important documents in your community. It's essential that you keep these items up to date and enforced, because policies, guidelines, and FAQs are the first places that new community members visit. A good general rule is to make a guidelines check part of your monthly housekeeping. (For more on establishing guidelines and policies, see Chapter 4.)

✔ **Offer a place for new members to check in.** Welcome areas should include a place for new members to introduce themselves and receive welcoming messages from the community manager and other members. This is mostly the case for forums, e-mail groups, and other communities allowing sticky (static) or threaded conversations. Facebook and Twitter don't allow for stickies or threaded replies and don't generally have Welcome folders.

✔ **Send e-mail welcome messages.** If your community requires signups and requires e-mail addresses, you can send a welcome letter to new members automatically. (See "Writing Your Welcome E-Mail," later in this chapter.)

✔ **Keep a calendar open.** Both new and old community members appreciate knowing any important dates to remember. If you have special promotions and contests coming up or you want to commemorate members' birthdays, launch dates, and other special events, use a calendar app that your members can check for key dates.

✔ **Make sure that content is appealing to all.** The most important way to welcome new members is to ensure that your content appeals to everyone (or at least to everyone within your niche). Don't take sides, don't join community cliques, don't allow prejudice, and keep negativity at bay. When a new or potential member comes in and looks around, you want him to think "Wow, I like this place" or "They're talking about all the things I like to talk about," not "Hmmm . . . no one is talking" or "No one has anything nice to say" or "They don't seem to want newcomers here."

✔ **Make introductions.** Online communities provide important networking opportunities. When you get to know the different members of your community, you can introduce members to those with whom they might build important and beneficial relationships. If you notice two or three members who have the same types of ideas, get them together to see whether they can work magic on their own. If two members of your community share a passion for fly fishing, for example, introduce them so that they can discuss it in depth.

The success of your community depends on a new member's first visit. Think about the best ways to make a great first impression and run with them.

Maintaining a Welcome folder

Unless you run a hobby community or a community for a special interest, such religion, parenting, or politics, the majority of the people who become members are there to network. They want to talk about themselves and benefit from relationships with other members of your community. If your community is big or extremely busy, it can be difficult for members to find out about one another as individuals. This is where your Welcome folder comes in.

In the real, noncyber world, if you start a new job, enter a new community, or go to an event where you don't know anyone, you either introduce yourself or someone else makes an introduction. This introduction doesn't always happen for online communities because people can't always tell when you enter the room. Moreover, you may be entering a community where no one knows you to make the introduction. In these cases, it's up to new members to introduce themselves.

Welcome folders don't work for every community, however. Facebook pages, for example, don't allow for a sticky type of folder. Also, introductions don't often work in normal Facebook conversations because after a few other conversations, each post falls from the page, and the introduction isn't the first thing that new members see anymore. Twitter chats also allow for only a very brief introduction; after a flurry of activity, the introduction is gone from the page, though the chat host might provide transcripts for folks to read later.

Online forums are perfect for Welcome folders because they allow you to pin a sticky folder to the top of the forum. This type of folder never moves, so the information never drops off the front page. Online forums are also perfect for introductory or Welcome folders for the same reason. Because most online forums now have Welcome or introductory folders, even new members know to look for these components upon entering the community.

Most Welcome folders are situated inside a forum's welcome area. To start the ball rolling, put up an Introduce Yourself Here folder. The title of your folder should make clear what it's about.

This approach works best for forums. For e-mail groups, these folders are kept on the group's home page, which means members have to check in every now and then to see new updates because they won't receive them via e-mail. Blogs are also set up to have a static page where members can introduce themselves, but most don't do this. Welcome folders are mostly used in forums.

Some forums have a single thread (discussion topic) where new members make their introductions. Others have a specific folder that allows each new member to start a thread for his or her own individual introduction. Each method has pros and cons:

✔ **Group introduction thread:** A single introduction thread allows for a single conversation. New members come in, introduce themselves, and add a few tidbits of what they feel is pertinent information. If they want to, veteran members respond to each new member by saying hello and adding a few words of welcome.

The problem with a group introduction thread is that a single conversation can become hundreds of pages long in a large community. I can guarantee that no one is going to start at page one to read every single "Hello" and "Welcome" comment. Sometimes, the first and last posts in the thread are several years apart, and many of the members aren't even active anymore. Also, members won't want to respond to a comment that's 20 posts away, so they're less likely to respond to old posts in a group discussion thread.

✔ **Individual introduction threads:** When newbies post their own threads, members can drop in at any time to say hello and leave a message. The benefit is that no one has to navigate a long discussion thread to catch up on new memberships and welcome messages. It's also kind of cool because members can pick out a specific aspect of a newbie's introductory thread, such as a job or hobby, and start a discussion based on that aspect. Each discussion is contained in one area and is easy to navigate.

The downside is similar to that of the group discussion thread. Because each discussion is a different thread, members have to navigate multiple threads to find out about new members and say hello. Also, many pages of discussion threads ensue, and it becomes impossible to read older members' introduction threads without investing hours to read each and every one.

Both types of introduction threads have their benefits, and new members love either option as they have the ability to introduce themselves and say a few words about who they are. Also, they don't feel funny about just jumping in to an established community discussion topic if they've already introduced themselves in another area.

Now, not every member reads or even cares about Welcome folders. With communities with hundreds or thousands of members, reading all those "Hello, my name is. . . ." and "Welcome!" posts gets a bit old after a while. It's perfectly normal to see only a couple of regular community members act as the official welcome wagon.

Even if regulars don't use forum introduction folders, it doesn't mean you shouldn't. As community manager, you should schedule welcoming new members as one of your daily tasks. Some days, you won't have any new signups. Other days, especially following a promotion or news, you'll have several. It doesn't take much time to say a few words to each new member.

Guiding new users through landing pages

If the purpose of your community is to sell or promote something or have members read certain content, you'll have to help members get to the places where they can accomplish these goals. Many communities use *landing pages* — pages where members have to achieve a specific goal, such as a subscription or a purchase. Landing pages can be any of the following:

- A sales pitch
- A welcome message
- Community policies and/or guidelines
- A newsletter or RSS feed subscription form
- An advertisement
- An article or blog post
- A Facebook page

Landing pages aren't always easy to find, which is where you come in. If community members didn't land on those action pages via a search engine and don't know that they exist, you have to use a little gentle guidance to get them there. Before you get out your megaphone and start herding, remember two important things:

- Community members don't like obvious sales pitches.
- Community members don't like trickery.

I'll even throw in a bonus tip:

- Community members don't like bossy community managers who tell them that they *have* to visit certain pages.

For new members, landing pages should be more about helping them get around the community than asking them to buy something. Eventually, if they have a positive experience, they'll be more open to subscribing to your newsletter or buying your product. For now, just make them feel comfortable and see to it that they have everything they need. You may find that they like to feel that they've discovered certain pages on their own, even if you gently showed them the way.

Your landing page should contain a Welcome folder. If new members are entering your community through a forum, the "Welcome!" folder should contain one section with links to everything they need. For example, all the rules, regulations and FAQS, plus contact info, brand About pages, and fun stuff.

Though you don't necessarily want to push signups and sales off the bat, it also doesn't hurt to have a couple of enticing links to newsletter subscription forms or sales pages.

Don't leave it up to the search engines to bring in new members or guide them to particular information. Take some time each day to answer questions and, if necessary, lead them to the proper pages and portals.

Forum, blog, or e-mail group landing pages

If you host a forum, blog, or e-mail group, your FAQs page in the Welcome folder is a perfect spot for introducing specific areas of your community or website. Simply create leading questions and use the landing pages to provide the answers.

For example, if you ask "How can I learn more about (insert name of brand here's) products and services?" your response could be, "Please visit the products and services area of our website for a full rundown of the experiences we provide." Now you've killed two birds with one proverbial stone. You answered a question your members will certainly want to know, and you guided them to a spot where they can take action, if they're so inclined.

Also, as many community discussions are centered around the brand, you'll want to take the opportunity to guide members to the most helpful landing pages. For example, if members want to learn more about nutritional information for a food product, let them know where they can go to find what they need. Also, if they want to sign up for your newsletter or the corporate blog, dropping links into the conversation isn't spammy because spam is unwanted information. However, it's ok to link to specific requests.

Facebook landing pages

Facebook landing pages are a bit different than other landing pages. You can create a Facebook landing page if you prefer to have at least one static page, especially if you feel actionable information will get lost among a lively conversation. A Facebook landing page can include one or more of the following:

- ✔ Your brand's logo
- ✔ Your brand's About page
- ✔ A newsletter or other subscription form
- ✔ A sales page

Keep in mind that a special Facebook landing page is optional. Not all members visit this landing page because that's not where the conversation is, and no one wants to hang out much on an obvious sales or signup page.

Many times, a brand has better luck driving community to action by using the sidebar on the left of their Facebook pages. By using links and text, they can guide members to action without being so obvious. Still, others swear by Facebook landing pages because they enable brands to put up a static page of information that shows both new and old members everything they need to know.

Though you want members to enjoy the conversation and they're under no obligation to buy, sell, or talk about you or the brand in any way, you do have an ultimate goal. For most online communities, the purpose behind the community is to get members to take a specific action, whether it's to click an advertisement in order for the brand to earn money or a commission, buy a product, share a link, or sign up to receive something. Your landing page shouldn't turn members or potential members off from socializing while still gently guiding them to action.

Twitter landing pages

It's a little trickier when it comes to suggesting landing pages to a Twitter community where the community is so wary of spam. In fact, it's gotten to the point where many of the people who use Twitter are afraid to mention certain words or key phrases because they're afraid spammers will pick up on it and tweet spammy links to them.

When you're making your rounds on Twitter, think before dropping a link to a landing page. If a member is talking about your brand because he had a positive customer service experience, the last thing you want to do is turn it into something negative by being pushy or spammy. Say thank you and invite that person to contact you with any questions or to learn more about the products or services you provide. If someone is looking for specific information — for example, "I love Brand X, but for the life of me can't find nutritional information online about this product" — you can reach out with a nice comment and a link to the information he's seeking. Sending links out randomly is considered spam. Even if it doesn't turn off most members or potential members, it'll get you banned.

Offering perks to newcomers

Here's a question for you: Though you want community members to take a specific action, what's in it for them beyond having a conversation with a brand? As awesome as you may think that you and your brand are, that general awesomeness won't always catch a potential member's eye and invite her into the community. If you're expecting sales, signups, or brand evangelism, you're going to have to have something to offer beyond conversation.

Unless your online community is one in which hobbyists and enthusiasts share their passion or come to find out about a specific topic, getting members to rally around your brand may be a hard sell. People enjoy certain brands, but they're generally aren't so enthusiastic that they'll visit the community each day or talk about the brand on the social networks. They need a little bit of enticement to visit your community, participate in the conversation, and especially evangelize your brand.

To generate this kind of brand loyalty, it's a good idea to offer perks and swag:

- ✔ **Offer T-shirts to everyone who signs up for your newsletter.** Everyone likes shirts. Even people who don't wear shirts with logos or words on them want to take them home to give to a family member or to sleep in. Because most Internet giveaways are inexpensive and even flimsy, a T-shirt is desirable swag.

- ✔ **Provide discount coupons for making a certain number of comments.** Most new members sign up for a brand's online community to receive free or discounted products. If you have a great product or service, and you can entice members to buy by using a discount code, they'll buy again if they like the experience. You may not get 100 percent return, but even 20 percent would be significant.

- ✔ **Announce different levels of perks for different levels of community commitment.** If new members know that they'll receive perks for participation, and that they'll receive more perks the more they participate, they're more likely to become active members of the community. They're also more apt to spread the news to friends, family members, and people they meet online.

- ✔ **Offer special badges and avatars for various levels of participation.** Community members love to show off their commitment. By giving them badges to display in their community profiles or widgets to display on their blogs, you not only let members show their level of participation and commitment to the brand, but also entice nonmembers to find out what all the fuss is about. When you award special badges for a certain number of comments or years of participation, members who earn them will feel super special, and members who aren't so active will want to achieve the same awards.

List the perks for all levels of participation on a specific welcome or landing page so that potential members know they'll receive cool stuff and freebies for various levels of commitment. Offer incentives for members to tweet about their rewards or post pictures on a special page so that nonmembers can see these perks and benefits and sign up as well.

People don't want pitches; they want perks. If you want them to buy your stuff or evangelize your product, you're going to have to offer something valuable in return. Suppose that your product is a newsletter. Truthfully, most people don't want to read newsletters, especially from a brand that's looking to sell products, but they may be inclined to subscribe to a newsletter if they know that they'll receive something worthwhile. Stickers won't encourage anyone to subscribe, but a T-shirt or coupon might. Moreover, if you continue to offer discounts in your newsletters, members won't trash the newsletters as soon as they receive their gifts.

Offering incentives to bring a friend

Like members of any good club or network, community members who enjoy the online socializing want to refer friends. It seems only fair to reward them for their good deeds. Here are a few possible rewards:

- Offer "Buy one, get one free" deals to a community member who brings in a friend.
- Give discounts and freebies to anyone who refers a friend.
- Offer higher levels of prizes for each friend referred.
- Pay a commission to member for every product purchased by a referred friend.

Writing Your Welcome E-Mail

Have you ever signed up at an online store or other e-commerce website and received a letter almost immediately afterward? This letter was the brand's welcome e-mail.

To receive this e-mail, you had to *opt in* — agree to receive letters, news, and updates from the brand. (For more on opting in, see the section "Asking Members to Opt in to Future E-Mail Campaigns," later in this chapter.)

The welcome e-mail reminds new members that they signed up for membership, lets them know why it's a good idea to be a member, and even offers an area where they can *opt out* — remove themselves from the mailing list.

Even communities that don't have stuff to sell often send members an introductory e-mail containing a welcome message, links to various important pages, and even a discount or other perk.

Many times, people sign up to be part of a community without realizing they've done so. For example, they may have registered at an online store while doing some shopping because they don't want to have to enter in the same contact information every time they shop at the same stores.

Other times, folks know exactly what they're signing up for and expect to receive correspondence, newsletters, and information for making the most of their experience with the community.

Welcome e-mails are important first communications between a brand or interest group and its members because it tells them what to expect and what benefits they can gain from community membership.

Writing welcoming form letters

Form letters are a convenient way to send messages to community members because you don't have to take the time to write a personal e-mail for each person. That convenience is also a problem. Everyone likes to feel special, and there's nothing personal about a form letter. Many people see form letters in the inbox and automatically delete them.

Still, if your community has a lot of members, you can't avoid using form letters. You probably don't have enough time to write a personal letter to everyone who joins the community, and you can't possibly know enough about every person to write a personal letter for each one. The trick is to create a form letter that looks and feels personal but is still a prewritten note sent to everyone who joins.

Here are a few form letter best practices:

- **Use first names.** Avoid using first and last names together or no name at all. The salutation "Dear New Member" or "Dear John Smith" is a sure sign that a member is getting an impersonal form letter. Though your members aren't dumb, and they know that they're going to be receiving form letters, the trick is to make it look like you wrote each letter just for them. Use an e-mail program, such as AWeber.com or ConstantContact.com, that pulls the first name from each signup page so that the salutation of a new-member e-mail reads "Dear John" instead.

- **Avoid using jargon.** Nothing turns people off more than smarmy sales jargon. It's unattractive for a couple of reasons: People may not understand all the terms, and it's apparent that you'd much rather sell than converse. Jargon is impersonal.

✔ **Provide directions.** Your welcome e-mail should also give direction to new members. The e-mail tells them what to expect and where to find all items of interest. If handled properly, the welcome e-mail directs new members everywhere you want them to go:

- Community discussion topics

- Promotional pages

- FAQs

- Comment policy and guidelines

- Brand policies

- Contact information

- Your About page

- Sales and discounts

✔ **Include contact details.** Your new community members appreciate knowing that you're an accessible manager. Make sure that you include a way to get in touch so that new members can reach out with questions and concerns.

✔ **Use a signature.** Sign your e-mails, even if you're only going to scan your signature or use a script font. Your members know that you can't sign an e-mail with a pen, but you can sign it with a flourish and make it seem more personal.

How can you do all this directing when you know that it's also important not to spam new community members? Remember that you're not spamming if you have permission to send the e-mail. New members must have agreed to receive this e-mail when they registered to be part of the community, so don't worry too much about being spammy, but do try to make your welcome e-mail more than just a bunch of links.

The point of your welcome e-mail is to remind your new members that they signed up to join in the first place and also to eliminate confusion. You want to guide them so that they find all the necessary information, without an obnoxious sales pitch or even pushing them into taking an action they're not interested in. The key is to invite or suggest, rather than tell someone where to go.

Reiterating the rules

Very few people will read your rules or guidelines word for word. In fact, those who do read them will scan in order to get the gist of what you're saying. The majority of members who make up your community couldn't care less about comment policies and community guidelines which is why there are so many rule breakers. The truth is most click "I agree" without even know what it is they agree to.

It never hurts to remind anyone of the rules. Pointing them to to your comment policies, FAQs, and guidelines doesn't hurt. Like the regulations posted in your forum, not everyone is going to stop by and read them but pointing them out will encourage some of your newbies to take a first or second list. Moreover, it holds you free from liability if you have to reprimand or ban a member who isn't playing by the rules. If anyone tells you he didn't know he couldn't say a certain thing or behave in a certain manner, you can point out that you sent him the guidelines in the welcome e-mail as well as posting them in the forum for all to see. While it's up to you to set rules and guidelines and past them in a prominent area, the onus of reading and behaving according to the rule falls on the member.

You don't have to point out the rules by lecturing. Simply have a paragraph on the welcome letter linking to the appropriate content. Lead up to it by saying, "Before you begin participating in community discussions, please read our comment policy" or "Please see our Frequently Asked Questions page before writing to ask question to be sure we haven't already answered them."

For more on rules and guidelines, see Chapter 4.

Watch your welcome-letter language

Try to make the letter sound more like news than a sales pitch. Write in a conversational tone to make new members feel comfortable and invite them to take part in your community's many experiences rather than push them into a sale. Use words that entice rather than pitch. Try these examples of enticing words:

✔ **Invite** ("I'd like to take this time to invite you to view this week's discounts.")

✔ **Enjoy** ("Enjoy the conversation with other members of our community.")

✔ **Experience** ("Why not experience the many positive benefits that come with participating in our community?")

✔ **Appreciate** ("We truly appreciate your faith in us.")

✔ **Welcome** ("Welcome to the Brand X community.")

✔ **Share** ("I'd love to share some of the many community resources...")

✔ **Community** ("As a community member, you'll enjoy...")

✔ **Thank you** or **thanks** ("Thanks for joining our community.")

✔ **Entertain** ("You'll find our discussion topics both enlightening and entertaining.")

✔ **Conversation** ("I hope you'll join the conversation.")

Asking Members to Opt in to Future E-Mail Campaigns

You're attracting new members who've signed up to be part of the community, and you're even sending out a welcome letter. Don't rest on your laurels yet, though. You still have a little more work to be done.

It's not enough to point members to a web page and leave it at that. You also want them to be apprised of all your news and updates, and the majority of your members won't be visiting your online community each day. That's where e-mail comes in. To make the most of your growing communities, you also want to be able to reach members via newsletter. However, you don't want to send them anything they didn't sign up to receive.

Behold the opt-in. Opting in is asking community members to sign up for newsletters and other mailings on their own accord. It means they checked off a box giving you permission to send them your newsletter.

For example, in your Welcome e-mail or folder, you should include text inviting new members to sign up for your newsletter by creating a check box with "I would like to subscribe to your newsletter so I can receive news and updates." Many blogs and Facebook pages also have opt in text or links in their sidebars.

If you have several different types of newsletters or mailings members should be able to sign up for each one individually. Most members don't sign up for every newsletter or mailing you put out, but, rather one or two.

No one likes to clog their e-mail boxes with stuff they don't have time to read, so don't take it personally if they don't subscribe.

For those who opt in, make sure that you set up your newsletter program to send a confirmation. This way, your members have an additional way to opt out if they changed their mind. Also, it ensures that no one is signing them up for something they don't want to receive and reminds them of their commitment.

Chapter 10

Encouraging Community Interaction and Involvement

In This Chapter

▶ Making your online community fun and interesting

▶ Figuring out what others are saying about your community

▶ Gaining popularity through word of mouth

There's nothing more rewarding than watching your community grow and its members interact. When a community clicks, it becomes a congenial and positive place to interact. This camaraderie doesn't always happen on its own, however. Sometimes, topics don't come easily, or participation isn't happening. At other times, a community is entirely too serious and needs some fun to liven things up.

In this chapter, I focus on fun ways to encourage community participation and feedback, while keeping the tone light and positive.

Creating an Upbeat Environment

An online community doesn't have to be a perpetually serious place. Cerebral topics and daily debates get old after a while. Wouldn't it be better if your members walked away each day smiling or inspired to take action? Not everyone has the talent to make people interact and even laugh, and that's where you come in. With some creativity, you can take your community from a place to leave comments to a lively haven that folks don't want to leave. It's human nature to want to have fun.

You can't force community. You can't put members in the same virtual room and expect magic to happen. Instead, you have to get the party started and keep it going. Many fun tools are at your disposal, and more launch each day. Take advantage of polls, contests, and other fun ways to gauge community interest. Your members will enjoy participation, and you'll receive important feedback in return.

Posting polls

If you're active on Facebook, you may notice that many of your friends and relatives enjoy asking fun questions and posting polls. They're not necessary into the answers; they're just looking for some lively interaction.

You can create a poll about anything, thanks to the assortment of polling tools available. It's not difficult to find an app that's easy to install and easy to use, with easy-to-see results.

Polls don't have to all be about your brand, either. Sure, you can fire them up now and then for feedback, but your members don't want to feel like guinea pigs. Instead, find some poll topics that everyone will enjoy talking about. For example:

✔ Personal (but not too personal) habits

✔ Favorite types of music, TV shows, or movies

✔ Hobbies

✔ Sports

✔ Summer pastimes

✔ Books

✔ Current events (but avoid heated topics unless you're looking for a heated discussion)

Offering polls is a good way to let members share interests and tell a little something about themselves, and the information gathered in polls is invaluable to you as community manager. Every bit of information, no matter how trivial, is important. You can do something with this stuff. If you work for a lemonade company, for example, and you find out that your community is made up of heavy readers, you can start a summer book club and offer a recipe featuring your brand to accompany a book discussion.

Holding contests

Contests keep your community members entertained and alert. If your idea is fun and upbeat, members will be more interested in the interaction than in the prizes. You can host different levels of contests. Contests with regular small prizes, such as discount coupons, keep members showing up each day to get their next opportunity to save. Contests with higher-level prizes take place less often but keep your members on the lookout for them nonetheless.

For example, some communities host limerick or haiku contests where members create odes to the brand or a product. Others draw random names out of a hat. Be creative with your contests so that members want to be a part of them regardless of the prize.

You can hold contests for a variety of reasons:

- ✔ **To draw traffic to your community:** When other people see your members interacting on the social networks or even offline, they'll want to know what all the fuss is about. They'll want prizes, too.

  If you have a button that enables your members to share the contest on social networks, they'll help spread the word for you, bringing in even more new members.

- ✔ **To give something back:** Rewarding loyalty with prizes and perks tells customers that their participation means something to the brand.

- ✔ **To gather information:** Contests can center on habits or product use to provide demographic information.

- ✔ **To defuse a tense situation:** Contests can help lighten up the atmosphere after a bout of negativity.

- ✔ **To create buzz about your brand:** People share fun, awesome contests.

- ✔ **To create content for your brand:** Contests create even more content for your brand, and this content will catch the attention of search engines and web surfers.

Interacting with Members through the Social Networks

Your community members aren't hanging out in one consolidated spot. They're scattered all over the web. They're not necessarily looking to interact with you, either. You have to seek them out rather than the other way around. Most people aren't hanging around on your forum or Facebook page all day, and it's up to you to find them, engage, and get them to act in one way or another.

Interacting online doesn't mean sending out links or annoying potential members with 140-character sales pitches. Following the proper protocol and etiquette will keep you from being laughed at, ignored, or (worse) blocked.

Also, remembering important rules of engagement mean you're never at a loss for words and you'll gain more friends and followers. The more fun you are on the social networks, the more interesting information you share (not necessarily about the brand), and the more personable you are, the more word will spread about what a fun person you are to follow. People will want to join your community because you have a reputation for creating a light-hearted, interesting environment.

Engaging others online

When you're engaging with current and potential community members, respect their space and privacy, but find common ground.

Here are a few tips for engaging with your community on the social networks:

- ✔ **Don't be aggressive.** No one likes pushy people. Chatting with people who may be a good fit for your community is fun, but making every interaction a push to join the community means you'll lose friends *and* members. Give the relationship time. When folks are interacting with you online, they know who you are, either because they've socialized with you before or because they read your profile before engaging with you. If they like you, they'll follow you to your community.

- ✔ **Ask questions.** If you're not engaging people in conversation, you may as well be talking to yourself. It's fun to make statements and share snippets throughout the day, but you'll get more response if you ask questions. Questions don't have to be about work or the brand. You can ask for tips, crossword-puzzle answers, and book recommendations. Every response is a discussion waiting to happen.

- ✔ **Share.** Sharing is what social networking is all about. People like to have fun, and sharing videos or articles and making them laugh will help you gain more friends and followers. Sharing discussion-worthy news items will help engage more serious types and show that your community isn't all fluff. Also, when you share something awesome, and your community members share in turn, it's almost like they get to take credit for the content because their friends and followers see them as being the original person to share the content.

- ✔ **Drop links sparingly.** There's a thin line between sharing and spamming, and if you're not careful, you can cross that line and drive people away. Sharing occasional bits of fun or news is fine, but making every comment or update a link back to your stuff is spam. Don't do it. You'll get a bad reputation, and so will your brand.

✔ **Make new friends (but keep the old).** Use the social networks to make new friends each day. Find a few who share your interests and friend or follow them. Respond to their questions and comments, and they may friend or follow you in turn. Don't neglect your old friends, however. It's equally as important to keep them engaged as well.

✔ **Let nonmembers of your community know what you're talking about.** If you have a fun promotion or interesting discussion happening on your blog or Facebook page, invite others to join in. It's not spammy to share your own fun once in a while.

✔ **Remember the little details.** Find out as much as you can about the regular members of your community. Make note of birthdays and send out birthday wishes. Find out about hobbies and share information of interest. Don't be afraid to call members out by name. If you want to share with a member of your community on Twitter, for example, you can say "Hey @twitterfriend, I saw this article about the migration patterns of tropical ladybugs and thought of you, since that seems to be your passion." If you don't have a long, drawn-out conversation, members appreciate it when you remember little personal things about them.

✔ **Retweet.** Retweeting is fun. It allows you to support a member who shared something awesome, and it may set off a wonderful chain of retweets, raising more awareness for the original commenter.

Avoid *vanity retweets* — retweets of nice things that people say about you — because they make you look like a fool.

✔ **Know when to take the discussion private.** Having a dialogue with another member or social-networking friend is the point of the whole thing, but sometimes other people get tired of reading your conversation. If a discussion gets too long or too personal, take it private.

✔ **Disclose.** Be honest with your community members. If you're using the social networks to sell, drop an affiliate link, or direct someone to a sales page, you have to let them know. It's illegal and unethical to be coy about selling.

Social networking pages and accounts are personal. Though you socialize with others online, you're not what your members would consider a close and personal friend. Members may be interested in following your brand on the social networks in order to learn news, participate in contests, and interact, but they're not necessarily looking to be your personal friend beyond all of that. Try not to invade their private space. If you develop a relationship that leads to a deeper friendship, by all means become a Facebook friend or a Twitter follower. Otherwise, leave the friendship on the brand pages only. It's nothing personal; it's like you befriending the Customer Service lady at your local telephone company. You're happy she helped and had a friendly time of it, but you're not looking to socialize on a deeper level.

The most successful online communities can run themselves in their manager's absence, but it's not recommended you stay away too long. You need to be there to help move the conversation along, create fun diversions, and put out fires.

Using conversational marketing to generate buzz and sales

When you're spending time on the social networks and visiting blogs, forums, and other communities to chat, what you're really doing is *conversational marketing.* By talking and building relationships, you're creating buzz about your brand, which may convert to sales. If you do it right, no sales pitch is involve. You may not even have to share links.

Very few people are going to respond to what you do. The majority of your community members aren't buying, selling, retweeting, promoting, or showing you any love for the cause. You don't have to give up on them, however. By being active in the social networks and maintaining a constant presence, you're staying on their radar. Even members who are less than active know who you are and what you want from them, even though you're not coming out and saying it in an obvious manner. If you're not a visible force and if your brand sort of fades into oblivion, members aren't going to remember you when it comes time to take action — whatever that action may be.

If people know who you are and what you do and remember you as someone who's nice but not pitchy or pushy, they'll reach out to you when they need help. Conversation isn't important just for the here and now. You also need it for the future.

Conversational marketing is more than just making sure that the lurkers don't forget about you, though. Probably the most important aspect of the whole thing is listening. There's a line in the movie *Pulp Fiction* that all community managers should think about often. In the movie, while having dinner, Uma Thurman asked John Travolta, "In conversation, do you listen or wait to talk again?" The sad truth is that too many people aren't hearing what's being said because they're too busy thinking about what they're going to say at the next pause, and this is a big mistake.

Some people look down on salespeople because many of them are all about the pitch. They want to find the perfect combination of words for the purpose of driving other people to buy. In-your-face pitches are fine for cheesy infomercials but not for growing a community. Listen and then talk, and then you can watch your community grow.

Listening opens a world of possibilities:

✔ **It puts you in touch with new trends.** By paying attention to what people are talking about and what they're buying or using on a regular basis, you get an idea of what the people in your demographic are into.

✔ **It tells you what's wrong.** This item doesn't always apply just to feedback about the brand. Listening can tell you why people aren't enamored with customer service or big business, for example. You need to know what turns people off in order to bring them the things that turn them on.

✔ **It makes you smarter.** When you listen, you learn — everything from trivia and pop culture to best practices for business and tips for success. Every day, people talk about things that you had no idea existed. How would you know about them if you're not listening?

✔ **It provides an opening for conversation.** Hearing what others are saying is a way of biding your time until the perfect opportunity comes along. When you hear it, you can add your own input or offer a suggestion.

Monitoring the social networks for feedback

As a community manager, you'll spend a lot of time on the social networks to see who's talking about your brand. It's important to have an arsenal of tools and networks ready so you can monitor feedback.

There's nothing a brand wants less than a public outpouring of negativity directed toward the brand. It's important to catch and respond to any brand negativity as soon as possible.

Consider the following tools for your arsenal:

✔ **Twitter:** The microblogging social network Twitter is a favorite haunt for community managers who want to collect feedback. Using a Twitter application, such as HootSuite.com, TweetDeck.com, or Seesmic.com, allows you to follow hashtags and search terms and receive updates as they come in. If you're searching for comments about Joe's Furniture Emporium, for example, type that exact phrase in your Twitter app or a search engine, such as `http://search.twitter.com`, and see results from everyone who has mentioned your brand recently. Because Twitter has so many users, it's almost impossible to see who's talking about your brand without using one of the handy apps.

✔ **Facebook:** Facebook is a gold mine of information. Everything your members talk about, no matter how trivial it seems, is an important nugget telling you who they are and what they want. Members of your Facebook community post notices on your wall to discuss why they're happy or why they have a bone to pick with you.

✔ **Google Blog Search:** You should use Google Blog Search (`www.google.com/blogsearch`) at least once a day. Many bloggers are very opinionated and like to rant about poor experiences. Monitoring blog posts and comments allows you to reach out to a disgruntled member and work on the next steps.

✔ **Google Alerts:** When you set up a Google Alert (`www.google.com/alerts`) by using specific keywords and phrases, you receive e-mail notices whenever your brand and other search terms are mentioned. The alerts include links so that you can read the content and respond accordingly.

✔ **Yelp!:** If your brand is a store, restaurant, or local business, it may have been reviewed on Yelp,com! It never hurts to see what people are saying, but there are also reports of trolling and unfair remarks from disgruntled ex-employees on this and other review sites.

Always make a note of who's saying what and why. Sometimes, banned community members will bad-mouth you or your brand, which comes with the territory, but you shouldn't always dismiss bad feedback as bogus. (For more on responding to feedback, see Chapter 7.)

Creating Advocates from within the Community

The best part about online communities is how once the word spreads, folks are just clamoring to join. They hear about others' good experiences and want to share in their experience. Once word gets out that you're providing a fun, online experience, the signups will be fast and furious.

When an online community is a positive experience, members will want to share with their friends. You can't buy authentic member advocacy, but you can certainly create it by providing a place members not only want to enjoy daily, but that they want their friends and relatives to enjoy it as well.

Here's how you and your fans can help spread the word about your online community:

- ✔ **Encourage members to bring friends.** Hosting a "bring a friend" campaign is a terrific way to welcome new members and reward older members for their support. Sometimes, just asking members to bring friends is enough, and you don't need to offer incentives. However, it's always nice to offer some type of prize, such as a discount or coupon for sales-oriented communities. Another option is to enter all participants in a drawing for a bigger prize.

- ✔ **Share pages.** It stands to reason if something is easy to share, people will be inclined to, well, share. Make sure that you have Share buttons where members of your communities can find them. These buttons are easy to install and allow one-click sharing for Facebook, Twitter, Google Buzz, and other social networks. Sharing is an "out of sight, out of mind" sort of thing, and if you don't put the idea out there, most people won't think to share.

- ✔ **Make joining easy.** Most online communities have simple, secure signup processes in place. If potential members want to join, they'll soon lose interest if they have to jump through too many hoops to activate their membership. Have a sign-on page and e-mail activation page is the norm; having to deal with a variety of CAPTCHAS (codes that must be typed to prove one isn't a spammer), check boxes, and long, informational forms will discourage new membership.

- ✔ **Remember the little things.** You know what makes people happy? When you remember them and make them feel special. Birthday or congratulatory announcements give community members the impression that you care.

- ✔ **Make it fun.** Folks want to share enjoyable experiences. Use polls, quizzes, and games to mix things up and add fun.

- ✔ **Provide value.** All community managers should ask themselves these questions: Why would anyone want to join my community? What value will I provide to members? Is the community a learning experience? Does it offer savings on a product or service? Does it feature intelligent discussion? A community can't just sit there; it has to provide something useful to its members.

True word-of-mouth marketing can't be bought. If you build an engaging community, your members will advocate on your behalf and bring in others.

Chapter 11

Attracting More People to Your Website

*W*hen I talk about community traffic, I'm not talking about cars, trucks, and motorcycles. Instead, I'm referring to the number of people who visit your online community each day. Your traffic is based on how many people drop by each day, and you want more rather than fewer.

In Chapter 13, I discuss how to measure your traffic. Here, I focus on how to bring traffic to your community by using the right kinds of keywords and content.

Gaining Momentum: Why Slow and Steady Wins the Race

Online communities aren't set-it-and-forget-it affairs. Though the best case scenario is to achieve steady, organic growth, the truth is, it doesn't happen overnight. You may be frustrated at first because you have only a few members at a time and your employer may not think your community is growing quick enough, but the truth of the matter is that very few overnight success cases occur.

A slow, steady growth can give you a better idea of who your community members are and help you tweak your online tools accordingly. A mob scene doesn't give a community manager the opportunity to get to know members on a more personal level. It's important to know exactly who is in your community, for several reasons:

✔ You can tailor content and social networking to meet their needs.

✔ You'll be able to offer the most appropriate types of promotions.

✔ You can write the types of content they want to read.

✔ You can easily work out discussion topics when you know who you're talking to.

Something else to consider is the experience of a community manager. This isn't true for every case, but sometimes it's easier for a new community manager to learn and grow with the community. If you've never managed a community, perhaps a crowded community scene isn't the place to start. A slow, steady beginning will allow you to get your bearings and learn as you go.

When a community is built around a mob, the mob rules. When a community starts out slow, there's more mutual respect between the members of the community and those in authority. The rules are established early, and there's no power struggle between the community and their moderator.

Does this mean you have to wait five years to see good results? Absolutely not, but instead of hoping for overnight success, work on bringing in a steady stream of new members. In time, it will almost seem as if the community is growing itself.

Taking Advantage of Search Engine Optimization

Search engine optimization (SEO) is the act of creating content that appeals to search engines. When you consider most people who are searching for certain websites look at only the first page or two of search-engine results, you need to do everything you can to put your community as high on the first couple of results pages as you can. To do this, you have to use the terms and phrases most people use to find your community. In short, SEO catches the attention of the search engines, which in turn catch the attention of potential community members.

Keying in on the right words and phrases

The search terms you want your community to rank high on are called *keywords*. If you want to use a phrase, it's called a *key phrase*.

You want to use the most important keywords and key phrases in your content without looking all obvious about it, but sometimes, this is easier said than done.

First, you have to determine the important words and phrases to use as your keywords. You can't just make up words and hope they lead people to your community. They have to be relevant and descriptive, and they have to make sense.

Many website owners make the mistake of using unnatural-sounding key phrases because of how people search. The problem is that most people don't talk like they search. A top search phrase, for example, is *buy new refrigerator,* but if you're looking to purchase a new fridge, you wouldn't use this phrase when you're talking to someone face to face. Instead, try something more natural sounding like "refrigerator sales," "discounted refrigerators" or even "appliance stores in New Jersey." Even though you want to choose keywords that will help you rank high, the last thing you want to do is use poor grammar, misspellings, or clunky-sounding examples, simply because that's what people type in to search engines.

The following list can help you determine how to find the right keywords for your community and content:

- ✔ **Use your stats.** Your stats program (see Chapter 13) tells you everything you need to know about the people who visit your website or community. Stats allow you to view the keywords and phrases that folks use to land on your website from search engines. If you work for Mattress King, for example, and your stats reveal people are finding your community by typing *affordable mattresses,* you know one important key phrase. Now enter that keyword in a search engine. Where is your community landing on the results page? If it's one of the top results, that's excellent; if not, you'll want to do what you can to get your site to the top of that list.

- ✔ **Do your own searching.** Search for your community online without using its URL or its title. Simply think of the terms you would use to find out more about your brand or community topic. Also, think of search terms that don't mention your brand. If your brand is Skippy, for example, search phrases may include *peanut butter, peanut butter recipes,* and *peanut butter cookies.* See where your community ranks in all the search results, and determine whether it can do better.

- ✔ **Find out what keywords competing communities use.** Using Skippy as an example again, find out what keywords competing brands such as Jif and Peter Pan use.

  Free tools available at Alexa (`www.alexa.com`) and Compete (`www.compete.com`) let you know some of the keywords your competitors use.

- ✔ **Use a keyword suggestion program.** You can use a keyword suggestion program to find keywords that relevant to your brand. Enter a keyword or subject, and the program offers you a list of keyword options, ranked by popularity. You want to choose the keywords that are the most popular and have the best results, of course. Some good tools to try are Google AdWords (`www.google.com/AdWords`), `Wordtracker.com`, and `SEOBook.com`.

Use different methods to keep on top of the keywords and key phrases that are being used to find your community as well as to find what's popular in your community. As keywords change every so often, it's a good idea to check them every six months or so and create your content accordingly. It's also a good idea to try new keywords and key phrases to try to reach a totally new audience.

Catching the attention of the search engines

When you have a good idea of the types of keywords to use in your content, it's time to write the content so that it looks natural. Too many people pepper keywords liberally around their blog posts, web articles, About pages, and other content, which looks silly and wrong. Although using keywords is good SEO, the best SEO is providing the best content available. Make sure that your keywords are relevant and that they make sense.

In addition, try the following tips when crafting your keywords and phrases:

- ✔ **Use keywords and key phrases in blog posts and article titles.** If you use the same keywords in a couple of different articles, your content becomes more attractive to the search engines. If you can, use them in titles which make them extra visible.

- ✔ **Use keywords and key phrases in at least one heading or subheading.** If your blog post or article features headings and subheadings, try to use your keywords in one heading. This will also make them attractive to the search engines.

- ✔ **Use each keyword or key phrase at least 3 times in a 500-word post or article.** If you can write a great article that uses a keyword at least three times, try to do so. You don't want to write content so that it seems unnatural, but you need to catch the attention of the search engines if you want your community to make their front pages. So if your keyword is "banana milkshakes," create content with this keyword in mind. For example, you can post a variety of banana milkshake recipes, discussion nutrition, or provide techniques for properly making said milkshake. Each article should use "banana milkshake" several times without it sounding overused and redundant.

Beware of *keyword saturation* — the practice of using keywords so many times that you turn off both readers and search engines. It was the practice in the mid-2000s to write articles so heavily laden with keywords that most people considered them to be spam. Keyword saturation led to an SEO bubble burst, and now writers and webmasters are a little more careful about what they put in their content.

Creating Reader-Friendly Content

Keywords are important, but content is even more important. In fact, content is king. No matter how many keywords you use, and no matter how hard you try to catch the attention of the search engines, people are more likely to stick around and see what you have to offer if you offer content that's informative, engaging, and useful.

Here's something else to consider: When you write something great, people will share your content. They'll send it out on Twitter, and others will retweet it. People who read good content also like to share it on Facebook, and bloggers like to lead discussions about compelling content that they read online, which also captures the attention of the search engines. Having content that attracts readers and encourages them to share is the best SEO possible.

How do you know what type of content to write for your community? Here are a few tips:

- ✔ **Spread the news.** If you have a company blog, use it to write news and updates about your brand.

- ✔ **Write content that relates to your community.** If you represent a sugar brand, write about the benefits of sugar, sugar cookie recipes, or home-made beauty products that use sugar.

- ✔ **Write evergreen content.** Content that remains relevant over the years is called *evergreen*. News items and fads that stay on the front pages for a short period aren't evergreen.

  Provide a balance of newsy and evergreen content.

The best part about good content is how it helps grow community. Web articles and blogs allow for comments. Write engaging comment, and your community will grow as they participate in the ensuing discussion.

Inviting Community Participation

The best testimonials can't be bought; they come from the heart. Here's the best part: Many of your community members may be bloggers and social-media enthusiasts who are more than happy to spread the word about a positive experience. If they really enjoy themselves, that experience turns into more than a one-off visit to your community and they become regular members.

You want people who are active in social media to be part of your community, and the trick is to appeal to them the right way.

Reaching out to bloggers

Bloggers do more than jot down ramblings of their everyday lives. Today's bloggers are web-savvy, tech-savvy, and generally savvy about a variety of topics.

Bloggers are your friends. I don't mean that in a "go out and find a blogger to use" sort of way, but in a community sharing way. Bloggers are community managers too — and they have the ability to drive traffic to your brand.

Bloggers cover a variety of genres and niches. They enjoying sharing tips, news, and even reviews. When you invite bloggers to participate in your community, there's a good chance that they'll recommend the community to their own network. They may write blog posts encouraging other people to join or make recommendations via Twitter and Facebook. If they become productive members of your community, you can share traffic both ways — a win–win situation.

Be careful with your outreach, though. There's nothing bloggers like less than receiving an obvious pitch, especially if it's not relevant to their niche. If you run an automotive community, you wouldn't want to reach out to a wine or food blogger. But if you run a foodie community, wine and food bloggers are exactly the people you want to reach.

You also don't want to seem as though you're trying to get something for nothing. Bloggers work hard. It's one thing to make them aware of your community and invite them to participate. It's something else to expect them to evangelize you and do a bunch or work for nothing. If you're looking for bloggers to write about you and bring in new members, you're going to have to give them something in return. Public relations professionals make a lot of money to promote brands, and too many brands look upon bloggers as some sort of cheap labor. If you want bloggers to pimp your brand on a regular basis, think about how they're going to benefit as well.

Research the blogs that are relevant to your niche. If you're with a sour cream brand, you can consider parent bloggers, food bloggers, recipe bloggers, and nutrition bloggers, to name only a few types. Read their blogs as far back as you can to determine whether they're a good fit for your own brand. Also make sure that they're the types of bloggers who share news and information about brands like yours with their readers.

When you have the ideal bloggers on your radar, reach out to them:

> ✔ **Send an invitation that isn't spammy and doesn't read like a sales pitch.** Let the bloggers know a little about your community and why they might enjoy participation. The goal is for them to have such a positive experience that they'll want to write about it on their blogs and share links with their other online networks. If you tell them that this is

your goal, however, they'll probably be turned off. I'm not saying that you should trick them; simply invite them to participate, and see what happens. If they do share links to your community or invite other people to join, see how you can reciprocate. Perhaps you can share their blogs and communities with your own.

- ✔ **Rather than invite bloggers to participate in discussions, do interviews with them.** Have them share their expertise with your community. Bloggers often promote their interviews, and this may help you to bring in new members as members of the blogger's own community come by to read the interview.

- ✔ **Let it be known that you or some interesting members of your brand are open to doing blog interviews.** During the interviews, you can mention the online community and invite people to join.

- ✔ **Find blogs that are relevant to your brand and offer to write guest posts.** A guest post has to be an informative article or fun topic; it shouldn't be promotional. At the end of your post, you'll have room to share details about your brand and issue an invitation to join your community. Don't forget to tell potential followers where they can find you on the social networks.

- ✔ **Attend blogging conferences and network with the other attendees.** Don't assault them with handouts and other paraphernalia, but do take the time to get to know as many bloggers as possible, and talk to them about how you can help one another.

Nothing makes bloggers angrier than to receive a request to do work, with no compensation. It's one thing to ask for an interview or invite them to stop by your community. It's a whole other deal to send them a letter with a long laundry list of ways they can promote your community with no benefit to them at all. If you're going to ask bloggers to promote your brand, offer some form of compensation. Bloggers aren't free labor.

Asking the community for reviews

The difference between evangelizing a brand and doing a review is that brand evangelists don't review: They promote, and they're compensated in exchange for their promotion. Reviewers, on the other hand, generally work for free, because their reviews come from the heart. Once you pay for reviews, you're actually asking for an advertisement or a paid post called a sponsored post. There's nothing wrong with reaching out to bloggers, writers, and other community members and asking them if they're interested in reviewing your brand or community.

If your community is a forum, people have to pay to join, so be sure to offer a free subscription to anyone doing a review. If your community is part of a brand, as opposed to a hobby community, you might also throw in some product or free service so that they can talk knowledgeably about the brand and fit in with your community conversations.

Make sure that you choose the right types of people to give reviews. If they have no interest in your brand, your niche, or your community, they're not the best people to contact; their reviews won't be enthusiastic and may do more harm than good, as people sometimes complain on Twitter that they received a pitch that isn't relevant to them at all. Always research the people you're pitching to.

You can mention in your community's Twitter or Facebook account that you're looking for reviewers, but you also want to reach out to people who aren't part of your community to get honest, credible reviews from people who haven't already bought in to your brand.

When you request reviews, you're really requesting honest feedback. Sometimes, honest feedback isn't what you want to hear, but don't get defensive. Even if the review wasn't as positive as you hoped it would be, thank the person who offered it and use it as food for thought for community improvement.

Creating an enticing Facebook page to attract new members

When you're building a community, you want to be where the people are, and at this time, Facebook is the best way to reach out to a vast community. People appreciate Facebook because they don't have to leave their own status pages to receive updates and discussion topics. Community managers love it because when friends see community members liking or sharing a Facebook page, they want to be part of the action, too. You're rocking a double win.

A Facebook page is made up of members who like your brand. The more likes you get, the bigger your community is. Every member represents a like.

Don't simply start a page, put up your brand's logo, and drop links to your sales pages. That method would ensure that you have the smallest community possible. Facebook pages should be appealing, engaging, and interactive, not clogged with boring updates. Moreover, when you offer nothing but sales pages or news updates, you're not leaving much opportunity for your members to interact. Your content has to be attractive for the entire community.

Here are ways to spice up your Facebook page:

✓ **Choose a profile picture that represents the brand.** Whether it's a logo or enticing photo of your product or service in action, your Facebook profile picture is the first impression that potential community members may have of your page. Make sure that the photo is positive, professional, and inviting.

✓ **Create open-ended content.** Engage with community members by asking questions or creating the type of content that inspires a discussion. Always leave room for a response.

✓ **Write in a conversational fashion.** Dull, antiseptic updates bore and discourage community members. Write the way you speak. Use a conversational tone and be pleasant, upbeat, and positive.

✓ **Share images.** Members love to see photos from staff events and conferences, as well as images of funny stuff from around the Internet. Sharing photos puts a human element on a brand page. Make sure that the photos are appropriate and relevant to the page.

✓ **Take advantage of Facebook's bells and whistles.** Facebook has many apps and widgets available at no charge. The Networked Blogs app, for example, allows your blog's RSS feed to appear on your Facebook status page automatically, and the Twitter app shows your tweets. Look at other successful pages to see which apps fit best within your community. AppBistro.com (see Figure 11-1) is a tool enabling you to search the available Facebook apps to find those best suiting your needs.

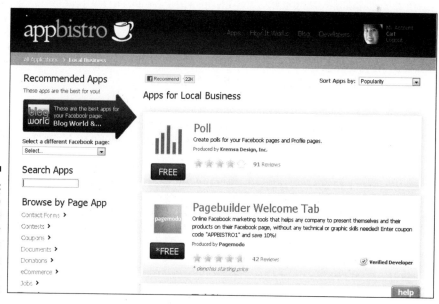

Figure 11-1: AppBistro offers an easy way to browse Facebook apps.

✔ **Share perks with members of the community.** Reward your loyal Facebook members with discounts, coupon codes, and prizes. They'll appreciate the gesture and may share it with their own networks, which may encourage other people to sign up.

✔ **Have some fun.** Facebook pages aren't only business. Have some fun with your community. Host limerick or haiku contests or invite members to caption photos and tell jokes. A congenial atmosphere attracts everyone.

✔ **Like similar communities.** Show your support of other Facebook communities by liking them (see Figure 11-2). Their logos and links will appear in your sidebar, and they may be inspired to do the same, driving members to both communities.

✔ **Encourage your members to share.** Though you don't want your community members to spam your Facebook page with their links, you can still encourage them to share. On a Facebook page that I manage, I invite members to *brag* about their blogs once a month — that is, I ask them to post links to their blogs and projects. In that thread only, members post links and descriptions of their blogs, and other members visit. The bloggers gain traffic and even new community members, and people outside the community see the Facebook page as a promotional opportunity.

✔ **Update regularly.** Post some sort of Facebook content every day to keep your members checking for updates. Here's something else to consider: When you post Facebook updates, they show up in your members Facebook statuses, which encourages them to share your content. When their friends see them sharing your content, or receiving cool perks from your brand's Facebook page, they may be inclined to join, too.

It's important to get a like from members, as they can't participate in your Facebook page unless they click the Thumbs Up or Like button.

Figure 11-2:
Members can't participate on your Facebook page until they like your page by clicking the Thumbs Up button.

Using promotions and discounts to attract new members

Many of the people who join a brand's community do so to receive some sort of perk, such as free promotional items like logo T-shirts and caps, printable coupons, or discount codes. The more perks you offer, the bigger your community will grow. In fact, many of your community members may be there more for the freebies and discounts than for the conversation. This fact isn't a bad thing if you work for a sales-oriented brand.

If your members are telling their friends and neighbors that they saved $10 on your brand's shoes because they're members of your Facebook page or Twitter community, those people may want to join too. If they find out that you use your blog to give out fun stuff and target a "commenter of the day," they may want to participate too.

 People don't always share the conversations they have online, but they're extremely likely to share discounts and perks. If you offer higher levels of discounts to members who refer people to your various communities, they're going to want to get even more involved. Done right, these campaigns have a way of going viral.

Don't think of offering perks as losing money. Ideally, the opposite will happen. An established community with lots of members can bring in so many sales through a promotional campaign that it becomes extremely profitable. If your community is new, offering discounts and freebies may be a way to bring in members quickly.

Getting a promotion going does take some work, though. If your community is large enough, most of the work is done for you as your members engage in a word-of-mouth campaign. However, you can't count on your members to do all your evangelizing for you.

Here are a few ways to spread the word about your promotion:

- ✔ Write about your promotion on your blog.
- ✔ Talk about your promotion on Twitter.
- ✔ Share your promotion on Facebook.
- ✔ Ask blogging friends to help promote your contest or promotion.

 Don't be a spammer. Talk about your promotion now and then, but don't make every single conversation a pitch. Ideally, when members and potential members see what you're sharing, they'll help spread the word.

Using Twitter to drive traffic

Twitter is a wonderful tool for driving traffic to your various online communities (see Figure 11-3). You can easily find people to follow your brand, especially if they like you as a community manager. In fact, some Twitter members are more into following a fun community manager than they are in following the brand itself.

Figure 11-3:
Use Twitter
to share fun,
pithy
comments
with your
community.

To find followers, find the people who have the most in common with your brand. If you're with a peanut butter brand, think about the kinds of people who would follow a peanut butter brand. Foodies might follow a peanut butter brand; people who blog about foods, review foods, and create recipes might follow the brand. If you have an all-natural or organic product, follow people who blog about organic food and health foods, as well as people who discuss these products on Twitter. Moms and dads also enjoy peanut butter; so might people who make their own jams, jellies, and breads. You might even consider some of the brands that go well with peanut butter, such as jelly, milk, and bread.

Now that you have a good idea of the types of people and accounts to follow on Twitter, how will you find them? Use a Twitter search tool (see Figure 11-4).

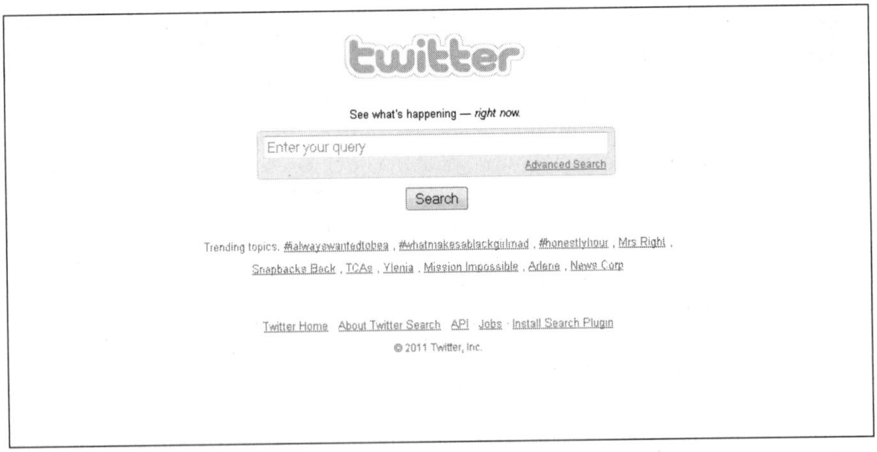

Figure 11-4:
Use Twitter
search to
find people
you want to
follow and
who want to
follow you
back.

Twitter search (`http://search.twitter.com`) allows you to search for people, names, phrases, and more. If you type ice cream in Twitter search, you can see all the people who are talking about ice cream at that time. By seeing what they're talking about, you can determine whether they'd be interested in your brand. If so, give them a follow; ideally, they'll follow you back.

Twitter search can be a little frustrating, because Twitter practices rate limiting. If you search more than a couple of pages, Twitter cuts you off from any more searching by notifying you that you've been rate limited (see Figure 11-5), which is Twitter's way of deterring spammers.

Figure 11-5:
If you search too much on Twitter, you receive a rate-limited warning.

If you're met with too many rate limit messages, it's a good idea to employ the use of a Twitter app such as Hootsuite.com, Tweet Deck.com, or Seesmic. com. The apps can help manage several social media accounts at once, plus they enable you to keep an eye on different Twitter accounts, hashtags (the pound [#] sign used to denote a Twitter conversation), and search terms.

When you have enough followers, you're ready to tweet and drive traffic back to your community pages.

First and foremost, the last thing you want to do is spam. People who tweet nothing but links all the time are considered to be spammers, and if you're reported for spam, Twitter will ban your account.

Use your account for fun things such as the following:

✔ **Start a Twitter chat.** Have a hashtag chat to promote your community. Use the hashtag #peanutbutter, for example, to lead a different discussion every week or two. You can also use a Twitter chat to ask your community members what they think of the brand, the brand's website, your online community, and anything else you want to solicit feedback on.

✔ **Have a conversation.** Without linking, share facts, jokes, recipes (if you can stay within Twitter's 140-character limit), and other fun-focus items related to your company's product. Don't make the conversation only related to your product, though. You can also talk about other interesting topics or just respond to discussions going on within your Twitter stream.

✔ **Retweet.** If you want to share someone else's tweet, you can retweet it (see Figure 11-6). To do so, click the Retweet button on your Twitter page. (It looks like two curved arrows forming a square.) From there, you'll be asked if you'd like to retweet the tweet to your followers, and you just click Yes. Some Twitter apps allow commentary with your retweet, so you can add a few words letting folks know why you're recommending that tweet.

✔ **Share.** Just because you shouldn't be spammy doesn't mean that you shouldn't share. As long as everything you Tweet out isn't a link, you're fine. Also, it's less spammy if you also share other relevant content with your community. So share links to discussion-worthy news articles and blog posts and fun links as well as your own stuff.

Figure 11-6:
Share with
your com-
munity by
retweeting.

Retweet this to your followers?   ✕

debng
Ok iPad geeks - riddle me this one...I can't get my screen to rotate. It's not locked, but it won't move. Thoughts?

Retweet   Cancel

New members are never hard to find. If you're active on the social networks, people tend to be curious and will follow you to see what you do and what your community is all about. If you have a truly rocking community, you might even find the members help to promote your community as well. Half the time, you don't even have to ask.

Provide good content, relevant content, keep the conversation flowing, and throw in some fun stuff. If you build it, they certainly will come.

Part V

Assessing the Health of Your Community

In this part . . .

So how do you know community management is working? How can you tell whether your promotions, outreach, and campaigns are effective? Part V shows you how to analyze specific data, gauge participation levels, and use your findings to continue to grow.

Chapter 12

Evaluating Community Participation

Community managers enjoy the social-networking and content-creation aspects of their jobs, but handling the nitty-gritty details usually isn't a favorite task. Who wants to talk about things like subscription numbers or community participation, and just how do you evaluate community management anyway?

In this chapter, I discuss some of the things that you need to track to determine whether your community is a success and you're achieving your goals as a community manager. The numbers stuff can be a little boring, but it can also be the most rewarding aspect of your job. After all, the boring stuff tells you how well you're doing.

Looking at the Bottom Line: Return on Investment

Every community has a purpose. If it fails to achieve its purpose, the community is unnecessary and a waste of manpower, resources, and money. Face it — if your community isn't bringing in results, there's really no sense in keeping it going.

As community manager, your job is to assess every promotion, event, activity, and bit of content to determine its success. How your community reacts to everything you do is an important indicator of success.

Return on investment (ROI) is exactly what it sounds like. If your community is achieving or even surpassing its goals, your ROI action is rocking and rolling. If you're losing money or campaigns aren't working, you're not getting a very good ROI, and you have to determine whether it's worth the effort to keep it going.

The tricky part is determining your ROI. It's more than sales figures; it's a whole collective of community reactions to the experiences you're putting forth for them. When you can determine how your community is paying attention and reacting to content or campaigns, you can determine what kind of return you're receiving on your investment.

When looking into whether you're receiving a good ROI from your community, consider the following facts:

- ✔ **Sales:** Did sales go up after launching your online community? Are they still going up? An active online presence should show positive sales growth and not the other way around.

- ✔ **Traffic:** Your various online communities — whether they're forums, blogs, Facebook pages, or Twitter accounts — should be driving traffic to whatever goal you hope to achieve with your community. If you created all these online networks to drive sales, for example, you should see a visible traffic increase to your website and sales pages from those networks.

- ✔ **Buzz:** If the word on the social networks is good and people are talking about your brand in a positive way, recommending that others join your community or buy what you're selling, things are going right. If the buzz is negative or nonexistent, you're going to have to think about some engaging ways to get people talking.

- ✔ **Subscriptions:** If your community outreach is successful, you'll see more people subscribing to your content. If you're missing the mark, not only won't you see new subscribers, but old subscribers may jump ship as well.

- ✔ **Comments and feedback:** A sure sign of a flourishing community is a rise in member participation. If you notice more members taking part in discussions, if each conversation is longer than the one before, and if everything that you post receives comments, you're doing something right.

✓ **Memberships:** Signups are funny things. Sometimes, you get dozens of them in one day; on other days, you have nothing but the sound of crickets. Though it's normal to have a dry period, if new members are continuing to sign up, that's a good indication that your community efforts are paying off. Do keep an eye on trends, however. If you notice that memberships are slowing, see whether you can pinpoint why.

✓ **Greater activity on social networks:** If your friend and follower numbers are rising, more people are becoming interested in your brand and in being part of your community.

✓ **Advertising revenue:** If you earn money by selling ads on your forum, blog, or website, you'll notice a rise in revenue along with growth in traffic and memberships. The more people who visit you each day, the more people are there to support your sponsors. Growth in advertising revenue indicates that your community efforts are working.

✓ **Goals:** If you or your team set goals for your community and your community efforts — such as raising sales by a specific percentage, having a specific number of new subscribers, or gaining a certain amount of growth in community participation — you'll want to measure progress toward these goals. If you have positive results to record, your community efforts are paying off, and you're getting a good return on your brand's investment. If you see no growth or negative growth, you're going to have to ramp up your community efforts to achieve a more positive outcome.

✓ **Customer loyalty:** When your customers use only your brand, that's some good customer loyalty right there. Also, when customers recommend you to their friends and relatives, that's an indication of loyalty. Having your members interested in your brand is only part of the plan. Getting them to be loyal to it every day is a much better goal.

If you're able to show positive growth in all your key areas, you can prove that your brand is getting a good ROI. ROI aside, if your members are happy, and if you're achieving or surpassing your community goals, your community should be around for a long time to come.

Logging Community Growth

Unless you have a good memory and a knack for numbers, it's a good bet that you're going to have to keep records of community milestones.

Keeping track of community data may involve using a spreadsheet program (see Figure 12-1). Logging all your community's activities and actions will help you determine how your community is growing and what areas need work.

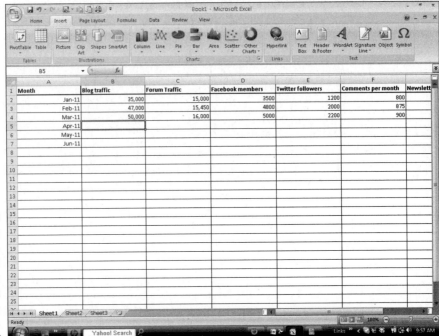

Using all the tools available, keep track of all community activity to see
whether your brand is getting a good ROI. These tools not only help you
gauge engagement and campaigns, but show you how many people are
clicking your links, retweeting your tweets, and mentioning your keywords
on Twitter.

Keep track of the following areas each month and log growth:

✔ Traffic to your brand's blog

✔ Blog comments

✔ Blog subscribers through RSS feeds, Facebook, and other sources

✔ Traffic to your brand's website via community pages

✔ Facebook membership

✔ Comments on Facebook pages

✔ Twitter followers

✔ Responses to Twitter questions, retweets, and comments

✔ Membership numbers for forum and e-mail groups

✔ Response to community promotions

✔ Sales as a result of community promotions

Ideally, you'll notice growth each month as you log in higher numbers. Some periods, however, are traditionally slow growth periods. For example, you may experience less traffic during the winter holiday season, on holiday weekends, and during the summer.

Many brands tend to run major promotions during times of slow growth to make up for the lack of visits.

Doing a month-by-month comparison is a good way to discover growth areas and the areas that need a little work. You can pinpoint growth further by noting weekly stats as well. Soon, you'll see where to focus your efforts. If you're not receiving as many comments as you feel that you should be, for example, spend more time engaging your members.

You can determine traffic numbers by using a stats program such as Google Analytics, which I discuss in Chapter 13. Google Analytics or FeedBurner (another Google endeavor) can help you keep track of all your RSS feeds.

Tracking Facebook likes

Your Facebook Insights page can help you determine how many people are liking your brand on Facebook and how many of those likes are leading to action or participation.

To check your Facebook numbers, click the Insights link to the right of the Facebook page. This link takes you to a page that provides graphs and statistics for your Facebook page (see Figure 12-2). Use the numbers and charts on this page to determine how well you're achieving your Facebook goals, and log the results on your spreadsheet.

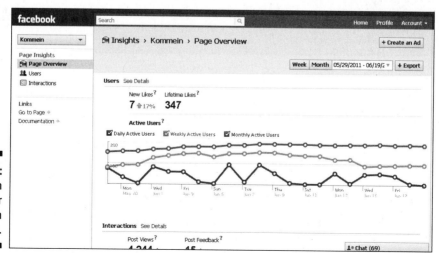

Figure 12-2:
You can check your numbers on Facebook.

Tracking Twitter mentions

You can use a variety of tools to determine how well Twitter is working for you. Klout.com notes growth and influence to specific accounts but you should use it as a number reference only, not as a measure of overall influence. Watching your score go up and down can help indicate how well you're engaging with your members.

TweetStats.com graphs your Twitter statistics. Alternatively, you can use a paid subscription-based service, such as Radian6.com, to measure your social-media campaigns.

Determining Whether the Community Drives Sales

If the goal of your community is to sell things, one area you'll want to pay special attention to is sales. You're probably hoping that sales are on the rise and your campaigns are working, but without analysis, you simply can't tell. By using special links and discount codes, you're better able to determine whether sales growth, or even sales in general, is occurring due to a positive community experience.

bitly and other URL shorteners not only allow you to fit your links to a character limit, but also let you create and track URLs if you create a special URL for a specific campaign by using bitly. For example, the bitly.com website will tell you how many people used that link.

Still, how do you determine whether how many people are using that link to drive sales? One thing you can do is use a special promotional code for members of that campaign only. So if you're selling sneakers, and 75 percent of the people responding to a sneaker promotion are from your community campaign, as indicated by the promotional code, you can tell that the bulk of your sales are coming from community efforts.

Using special URLs and promotional codes, you can even determine which campaigns bring in the most results. For example, if your Facebook page,

Twitter account, forums, and blogs each get their own promotional code and URLs, you can see how many people react from each community.

Also, you can measure general sales growth. If your sales numbers grow as your community numbers grow or fall after a bad community experience, compare them with the overall community numbers for that same period.

Don't overlook community discussions. Members often like to mention when they received a good bargain or enjoyed a certain product. Monitor these conversations to determine what community members are buying.

Evaluating Feedback

Community managers have a love/hate relationship with feedback. It's a good feeling when you hear from community members that you're a wonderful community manager. It's also a great ego boost to discover campaigns and promotions are paying off or that your members feel good about participating in such a positive atmosphere.

This kind of positive feedback is helpful because it tells you where you are in achieving your goals for the community and also that your campaigns and other community efforts are paying off. Plus, you know you're doing something right and can work on ramping up your community plans to see how to make it even more positive.

When you're doing something right, you want to continue doing it right. If you hear that a particular giveaway was a huge success, are you going to leave it at that? No, you're going to plan more giveaways! The last thing you want to do is have one successful campaign and leave it at that.

On the flip side of the coin, you have your negative feedback. No one likes hearing or reading something bad. It's even more embarrassing if negative feedback is left as a public comment on a blog post, written out as a whole blog post, or posted on social networks such as Twitter or Facebook. (For more on receiving and reacting to feedback, see Chapter 7.)

Responding to bad press

Not all of your feedback is coming from community members. Outsiders — though I prefer the term "potential community members" — also like to add their feedback, and sometimes they give you bad press. This feedback is interesting because it's coming from someone who may not have a vested interest in your community or doesn't experience the positive vibe your members receive from participating. It doesn't mean this type of feedback isn't valuable — just that it might be different from the feedback coming from folks inside your community.

There's a saying "There's no such thing as bad press," but I'm not so sure it's true. I think bad press can lead to some bad results — for example, a drop in sales or lower community numbers. However, I also believe that all feedback is valuable feedback, regardless of whether it's positive or negative.

Now, here's where it gets tricky. Unless it's a very positive piece, feedback from the press can be a bit scary. You don't want anyone writing any bad things about you, right? And if it's in a major newspaper or top blog, a lot of people are going to read it.

Handling reactions to your community from the press, whether positive or negative, takes a bit of finesse. Most likely, you're going to be acknowledging the feedback in public in the form of a comment under the article or blog post. You may even be asked in a follow up for a response.

Here's what you need to do when you respond to bad publicity:

- **Say thank you.** Whether the press is positive or negative, thank the writer for taking the time to offer thought-provoking comments. Let her know you will take the criticism into consideration.

- **Note areas of concern.** Don't sweep anything under the rug and don't make a lot of excuses. If you're aware of an existing issue, acknowledge it and say that you're working to fix it. If you're not aware of the issue, let them know that you're going to look into their concerns and take any necessary steps. Don't minimize any of the author's concerns, even if you feel he's off base.

- **If you disagree, do so respectfully.** Don't be afraid to voice disagreement but don't turn it into a debate. Respectfully discuss your reasoning and don't turn it into a spitting mix. Stay pleasant and positive throughout the exchange.

- **If you agree, stay loyal.** If the writer raises good points about a bad experience, don't throw your team members under the bus. Saying that it's someone else's fault or that you have inexperienced staff members only serves to make both you and your brand look bad.

- **If the writer says something nice, and you agree, do so without being self-righteous or sanctimonious.** By all means, agree that your community is the best, and your team really knows their stuff, but don't make it sound like it's coming from your ego.

- **Don't ignore feedback.** If someone writes about you, do take the time to write back in response. It doesn't matter if it's positive or negative; your community wants to know you know what's being said about you and that you're listening and working to make improvements.

Hopefully, the kind of press you receive is the good kind, but whether it's positive or negative, you still want to acknowledge it. Say thank you, make any specific comments you feel need to be said, and keep it positive and friendly. With any luck, the positive press will keep on coming.

Using Google Alerts

If anyone is talking about you on the web, you'll hear about it if you use Google Alerts (http://www.google.com/alerts). This free service allows you to sign up for specific search keywords by filling out a quick form and receiving the results in your e-mail inbox.

As Figure 12-3 shows, you can use Google Alerts to see who's talking about this book online.

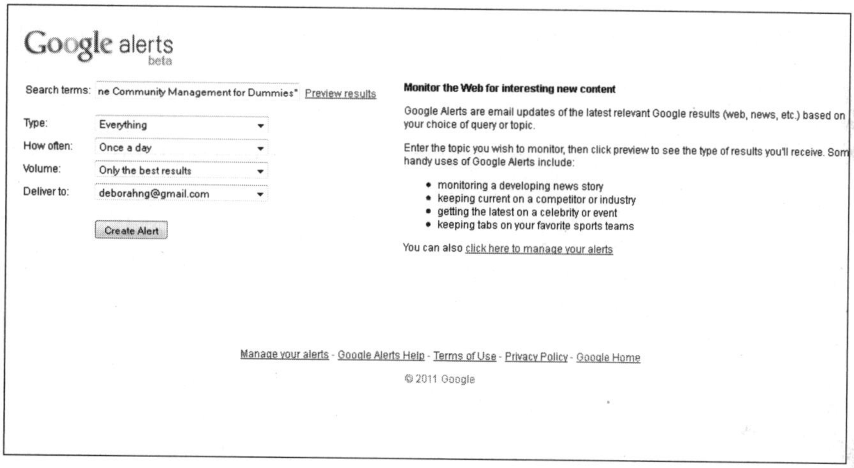

Figure 12-3:
Use Google Alerts to see who is talking about you online.

Google Alerts is a good way to find out what's being said about you, your community, and your brand, as well as what's being said about your competitors. Here's what you need to do to set up a Google alert:

1. **Go to the Google alert site.**

   You're taken to a form with self-explanatory fields.

2. **In the Search Terms field, indicate what word or phrases you'd like to search for.**

   You have several options:

   - Keywords related to your product or brand
   - Your blog, website, and community URLs
   - The names of prominent members of your team or organization
   - Your name
   - Your competitors' names and URLs

3. **In the Type field, determine what kind of results to receive.**

   For example, you can choose to receive all results (that is, every result Google Analytics has for your search term on that day) or all the best results (the most popular and most relevant to your search).

   Try receiving all results and see what happens. If you receive too many results that aren't relative, you'll want to tweak it a bit to give you the best results.

4. **Indicate how often you want to receive alerts.**

   If you have more than one alert set up, and it's a popular search term, you're going to receive quite a few e-mail alerts during the day which can be inconvenient. My preference is to receive one daily e-mail with all the alerts.

5. **In the Volume field, choose what kind of results you want to receive.**

6. **Choose where you'd like the results delivered, such as your personal e-mail address.**

You can set up as many alerts as you'd like. After you enter your information, Google will send you e-mails every time these items are mentioned on the web.

When you receive the alerts, they'll tell you what is being said and where. Now you need to determine whether each mention is worthy of investigation. Your e-mail alert will consider an excerpt from the mention. It may be a blog post or forum entry having nothing to do with your brand at all and someone is using a similar term in their content. However, if it's obvious you're being discussed online, click through the link to view the content and determine whether the content is worthy of a comment or action.

Searching Facebook

The social networks are important tools for determining who is talking about your community and your brand online. If you search for your community name in Facebook, the Facebook search engine will bring up results about your community but it will also bring up results if someone shared news about your brand (see Figure 12-4). Also, sometimes people start online communities on Facebook having to do with your brand or product, independent of your brand. For example, if your brand produces a popular hair care line, you may find a few fans start their own pages in tribute.

If you work for Joe's Peanut Butter, for example, and your Facebook search turns up a Facebook group called Joe's Peanut Butter Sucks, it's worthy of investigation. You need to know why there's a whole online community devoted to the suckage of your peanut butter. Likewise, if there's a community called Joe's Is the Best Peanut Butter Ever, you'll want to visit it.

Knowing who is talking about your community and why is a major part of a community manager's job.

Figure 12-4:
Use a
Facebook
search to
bring up
results
for your
brand or
community.

Searching Twitter

Searching Twitter — or using an app such as TweetDeck, Seesmic, or HootSuite to search it (see Chapter 10) — allows you to monitor online conversations on Twitter. When you enter various search terms, you'll receive results from members both inside and outside your community. Definitely take some time to analyze the conversations and respond to them. Being responsive is one of the most important parts of a community manager's job, and it's also something that people online will notice, which may encourage them to join your community.

Searching other social networks

Twitter and Facebook aren't the only games in town. You can also search other social networks and bookmarking/sharing tools, such as the following:

- ✔ LinkedIn
- ✔ YouTube
- ✔ reddit
- ✔ StumbleUpon
- ✔ Friendster
- ✔ orkut

For more information about monitoring the social networks, see Chapter 9.

Chapter 13

Paying Attention to the Numbers

Statistics and analytics programs can tell you everything you need to know about how your community members spend their time online. You can find out how many visits a given website gets each day, where those visitors come from, what browsers they're using, what they're doing when they land on your website, how long they're staying, and much more. As you can imagine, all this stuff is important for you to note and analyze.

Without a good stats program and a regular analysis of your community's habits, you won't be able to succeed as a community manager or move your community forward. Your stats give you an important peek at your community members' habits.

Choosing an Analytics Program

Many analytics programs are available, some of which are free. With the exception of Google Analytics, which is probably the most comprehensive free stats tool available, many of the free services are bare-bones products that require you to pay for an upgrade. When you're searching for a stats package, do your research. These programs aren't created equal, and you want to find the one that best suits your brand and your community's needs. Some of my recommendations are

- ✔ Google Analytics
- ✔ Site Meter
- ✔ Performancing Metrics

✔ Omniture

✔ StatCounter

✔ Webtrends

Take some time to check your stats and analytics tools each day, but save time once a week to look at the results and do some heavy analysis. Note trends, how campaigns are working, where people are coming from, and anything else that you feel is significant and noteworthy. Use your notes to tailor future content and campaigns.

For example, if you notice you're receiving traffic from other websites talking about a promotion you're doing, consider future promotions appealing to the same groups of people.

Using Stats to Find Out about Your Community

When you use an analytics program such as Google Analytics (see Figure 13-1), you can find out about your community members' habits and tailor campaigns and promotions to their needs.

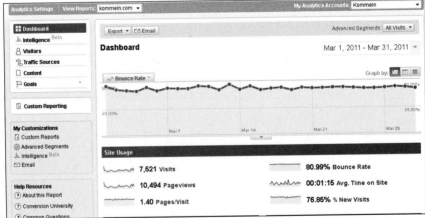

Figure 13-1: You can use an analytics program to help you target your members.

Without a solid stats or analytics package in place, you won't know enough about your community to manage effectively. Your stats offer a wealth of information about the traffic patterns in your communities:

✔ How many people visit your community each day

✔ How much time the average person spends visiting your community

✔ What your most popular content and discussion topics are

✔ Where your visitors are coming from before they land on your site

✔ Who is linking to you from other blogs and websites

✔ Which days and months yield the highest and lowest traffic

✔ Which content interests your community least

✔ What search terms members or potential members are using to land on your pages

Your stats may reveal details that you didn't even consider. You may not think that it matters if one hour of the day is busier than another, for example, but it matters for sure. The more people are online at any given time, the more of them will react to your content, perhaps sharing it on the social networks or even buying what you're selling. If you drop important news or launch a promotion during a time that isn't so busy, your campaign may start with a whimper. Because online content doesn't stay relevant for long, you want to post and interact during the busiest times possible. You can't tell what times are busiest without your stats.

The purpose of many of your social-networking campaigns is to drive your community to take a particular action, whether that action is blog traffic, sales, or a charitable campaign. Your analytics program will help you to determine if those social campaigns are working.

Gathering details on your visitors

Stats reveal many more important details about the people who visit your blogs and website.

Figure 13-2, for example, shows that the majority of visitors to this blog come from the United States, the United Kingdom, and Canada, so the blog's content should be written for a primarily English-speaking audience. Knowing the top cities in which members reside helps you tailor content even more.

✔ **Where your members live:** Your stats tell you not only the countries in which your members live, but the cities, states, and counties as well. Location is relevant because if large chunks of your members live in the same area, you can tailor content and promotions to that area. If most of your members come from New York City, for example, you can create discussions that are relevant to New Yorkers, such as nightlife, cuisine, or life in the boroughs.

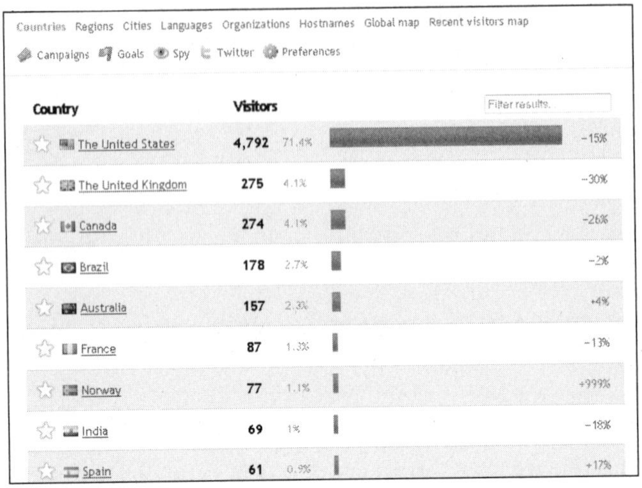

Country	Visitors			
☆ 🇺🇸 The United States	4,792	71.4%		−15%
☆ 🇬🇧 The United Kingdom	275	4.1%		−30%
☆ 🇨🇦 Canada	274	4.1%		−26%
☆ 🇧🇷 Brazil	178	2.7%		−2%
☆ 🇦🇺 Australia	157	2.3%		+4%
☆ 🇫🇷 France	87	1.3%		−13%
☆ 🇳🇴 Norway	77	1.1%		+999%
☆ 🇮🇳 India	69	1%		−18%
☆ 🇪🇸 Spain	61	0.9%		+17%

Countries Regions Cities Languages Organizations Hostnames Global map Recent visitors map
Campaigns Goals Spy Twitter Preferences

Filter results...

Figure 13-2:
Knowing where your members live can help you tailor content toward them.

Don't alienate your other members. Target locations, but make sure that you have enough content to include everyone.

✓ **What browsers they're using:** Web content and design don't look the same in every browser. Sometimes, what looks good in Mozilla Firefox doesn't look good in Google Chrome, for example. Knowing the browsers that your members use allows you to adjust your design to work well with every browser that your members are using.

As you see in Figure 13-3, this community's visitors primarily use the browsers Firefox and Internet Explorer. You should test content and design in both browsers to make sure that users get an optimal experience.

✓ **How social-media campaigns are working out:** If you're using Twitter, Facebook, Google+, or another social-networking site to drive traffic to your community, you'll be able to pinpoint the success of each campaign by using your analytics. Also, seeing which networks most of your visitors are coming from gives you an inkling of where you should be spending the most time. If most of your community members are on Facebook, for example, spend more time on Facebook.

✓ **Why people are joining your community:** This fact is the most important one you can gather from your analytics tool. Knowing why people come to your community enables you to find the means to bring in more people and turn visitors into community members. Knowing the types of content and promotional opportunities that bring in the most people encourages you to create more of this type of content. If folks show up only when you offer freebies or post a controversial topic, this information is important to know; you want more than just freebie hunters, and you definitely don't want to be controversial for controversy's sake.

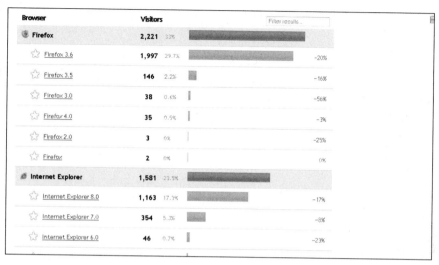

Analyzing content

Next to your community, your most important online asset is your content. Your content brings people in and keeps them coming back. When you begin your community, content is trial and error. As you evolve and as your stats pick up more details, you can determine the types of content that your members and visitors enjoy most and create more content accordingly.

A good stats program, such as Performancing Metrics shown in Figure 13-4, shows your most popular content. Use this information to create more relevant content.

Your content is more than just blog posts and articles. It's also made up of comments, Facebook posts, Twitter updates, promotions, video, podcasts or online radio shows, images, and anything else that you post online. Try a variety of content to see how your community responds.

Because your stats program lists all your website and blog content by title, as well as how many people visited each piece of content, how long they stayed on each piece of content, and what they did afterward, you have a golden opportunity to create the types of content that your community clamors for most.

Your stats also reveal other important content-generating information. If the majority of your visitors are landing on your page because of a particular search term, you want to be sure to write more content that includes that search term. Also, if you find that you receive more visitors on the days when you post funny photos, you'll want to do more of that in the future. When it comes to content, let your stats and your community be your guides.

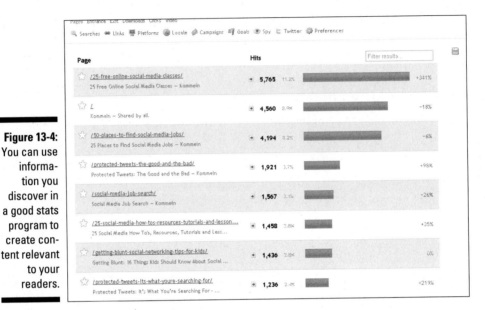

Figure 13-4:
You can use information you discover in a good stats program to create content relevant to your readers.

In Figure 13-5, the stats show that the top search terms for this period were *google+ tips* and *social media jobs.* Creating more content about these topics will lead to more searches and perhaps to a higher search-engine ranking.

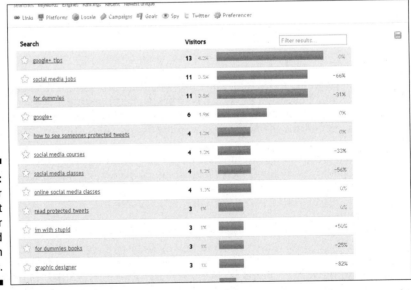

Figure 13-5:
Focus your content on your top-ranked search terms.

✔ **Take advantage of search terms.** Your stats give you a good idea of the top search terms used to find your community or website. Don't write unnatural content to include these terms, but create topics that relate to them. If the majority of your members or potential members are searching for those topics, give them what they want or risk losing them to another site that's providing them.

✔ **Note the most popular content.** The best way to see what your community is responding to is to check your stats or analytics tool. All stats tools have sections for content. Set up a date range to see which content is most popular. When you know the best-received content, you have a good idea of your members' tastes and habits; write with them in mind.

✔ **Note the least popular content.** Also check the least popular content by scrolling down to the bottom of your stat tool's content page. There, you'll find the content that is least well received by visitors to your community. Use these topics sparingly, or find a way to repurpose them so that they work to your advantage.

✔ **Note who is linking to you and why.** Your stats program reveals other blogs or websites that are linking to you. (See the section "Discovering who is linking to you," later in this chapter.) It's in your best interest to check out these links. If you're receiving a number of people are linking to your content, it could be you have others in agreement or you touched a nerve. Read what others are saying and find out why they're linking. Knowing how your community and other communities react to your content helps you determine appropriate future content. In addition to using your stats to write content for your blog or website, you can determine the content that your community responds to best on the social networks. If a single post on Facebook sends hundreds of people to your main website, for example, this information shows up in your stats, and you can use it to determine how to post to Facebook and the other social networks moving forward. You shouldn't post about the same thing every time, but knowing the types of social-media campaigns that your members are responding to helps you shape future content. The same thing applies to the content that receives the lowest response. You'll want to discontinue or retool that content in the future.

Your content and your community are your brand's most important assets. Don't lose them by providing inappropriate content. Use your stats to guide you.

Understanding your bounce rate

Your stats reveal a few other secrets that may seem to be insignificant but are important nonetheless. One example is the *bounce rate,* which tells you how long people stay on your website before bouncing out again. If you have a lower bounce rate, your visitors are sticking around for a while. A high bounce rate indicates that people are turning tail and leaving as soon as possible.

Most websites average a bounce rate of about 60 percent. The lower the bounce rate, the better. A low bounce rate means that folks are not only sticking around, but also exploring and taking part in what you have to offer.

The bounce rate of the blog shown in Figure 13-6 is relatively low.

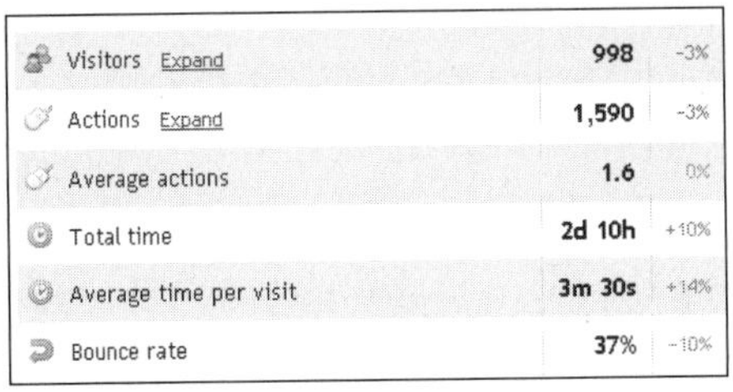

Figure 13-6:
A low bounce rate means that visitors like what they see and are sticking around to explore your site.

Visitors Expand	998	-3%
Actions Expand	1,590	-3%
Average actions	1.6	0%
Total time	2d 10h	+10%
Average time per visit	3m 30s	+14%
Bounce rate	37%	-10%

If your bounce rate is extremely high, you need to do some heavy analysis to determine why folks aren't sticking around.

Take a look at some of these common problem areas:

✔ **Content:** Analyze your content. Are your members using Share buttons to recommend the content, or are they commenting on it? If your community is reacting well to your content, then it most likely isn't the reason why people aren't sticking around. But if every time you write something, all you hear are some virtual crickets, you need to retool your content strategy.

You also want to make sure that you're not misrepresenting what you're offering. If your content about choosing hair color is great, but readers are going to the site because they think they're going to see some popular short hairstyles, then you're not meeting the expectations you set out.

✔ **Design:** Believe it or not, design for a website, blog, or online community counts a lot. Suppose that your community is primarily an online forum. If the forum site is a dark color and the font is hard to read, very few people are going to stick around because the content is too hard to read. If you have a cluttered design with lots of flashing ads and widgets that distract community members from their conversation, your members are going to pack their bags and head to a less cluttered community. A clean, uncluttered design is pleasing to the eye, and your members won't feel that their senses are being assaulted every time they visit.

✔ **Comments:** Sometimes, the caliber of the comments keeps potential members from sticking around. If existing members are nasty and the overall tone is negative, few people are going to want to stick around for more abuse.

✔ **Engagement:** Maybe folks don't stay long because they have no reason to stay. They may stop in and have a look around, but nothing is telling them to stop and interact. The content isn't open-ended, and no one is commenting. Keeping your community engaged and intrigued means that potential members are going to be intrigued as well.

Play around with your design and content and see whether the changes lower your bounce rate.

Keeping track of subscribers

A good stats program helps you determine what subscribers to your content are doing. For example, if you have a newsletter, and the newsletter features truncated or shortened content from your website with a Read More link that readers click to finish an article, the stats for your newsletter subscription service can show you how many of your readers actually clicked the link to read the whole article and which articles received the highest numbers of click-throughs.

You can even use stats programs to track your RSS feeds. An *RSS (Really Simple Syndication) feed* is what people use to subscribe to a blog, website, or online news service's updates. They view updates in a feed reader such as the one provided by Google, or even Facebook, Flipboard (on the iPad), and other tools on mobile devices.

If you use a stats program for your RSS feeds, such as Feedburner, you can link it to certain stats tools such as Google Analytics and Performancing metrics. You can also check your feed's stats using Feedburner itself. The tracking tools for RSS feeds also tell you interesting things about your community and their habits.

When people read your content through a feedreader, the goal should be for them to click through the content to the place where it's originally posted. From there, they'll take specific action whether it's to comment, share with the content with others, or buy something. Your feed stats tell you how many people read the content, and how many click through to the original consent. Learning the types of content your subscribers respond to most is essential for creating new content and programs.

Finding Out Where Traffic Is Coming From

Your members don't show up at your community out of the blue. Your traffic has to come from somewhere. Whether you led a social-media campaign to bring in new members or your community was found through a search engine, a variety of factors drive traffic to your community. Understanding what drives traffic helps you plan future content and campaigns.

Knowing where your visitors come from presents two challenges:

> ✓ **When most of your traffic is coming from a single source, your challenge is to continue having this source drive traffic.** New campaigns, discussion topics, and promotions keep content from going stale, and the traffic continues to flow. Not stepping up your efforts simply because you feel that you have enough traffic from that one source means that you're risking that traffic. Eventually, people get bored, and traffic drops off. Your challenge is to keep the same amount of traffic, if not more, flowing to your community.

> ✓ **When other sources of traffic aren't sending enough people your way, your challenge is to work harder to get traffic from other sources.** You may have to tailor campaigns to appeal to different social networks or community groups, or toss out or overhaul campaigns that aren't bringing in good results. Spend time at your various sources of traffic to understand what drives your community and what doesn't.

Pay attention to stats and especially note traffic patterns. A significant increase or decrease always has a reason, so take the time to investigate both.

Determining who makes up the bulk of your traffic

Your incoming links, or *backlinks,* tell you a lot more than who is talking about you. They also tell you who is visiting you. Traffic has to come from somewhere, and those locations can be very revealing. You can discover

> ✓ **Likes and interests:** Backlinks reveal a lot about how your visitors spend their time. If you manage a crafting forum, and a good chunk of your links come from knitting and crocheting communities, you know that the majority of the crafters who visit your forum enjoy knitting and

crocheting over all else. You should make sure that you have plenty of content and discussion fodder to keep the knitters and crocheters amused, but you also want to be sure that you don't leave out other types of crafters. This is your cue to reach out to scrapbooking, cross-stitching, woodworking, and other crafting communities to see how you can bring in traffic from those niches as well.

✔ **Ages:** You may be able to estimate the median age of your community members by visiting their haunts. If you're receiving links from a cloth-ing website, take note of the types of clothes that the website is offering, as fashion choices differ between 20-year-olds and 50-year-olds and also between men and women.

✔ **Locations:** Maybe a restaurant in Muskegon, Michigan, is linking to your peanut-butter community because it uses your product in one of its recipes. If you receive a staggering amount of traffic from the Muskegon area, you'll want to create some content for that region. This is a good opportunity to welcome the newbies to your website too. Many com-munities have a special greeting for major traffic, such as "Welcome to everyone who is visiting from Joe's Family Restaurant. Have a look around, make yourself at home, and join the conversation."

✔ **Social-network use:** You may discover you have more traffic from Twitter than from Facebook, or that Google+ is starting to send some traffic your way. Now you know to spend more time building relation-ships on these networks. Find out where the majority of your commu-nity members spend their time, and spend a good portion of your time there as well. Then visit the other places, and work to build up more of a presence there too.

✔ **Purpose of visits:** If you often host giveaways or offer discount codes, you may notice a spike in traffic from freebie and deal-seeking communi-ties whose members like to share deals from around the web. Visit these communities to determine appropriate content, and see how you can convert the traffic from those communities from deal-seeking visitors to full-fledged members of your own community.

Discovering who is linking to you

Backlinks are good for both SEO and traffic. If a high-ranking website or blog is linking to yours, you may even experience a huge increase in traffic.

Use your stats program to find out where your traffic is coming from (see Figure 13-7). If it's coming from a specific blog post or website, investigate to see what's being said about you.

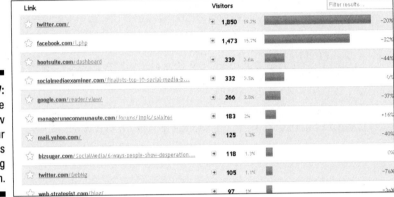

You may find that traffic is coming from Facebook and Twitter without know-ing exactly what had people coming to your community. But you may notice a spike in traffic from the social networks on days when you release a new community feature or launch a promotion. If you notice changes in traffic patterns, see whether they coincide with promotions and announcements.

Many of your incoming links are specific to a certain blog post or web article, or even to comments from other forums. Don't disregard these links, even if they show only one or two hits. Take some time each week to investigate. Someone is linking to your brand or community for some reason, and it's in your best interest to find out why.

Your brand may be the subject of a positive discussion, and if so, this infor-mation is important. Monitor the discussion carefully and read all comments, and don't forget to thank everyone involved. Or your brand may be the sub-ject of a not-so-positive discussion, and this situation is worthy of investiga-tion as well. Report all feedback to the appropriate departments, and monitor negative feedback to be sure that there's no crisis in the making.

Your community wants to know there's a human element to the brand. If people are talking about you online, they like to know that you're paying attention. When you take the time to investigate a mention, you're telling your community that you hear them loud and clear.

Chapter 14

Making Decisions
Based on Your Findings

In This Chapter

▶ Driving traffic to a target

▶ Keeping people talking

▶ Retaining members

▶ Walking away gracefully when something isn't working

*Y*our stats do more than just tell you how many people visited your site each day. They also help you identify problem areas, shape your content and community, and provoke some "Eureka!" moments as you get a peek at the habits of your community members. (For a discussion of stats and analytics — what they are, how they work, and why they're important — see Chapter 13.)

In this chapter, I discuss how to use your stats to achieve positive community-building results. If you're not going to act on your findings, it doesn't make sense to go to all the trouble to install a stats program and spend hours analyzing the data.

Generating More Traffic

As a community manager, regardless of the purpose of your community, you're expected to grow traffic on a regular basis. This goal is important because community members are fickle. They come by for a while, but eventually, they get caught up in something else. Very few people stick around for years. Without a fresh crop of new community members coming in, your community will turn into a ghost town.

You also have to drive traffic to a specific target. The goal of a product-based community, for example, is to achieve sales growth. Without knowing your community's traffic habits, you won't be able to drive traffic anywhere, let alone to a sales page. That's why those stats are so important. They tell you where your traffic is coming from, what visitors are doing when they reach your community or website, and how long they stick around. Take that information from your stats, and see what you can do to raise the bar.

Develop a content strategy

One of the most important things you can learn from your stats is how readers are reacting to your content. By *content,* I mean your blog posts, articles, comments, videos, webinars, and anything else that your readers see or hear while they're on your site. Your Facebook posts, Tweets, Google+ updates, and forum discussions are also content.

Your stats and analytics programs show you your top content of the day, week, month, or year, and even how well it fared for all time. Most of your potential members probably found your community's content via search engines, so it's imperative to develop a strategy that uses your content to lure in even more readers — readers whom you hope will become productive members of the community. (I cover developing a search-engine strategy in the next section.)

Make note of the most popular topics, as well as the types of content that your community members enjoy most. If they react best to video, create more videos. If a certain topic brings in a flood of traffic, create more content in that vein. If certain discussions bring in the most comments, plan future discussions on the same subject matter.

Don't fall into the trap of posting negative or controversial content simply to bring in readers. You'll lose your loyal community members.

Also note new trends. If certain search terms are starting to attract attention, use those terms to create similar content to further attract searchers and search engines. That isn't to say you should write the same article one hundred different ways, but do plan content around the types of things your community reacts to best. Avoid the topics getting little or no reaction from your community.

Create a search-engine strategy

Just as you want to have a strategy to attract new members, you want to have a plan to dominate the search engines. As I discuss in Chapter 11, the higher you rank in the search engines, the more traffic your content will bring in, and the more your community will grow.

Use your stats to pinpoint the most popular search terms for your community. Knowing what search terms visitors use to find you in the first place will help you understand why they're coming to your community. If you notice that most searchers are looking for an inexpensive product or service, this information is your cue to create campaigns that attract bargain seekers. Moreover, knowing what types of content, products, and services people are searching for allows you to create the kinds of products and services that they'll not only investigate, but also spend money on.

Plan promotional campaigns

When you know a lot about your community, it's easy to plan campaigns that build both traffic and community. If your stats indicate that the majority of visitors to your community are coming for an educational experience, give them one. Bring in experts to answer questions and give interviews, give webinars, and write how-to articles.

If the majority of your community members are reacting to your offer of free samples, invite them to test more products or offer discounts. If your community members are music lovers, have a song-lyric contest. If it's summer, invite your members to a virtual picnic, and have them post images of the dishes they'd like to bring.

Your stats enable you to give the people what they want. All the clues into their habits, usages, wants and needs are right there at your fingertips.

Stimulating Conversation

You can create intriguing discussion topics based on what your community members are most interested in. The people who visit your community leave behind a variety of hints about what they want to talk about most:

- ✔ If they join your community because you regularly offer discount codes, talk money. Discuss ways to save in products, as well as in other areas around the house. A huge response to a bargain tells you that your community members want to save. Encourage them to share their money-saving ideas as well.

- ✔ If folks are landing at your community after you post a job on your website's corporate page, you have some job seekers in your audience. Talk about the current job situation, and share tips for finding jobs, interviewing for jobs, and making the best career choices.

✔ If folks are landing at your community via a search for *dorm decorating ideas,* it tells you that your community has college-age members. If you're receiving a large number of these searches, plan discussions that are age appropriate (of interest to people 18 to 25 years old).

If you notice that traffic is down on the days where certain topics are being talked about, you know that this topic isn't of interest. On the other hand, if bloggers or other communities are linking to something that's posted at your community and driving traffic to you that way, this topic is worthy of discussion.

Lowering the Bounce Rate

The *bounce rate* (see Chapter 13) is the percentage of people who visit your site and bounce off to another site or community right away. You don't want that. When it comes to bounce rates (see Chapter 13), less is more. The lower the bounce rate, the longer people are staying on your site.

An average bounce rate is about 60 percent. If your bounce rate is 70 percent of higher, folks aren't sticking around after they land on your pages.

There's only one way to lower your bounce rate: Make sure that the folks who visit your community stay for a while.

Make your content appealing

The average person knows all he wants to know about your community in the first 10 seconds. If a visitor lands on your community pages, looks around, and leaves within a few seconds, something is wrong. Your landing pages have to be intriguing enough to keep potential members interested longer than 10 seconds and encourage them to check out other areas of your community.

Your community needs to be visibly appealing, with intriguing and eye-catching subject or topic headlines. That isn't to say everything needs to be a scandal, but it does mean you have to take care to make things interesting.

For example, an article entitled *Crochet Tips* is kind of generic, but *10 Tips for Taking Your Crocheting to A Whole Other Level* is more appealing, intriguing, and discussion-worthy. Not only will it draw in members who want to discover new tips, but it will encourage them to offer their own as well.

Likewise, *Peanut Butter Coupon* is sure to grab some attention, but *Save 7 0% on Peanut Butter!* goes beyond casual couponers into serious bargain-hunting territory.

Avoid the exclamation point trap. One is eye-catching; more than one is over-kill and spammy.

Ask questions

If potential members are landing on your community pages, they're some-what intrigued, so suck them in a little more by asking the types of questions that people want to answer, you're asking them to commit to membership. For example, if your primary source of communication with your community is your brand's Facebook page, potential members have to like your page in order to comment. If you host a discussion forum, they'll have to sign up to become members to respond.

Asking about the weather is going to cause a few eye rolls, and but won't stimulate discussion. Most members won't care what the weather doing out-side in Oshkosh, Wisconsin. Instead, ask the kinds of questions that require further investigation.

Asking questions that require one-word answers, such as the Facebook discus-sion shown in Figure 14-1, allows members to participate in a fun discussion without having to commit to typing a long response.

Figure 14-1:
Ask ques-tions with
one-worded
answers,
whenever
possible.

Keep the conversation going

No one wants to hang out in a virtual ghost town. If a visitor lands on a Facebook page and find that the last conversation took place two years ago, she's not going to stick around. Thriving communities are updated every day. If your members aren't creating conversations, that job falls to you.

Limit advertising

Ads shouldn't overpower content. If yours is an advertising-powered community — that is, if you have to rely on ads to pay the bills — those ads shouldn't be so distracting that they take precedent over content. By all means sell ad space on your community pages, but don't make them more important than the community itself.

Cutting Your Losses

Your stats are valuable for another reason: They let you know what's not working. Finding out that a campaign or idea didn't turn out as you planned isn't appealing, but it's important. It's better to realize what isn't panning out and try something else than to waste time and resources to keep a failed idea going.

Not every case of low turnout or negative reaction is a reason to cut bait and run, but it's good to know when to breathe life into a lagging campaign and when to give up the ghost. Here are a few signs:

- ✔ If the same topic gets little or no response every single time, bag it. Create projects, conversations, and campaigns on the subjects that folks respond to best.

- ✔ If sales of a particular product or service are dismal no matter how much you push, promote, or discount it, face reality, and drop the campaign.

- ✔ If you're not receiving a response to community-building efforts on the social networks, analyze your content there to figure out why. If all you do is tweet links, for example, you're spamming, not building a community. If outreach on a particular social network isn't working despite repeated efforts, put your effort into the networks that are working while you figure out a new strategy.

Admitting that something isn't working doesn't mean that you're a failure. It's better to implement new ideas and find out that they're not working than not to try anything new at all.

Pay attention to your stats and feedback. They give you extremely valuable insight into how new members are coming into your community, and what they're doing once they get there. Learn from both the campaigns that are working and those that aren't turning out as planned.

Part VI
Taking Your Community Offline

In this part . . .

Online communities are great online fun, but they can flourish offline as well. In this part, I discuss bonding with your members in real life as you meet at offline events. I also talk about why conferences and even speaking engagements are vital to gaining your community's trust. I even throw in tips for creating your own community events.

Chapter 15

Fostering Community Growth with Offline Activity

*Y*ou may think that as an online community manager, all your work will involve online endeavors. Actually, though, you'll want to make sure that you're not overlooking offline efforts to attract members to your online community.

In this chapter, I tell you what you need to know to use speaking engagements, events, classes, and more to grow your community.

Why You Need to Go Offline to Grow Online

There may come a time when you'll feel that your social networking and other online outreach has hit a plateau. It happens, and it's not a reflection on you. Summer months in particular are notoriously slow, for example. Still, your job as community manager is to grow a community, and you can't do that if no one is biting.

At other times, you want to bring in new members regardless of plateaus and traffic numbers. New members liven up the conversation; the same people talking about the same thing gets old quick. Bringing in new members keeps the conversation and atmosphere fresh. There's a fine line between community and clique. By bringing new members in, you're ensuring you have the former, and not the latter.

Your members aren't always online. Not everyone is doing an online search for your brand or looking for a place to hang out on the web. If you can't bring members to the community, you have to bring the community to potential members. Sometimes, your community outreach has to hit the road and go live.

No rule in the online community management handbook states that community managers must have both an online and offline presence. Some community managers guard their privacy, while others enjoy meeting the people who make up their communities in person. However, members of tight-knit communities often bring up the idea of socializing offline, with or without you. Entertaining the idea of personal meetings is a good move you and your brand because members see you as someone who is accessible and involved in the community. Also, many community managers are respected and almost viewed as celebrities to their members. It means a lot when you take some time out of your schedule to get together.

In addition, your job may require public appearances from you anyway, and you may find yourself in charge of organizing community events, such as meetups, parties, and even conferences. Community outreach of this kind occurs all the time, and plenty of professional and niche-related opportunities give you an opportunity to meet your members.

Use your imagination and keep your eye out for the types of events appropriate to your community. You may find you enjoy offline outreach as much as your online community management.

Using Offline Outreach to Recruit New Members

Community managers recruit new members (while offline) in a variety of ways. Party-like meetups and tweetups are popular, and I cover them in Chapter 16, but they're not the only game in town. You can also meet potential members at professional and educational events.

The point of offline recruiting is twofold. First, depending on who you work for, not everyone who uses your brand is socializing online. How will they know about your community? You want to find your brand's fans and encourage them to come and interact with other like-minded people.

The second reason is to find the people who enjoy your brand and enjoy socializing online but may not know about your community. When you consider how many people are online, only a small fraction know about your online community.

Millions of people may enjoy your brand or the topic of your community. If you only have a few hundred or few thousand members, you have your work cut out for you.

Bringing in Followers from Public Speaking Engagements

Many community managers are discovering the benefits of speaking opportunities. By sitting on panels or giving solo presentations at professional or educational events, they're establishing their expertise, promoting their brand, and even creating community awareness. Public speaking engagements aren't as boring and stuffy as they sound. Many conferences bring in thousands of attendees who come to network with other like-minded people. What better way to draw them into your community than attending a niche-related event?

Finding speaking opportunities isn't very difficult. Conferences and professional events post their calls for speakers on their websites. In most cases, you have to fill out an application and submit a proposal stating what you'd like to talk about. Do searches for appropriate conferences. If you manage a community of writers, for example, look for calls for speakers for writing, journalism, and book conferences. Because you use the various social-media tools in your community outreach, it's also appropriate to look into blogging and social-media conferences.

If you're nervous about speaking to a crowd, get your feet wet by speaking on a panel. You can go about it in a couple of ways. The first is to contact conference organizers and let them know that you're interested in speaking on a panel. Tell them why you're a good fit and the different topics you can speak about. Be sure to attach a brief professional bio so that they know your background and can put you on an appropriate panel.

You can also research appropriate conferences to find how to respond to their calls for speakers. Many list opportunities for speaking on their websites and ask for a proposal and some details about your experiences.

Most people who come to hear a public speaker aren't doing so to receive a sales pitch. They want solid, tangible information such as how-tos or inspirational anecdotes. In short, they're interested in learning. It's not uncommon for speakers to have attendees approach them after their presentations to ask questions. Use that time to network. If attendees like what they find out about you, there's a good chance that they're going to explore your community.

Many of the speakers at conferences are there because they have something to promote, such as a book or a business. Don't feel bad about speaking at events to raise community awareness. As long as you're not pushing the hard sell, speaking for that reason is okay.

Attending Conferences and Other Events

Many community managers are taking advantage of the benefits of conferences. No longer stuffy professional events, today's conferences provide educational experiences and ample opportunity for networking with current and potential community members. They're also terrific for sharing tips and ideas with other community professionals.

Because you spend a large chunk of your time using the various social media tools, you may especially find value from attending social media conferences for the learning. Many of your peers even speak at such conferences. However, they also attend a variety of industry and niche-related events on behalf of their brand.

Reasons to attend conferences

I encourage you to attend conferences for a variety of reasons:

- ✔ **To interact with others in a niche.** Suppose that your community is for professional writers. Attending events for writers, journalists, and bloggers enables you to interact with other writers and invite them to join your community. Not everyone you meet will want to become a member, but there's no reason why you shouldn't walk away with at least a few signups after attending a conference.

When recruiting new members, watch out for being too sales-pitchy. The idea is to get to know the attendees and interact with them. Carry on a conversation and talk about what you do, while being careful not to make the discussion all about you and your brand. This can pique the interest of potential members who might ask for a business card or the web address for your community. If you're pushy about recruiting new members, all you'll do is turn them off. By having a conversation and learning about potential members, while discussing what you do, you're letting them make their own decisions — and there are sure to be some people who are intrigued enough to take your community for a test drive. You're conversation doesn't even have to be work-related. Meet people and chat, and you'll find it all fall into place.

✔ **To find out more about a particular topic:** Because you're expected to provide discussion topics for your community and answer questions related to your niche, you should stay on top of the latest news and techniques. Definitely attend learning sessions to stay updated. Community members appreciate a knowledgeable community manager. If you're viewed and talked about as someone who knows her stuff, you're sure to attract new members.

✔ **To mingle with other community managers:** Both online and offline communities, clubs, and groups are available for online community managers to network and share with their peers. Interacting with other community managers enables you to discuss methods for community management and commiserate on issues you all face. In addition to potentially becoming members' of each others' communities, you can also discuss ways to build your own networks.

✔ **To meet with their community:** Members of your community may attend the same events as you. If so, do take time to say hello. They'll appreciate your taking the time out, and you'll find out more about the people who make up your community. Knowing as much as you can about your members is important for community growth and content and promotional strategies.

✔ **To work for their brands:** Brands send community managers to industry-related events for many reasons. They want to educate their managers and have them evangelize the product or service. While there, they also hope to grow community. For example, if your brand is a yarn company, attending a craft fair is a terrific way to meet the people who use or may use your products. Talk to them about their needs and learn about why they're looking for in a brand, all while talking up your community.

Benefits of conferences

Conferences can be expensive to attend, but they're a good investment in both your business and personal brand. You see, you're not only there on behalf of your company, but your name is also getting "out there" among peers and potential community members as the voice and face behind the brand. It's good for people to get to know you personally because it instills trust to see a real live person and not just a social networking account. Some community managers are very well known, and if they're ever in the market for a new career opportunity, it serves well in their favor.

When your name is synonymous with your brand, your community, and community management in general, some interesting things happen:

- People who like you in person want to follow you to your community.

- When people see your name on a social network such as Twitter or Google+, they want to be friends online.

- People who have heard you speak in public at a conference or professional event may follow you online to learn more about what you do.

- When people meet you in person, they feel more connected, as if you're their real-time friend.

- When you have good personal connections, you have good community connections. In fact, some of the people you meet may not be in the market to join an online community, but will join yours as a show of support.

When you attend professional or consumer events, either as a speaker or attendee, the people who use your brand feel they know it better. If you're warm, genuine, and outgoing, they're going to equate you with the brand and want to be a part of your community. They're going to want to follow you online and participate in your conversations. This type of trust goes a long way as you grow your reputation as a community manager.

Exhibiting at Trade Shows and Conferences

Though conferences are good educational and networking experiences, you can also use them to promote your brand in a matter that befits such an event. Many conferences have trade-show areas where businesses can purchase booths and use those booths as platforms to discuss their products or services and even their communities.

The terrific thing about exhibiting at a trade show is that you're not being spammy or overly promotional if you talk about your brand and your community. People come by your booth expecting to find out more. In addition to having your salespeople promoting the brand's products and services, you can set up a computer screen to show potential members what the brand's community has to offer.

Trade shows can host thousands of people, many of whom will walk by your booth to familiarize themselves with your brand or request more information. A trade-show booth is a perfect place to recruit new members because visitors are voluntarily requesting information from you and have time to discuss the benefits of your online community in depth.

Because trade shows target specific markets, you can pick the shows that best fit with your brand and community. Potentially, everyone in attendance may have an interest in your community.

Offering Classes and Courses

One way to bring in offline members is education. Whether you have a hobby community or are representing a brand, you have information to offer, so why not teach classes?

This method is used more often than you may think. My local library, for example, features classes put on by businesses and individuals all the time. I've attended several classes whose instructors recommended that students connect with them online as well.

Figuring out the details

Classes don't have to be academic. Craft communities can give scrapbook or woodworking lessons. The hardware-emporium chains Lowe's and Home Depot are good examples of brands that offer classes for children and adults as a way to grow their communities and generate sales.

Consider what you have to offer your community:

- ✔ A wine brand can offer wine tasting or pairings classes.
- ✔ A food brand can give cooking lessons.
- ✔ A camping-goods brand can teach gourmet cooking on a camping stove.
- ✔ A writing forum can teach the fundamentals of novel writing.
- ✔ A social-media firm can give blogging lessons.
- ✔ A pet brand can offer grooming or training lessons.

Offering these types of classes is inexpensive and fun, and you don't have to give up more than an hour or two of your time on a night or weekend.

Chances are that your community members don't all live in the same neighborhoods, so test your classes on a local level so that the expense is minimal. See whether a local high school, recreation center, clubhouse, library, municipal building, or other space will donate a room or let you rent it for a couple of hours.

After you have a subject and space, you need a teacher. That part is trickier, because you want to make sure that the person giving the lessons knows her stuff, and many experts come with a high price tag. If someone on staff with your brand can teach, that's the best-case scenario. Otherwise, see what you can do about getting some local experts to donate their time.

Advertising the classes

You also have to promote your classes. Advertise them on all your community pages and create a Facebook event page specifically to invite members of your Facebook community to attend. Use a Facebook event invitation (see Figure 15-1) to spread the word among members of your online community. Ideally, the invitation will trickle down to some potential members as well.

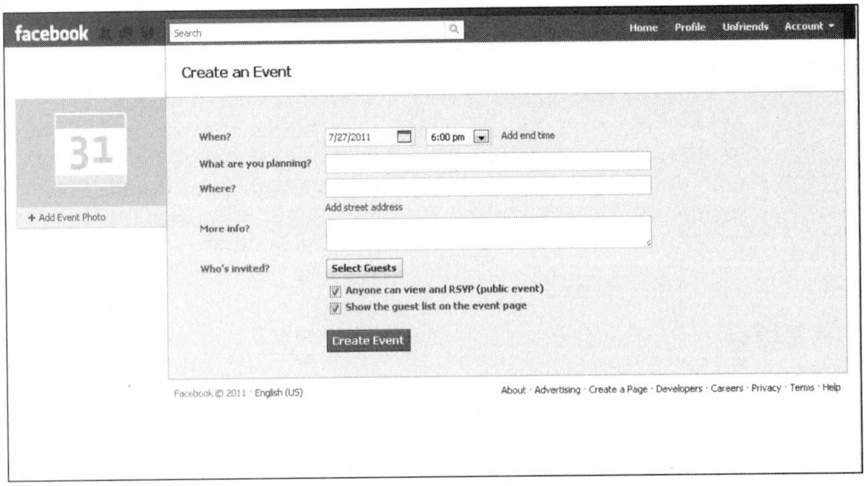

Figure 15-1: You can use a Facebook event invitation to invite people to your class.

Even if most of your community members live in other towns, sending a Facebook event invitation accomplishes several goals:

✔ It gets the word out to all community members. Even members who can't attend may have friends or family members in your area who can attend, and they can share the invitation with those people.

✔ The invitation appears in your members' Facebook streams. Nonmembers may see it and become intrigued enough to want to investigate.

✔ When you make the invitation public, nonmembers may come upon it in a search and come to the class.

Many of your potential members aren't hanging around online, of course, which is why you need to create offline events. And if they're not online, they won't know about your classes if you're advertising only on Facebook. Sometimes you have to go offline with your promotional efforts as well. Here are a few examples:

✔ Place ads in local newspapers and magazines.

✔ Post flyers on community bulletin boards.

✔ Advertise at the place where the class is being held.

People like free things. If you announce a free event in the neighborhood, folks will come to it. If you have classes on a regular basis, word of mouth spreads, and more people show up for every event.

Your classes should be 99 percent about education and 1 percent about promotion. Though the speaker or instructor won't be giving a sales pitch every few minutes, the brand logo should be apparent on signage, staff T-shirts, or handouts. Attendees shouldn't have any doubt who's sponsoring the class.

At the end of the class, you or the teacher can tell attendees where they can go online to find out more. Don't forget to talk about your website and your community and invite everyone to join. Print some literature with your community's URLs listed and distribute it.

Giving Potential Members a Reason to Sign Up

A bunch of people who you met offline liked you and liked what they heard about your community. Don't be too excited, though; only a small percentage of the people who you spoke to will become actual members. Sure, they seemed interested and gladly took your business card, but a few days later, they don't always remember why there were so excited about your community or your brand.

You have to make signing up interesting for them. You have to give them a reason to sign up, beyond the good vibe received at a conference or networking event:

✔ **Trial membership:** If you have a pay-to-play community or your community is centered around a subscription-based service, consider offering a trial membership to potential members. They can sign up, look around, participate, and, hopefully, become more permanent members. Not everyone who takes part in a trial membership commits to a full-fledged membership, but if you get a one commitment for every ten trial memberships, you're doing well.

✔ **Swag:** Make it so that members can't forget you. Entice them with a perk. Use a trick many Internet marketers are now using and offer potential community members something of value for being a part of your community. T-shirts, Internet apps or programs, ebooks, or any other product or service entices potential members enough to have them sign up for your newsletter, join your forum, or commit to another aspect of membership.

✔ **Discount or freebie:** You know what attracts potential members? The feeling that they're getting a bargain. Everyone loves discounts, and everyone loves to save. Whole communities are devoted to discounts and freebies; every time something is offered at a lower rate or a free sample is up for grabs, members of these communities share them with other members, and thousands of people will come by to see what you have to offer. Even if your discount isn't shared in deal-seeking communities, when you offer a perk during your offline recruiting, you're sure to bring in a few new members.

When potential members sign up for promotions and offers, you can offer a spot for them to opt in for future mailings. As your mailing list grows, so will your customer base.

Chapter 16

Hosting Meetups and Tweetups

. . . .

. . . .

After socializing online for a while, members become curious about one another. They're especially curious as to whether the relationships they're cultivating online hold true in the real world. Online communities are important to the people who visit them every day. Members feel a personal connection to both other members of the community and the team behind it. It's only normal that they want to meet in person. You may want to consider hosting some fun mixers and meetups to bring everyone together.

Online meetups and tweetups are a fun way for community members to meet offline and build on their relationships. They establish faith and trust in the brand and renew community bonds. Your members will love them . . . and so will you.

In this chapter, I discuss why meeting offline is important and the benefits to your community and your brand.

Fostering Community Offline

You're indebted to the members of your online community. They talk to you about your brand, share feedback, and do some word-of-mouth marketing for you. Why not reward them for their evangelism with some fun offline events?

Meetups and parties give them a place to let their hair down and carry on a discussion beyond the limitations of a web platform or social network. When members sit down together to share some chat, food, and drink, they become more than a community; they become friends. Some people even form close lifelong friendships.

Meetups are like mixers or parties where people don't necessarily know one another personally, but enjoy getting to know others face to face. *Tweetups* are similar to meetups except that they're planned via Twitter; most of the people in attendance are people who communicate via that network and are looking to take their relationships to the next level.

Meetups and tweetups also create renewed fondness for the brand and are great marketing tools as well, because your members take to social networks before, during, and after meetups to thank you and your brand for bringing everyone together. In fact, your members may even write about their experience in their blogs.

When members feel good about being part of the community, positive things result:

- ✔ **Sales:** When you host an event for your community, and it turns out to be a positive experience, members want to show your brand the love in return. Not only will some of them want to buy what you're selling, but they'll also want to recommend your community and products to nonmembers.

- ✔ **Interest:** Meetups, tweetups, and other events put together for online communities are rarely private affairs. Most are open to all, and most are discussed on the various social networks. Members post pictures on their Facebook and Google+ accounts and offer updates on Twitter and their blogs. Nonmembers wonder what all the fuss is about and investigate. Don't be surprised to have new community members after meetups and tweetups.

- ✔ **Brand evangelism:** When a meetup or tweetup goes well, members feel great about the experience, and a spontaneous marketing campaign happens as they talk online about their experience.

- ✔ **Community renewal:** You may notice a surge of traffic in the days following a community event. Members want to keep up the good vibe, so they come back to the community networks to share stories about their experience.

Planning Meetups and Tweetups

Though there have been instances of successful spontaneous tweetups, the best parties are planned:

1. **Choose a venue for your event.**

   Most meetups are held in restaurants, coffee shops, or pubs. Choose a place where crowds can gather. If you're not going to need a huge space, see whether a restaurant has a private room you can use, but always leave enough room for unexpected guests. Meetups mostly include your community members, but you may get a few potential members who want to know more about the community.

2. **Create an event page.**

   Using Facebook or a network specifically designed for creating events, such as Evite.com or Eventbrite.com, create a page where members of your community can sign up for your meetup. Though you should always leave room for a few guests who didn't RSVP, you want to get as accurate a count as possible. An event page shows you exactly how many people are coming and when you need to cut off invitations. (The last thing you want to do is exceed a restaurant's maximum capacity.)

3. **Determine whether you should serve food and drink.**

   You should serve light refreshments if you're hosting a meetup or tweetup. You don't have to have a full meal; snacks or appetizers will do. Also, you can offer each attendee a ticket for a complimentary drink rather than provide an open bar.

   Attendees aren't coming for the refreshments; they're coming to meet people, network, and have a good time. Light fare is fine.

4. **Decide whether to bring in a speaker or presenter.**

   Some meetups have speeches or presentations, and yours can too. A comedian can do a funny routine; an executive from your brand can discuss your community and how far it's come; someone can speak about a topic that's of interest to all attendees. A speaker or presenter isn't necessary — just something to consider.

5. **Figure out what equipment you need, if any.**

   If you need a microphone, a laptop, a screen for a presentation, or anything else, make a list so that you don't forget anything.

6. **Consider whether to have outside sponsors.**

   If budget is a concern — for example, you're a small brand and lack funds — you may want to bring in *sponsors* — brands that help defray the costs of your event in exchange for advertising.

7. **Think up a hashtag.**

   A hashtag uses the pound symbol (#) to denote a particular search term on Twitter. If you work for Joe's, for example, you might use the hashtag #Joesmeetup. Then everyone who attends the meetup and posts updates on Twitter about it will use that hashtag to make it easier for people to find news about this event. For larger events, some event organizers even bring a projector, laptop, and stream to show off the hashtags live.

8. **Invite your community members, using the social networks, newsletters, and other channels.**

   Post details about your tweetup on all the channels you use to communicate with your community, including forums, Twitter, Facebook, and newsletters. Make sure that the information about your event signup page is easy to spot.

9. **Count the RSVPs.**

   Your event page (refer to Step 2) lists all the members who said they'll be attending the meetup, everyone who said maybe, as well as everyone who said no.

   When you present the head count to the venue staff, caterers, and anyone else who needs to know how many people are coming, be sure to add a few extra heads to cover a bunch of the "maybes."

10. **Print name tags.**

    Name tags are ice-breakers. They take away the need for awkward introductions by enabling members to see names rather than ask for them. Make sure that you have a name tag for every RSVP. You don't need anything fancy; peel-and-stick labels that you can print on any printer work just fine.

    Be sure to bring blank labels and markers for any names you may have missed and for anyone who wasn't on the RSVP list.

11. **Put together gift bags.**

    It's not mandatory but nice to hand out gift bags or favors to attendees. A gift doesn't have to be anything fancy or expensive; it can be one of your brand's products or a T-shirt with the brand logo on it.

    If you have sponsors, you can also ask them to provide swag to your attendees.

12. **Print signs and literature.**

    You may need to print signs (with your brand's logo on them), or perhaps you want to print a promotional card that provides a discount code for your latest service. Don't wait until the last minute to visit the printer. Do the printing it at least a week in advance in case something goes wrong and the material needs to be reprinted.

Should you have free Wi-Fi at your event?

Many meetup organizers look for places that have free Wi-Fi so that attendees can update their social networks and live-blog, if they're so inclined. But Wi-Fi access is a double-edged sword. The more access attendees have to Wi-Fi, the more likely they are to be distracted from the event. Most people can update from their smartphones, so Wi-Fi shouldn't be a priority unless you want people to bring laptops.

Setting Meetup and Tweetup Rules

Planning a meetup is fun, but the actual event trumps the anticipation leading up to it. There are no serious, hard-and-fast rules for having a meetup, but keep a few things in mind:

- ✔ **Make sure that you're accessible.** Don't spend all your time in a corner or with one group of people. Your attendees want to meet you, so be as accessible as possible. Shake hands, have conversations, and spend as much time as possible with your community members.

- ✔ **Bring the team.** Make sure that representatives of your brand attend the meetup. Your community members will be disappointed if other members of your team aren't in attendance. They want to be able to talk to the brand team and ask questions. When executives and team members come out to say "Thanks for being part of our community," it show that they care.

- ✔ **Don't have a boozefest.** Open bars are bad ideas. They're expensive, and you always have a couple of people who overindulge. You can buy the first round or two, but no one should expect you to keep 50 people in booze all night.

- ✔ **Take lots of pictures.** Post lots of photos of the event on your Facebook page or in your forum. Members like to see themselves interacting, and those who couldn't make it will feel almost as if they were there.

Meetups show your community you appreciate their support and loyalty and that you're encouraging the bonds they've made with each other.

Planning an Out-of-Town Meetup or Tweetup

You just hosted a meetup in the same city as your brand's home base, and it was über successful. Guess what? If your community is national or global, you missed out on a great big group of people who'd like to get together, too. Not everyone has the budget to travel just for a three-hour meetup, and some people may feel a little left out because there was no brand-sponsored event in their area. Hardcore members especially may feel that they're missing something.

Members of online communities come together from around the world, and many of them want to meet offline as well. No one is saying that you have to travel the world making everyone happy, but if you visit different parts of the country hosting meetups for your attendees, those who didn't make the original event won't feel overlooked. If budget permits, consider visiting a few key locations.

Choosing a location

Despite what it sounds like, going on the road doesn't mean spending long days driving around the country in a Winnebago. Instead, target the areas where the most members are concentrated and plan to have meetups there. Your stats, which I talk about in detail in Chapter 13, give you a good indication of where your members live. You can also discover more about them and their geographic locations from their conversations.

Announcing a community tour

A community tour is certain to create a little buzz around the web. Existing members can't wait to meet members from their area, and even potential members may wonder what all the fuss is about.

In addition to the buzz and attention that a community tour might attract, meetups are a terrific way to gather feedback from your community.

When you talk to members in person and establish face-to-face trust, they'll tell you how they really feel about your community, your brand, and your products and services. Consider using the meetup as a sort of focus group where you gather in-depth information from members about what they like, what they don't like, and what they'd like to see in the future.

Research your members to find out whether high concentrations of them live in certain areas (see Figure 16-1). Usually, more members live in cities and bigger towns, though niche communities may be more regional, suburban, or rural. Target the areas that have the most members.

Figure 16-1:
Stats can help you pinpoint where most of your members reside so that you can choose a location.

Choosing a venue

Putting together a meetup in an out-of-town location involves the same procedure that I describe in "Planning a Local Meetup" section, earlier in this chapter. Because you're not local, however, you'll have to do some research to find locations in those out-of-town areas to host your event. One solution is to use the Internet to find a pub or restaurant that can host your meetup. Many restaurants have websites showing their menus and even photographs of their facilities. Also, read online reviews to find places that seem to be a good fit. Make a short list of the places that appeal to you and contact the managers to find out how you can hold a meetup there.

Another solution is to recruit a trusted member of your community to help you find a venue. People who live in that area know the best places to go. They can present a list of recommendations and prices, and you can make your decision based on their suggestions.

If budget permits, you can even fly to the area yourself to scout locations.

Encouraging the Community to Host Its Own Events

If you can't host meetups in different locales, not all is lost. Community members can still host their own meetups in their own areas with or without your involvement. If community members approach you about bringing your meetup to their area or hosting their own meetup, consider giving your blessing. Talk with your team and your superiors to see whether they're okay with lending the brand name to an outside meetup.

This situation is kind of tricky, because you don't want your brand's name associated with drunken affairs. For brand-sanctioned events, you may want to provide an official application (see the next section), on which members have to let you know as many details about the event as possible.

If your brand would rather not get involved in community events, you can still give your blessing to meetups within the community. Make it clear that the brand isn't sanctioning the event, however, and that the organizers can't use your signage or anything else that would hold the brand liable for an accident or other incident.

Many online communities hold their own unofficial meetups and tweetups, where members pay for their food and drinks out of their own pockets. You shouldn't discourage these meetups because if members want to get together, they're going to do it with or without your blessing. If they have your blessing, even for an unofficial event, they'll still have a good feeling about the brand. If the brand discourages meetups and tweetups, however, members may feel that they're being stifled or censored. Anything you can do on behalf of the brand to encourage community harmony and support is always helpful.

Requiring an official application

You're requiring an application to hold brand-sanctioned meetups because you have to protect the brand. Before approving outside meetups, your legal team will probably want to discuss all possible scenarios and situations and what the brand is liable for if an accident or negative situation occurs.

It may be a good idea to have organizers sign an agreement spelling out the brand's involvement, liability, and the areas which members are on their own. This agreement should include the answers to these questions:

✔ **Who's putting the meetup together?** Find out which member of your community is handling the details and whether she will have help. If the organizer is someone whom you know is responsible and will act in the best interest of the brand, go ahead and approve the application. If the organizer is someone who causes trouble, picks fights with other members, and generally is a troublemaker, you may have to think about whether this person is acting in the best interest of the brand. If your name or your brand's name is attached to the event, you have a responsibility to put on an appropriate event, not a drunken party.

✔ **Where will it be held?** Members can hold meetups anywhere. They can have "bring your own" (BYO) picnics or barbecues at a park, or they can reserve a room at a restaurant. If you're lending your brand's name to an event, the venue is important. You wouldn't want to approve an event held in the back room of a local "gentleman's club" or a place that's so exclusive that some of your members wouldn't be welcome. For this reason, it's important to research proposed venues.

✔ **Who's paying for it?** Assume that members are paying for their own food and drinks unless you want to offer a certain amount of refreshment funds to the event planner. The last thing you want to do is provide unlimited alcohol for a meetup because drunkenness can lead to all sorts of problems and complications.

✔ **What's the purpose of the meetup?** Find out whether the purpose is simply for community members who live in the same area to meet or whether the groups wants to bring in speakers or raise money for a cause. Be careful about allowing a meetup to turn into something else entirely. When you have to bring in the legal department, you're probably starting to move into territory that's more complicated than originally planned.

Creating a meetup or tweetup kit

For approved meetups and tweetups, consider putting together a meetup kit so that members will have everything they need. Although such a kit is optional, it makes members feel that they're part of the brand, and it turns the meetup into a true community event.

The kit should contain items that all meetups can benefit from:

✔ **A banner or signs:** Give the meetup organizers the means to put up signage so that there's no mistake who the community represents. The signs should be simple — just a printed logo with the words *Community Meetup* below it, for example — and easy to print on a home computer.

You can either print the signs yourself and send them as part of the kit, or you can provide the paper and the template for your members to print.

✔ **Printable name tags:** Name tags are essential for any meetup. Create branded labels with your logo in the corner so that members can print or write their names and Twitter handles.

✔ **Gifts or door prizes:** Provide inexpensive door prizes or gifts for meetup attendees — perhaps branded products such as T-shirts and caps.

✔ **Meetup guide:** It's a good idea to prepare a nicely worded list of rules and regulations or instructions for hosting a community event. Be careful wording it, because you don't want to seem too strict. But because the meetup is representing your community and brand, don't be shy about providing a list of do's and don'ts.

✔ **Social-networking tips:** You want members to be able to talk about the meetup on the social networks. In addition to providing instructions for inviting members on Facebook or Eventbrite, you should provide a Twitter hashtag to display the brand affiliation for all the meetups. If your brand is called Harry's, for example, and you're holding a meetup in New York City, #HarrysNYC could be the hashtag.

✔ **Refreshments:** If yours is a food or beverage brand, consider providing refreshments. In fact, if you have new products on the market, meetups are a good way of launching them, eliciting some feedback, and getting a word-of-mouth marketing campaign going. If yours isn't a food or beverage brand, consider a partnership with a company that can provide refreshments; otherwise, indicate that members are on their own for those costs.

Ensuring Meetup and Tweetup Safety

No one likes to admit it, but not everyone who's part of an online community is who he says he is. Grownups pretend to be youngsters; youngsters pretend to be older; men pretend to be women, and vice versa. If your community has ever had a bad experience with trolls or other abusive members, you know members can hide behind their anonymity despite your best efforts. So if your community is talking about wanting to get together offline, or if individual members are interested in meeting, you may want to discuss offline safety issues. You don't want something bad to happen to a member who met another member offline and have your brand associated with the incident.

As someone who attends conferences and meetups all the time, I can assure you that I've met hundreds of people with whom I interacted online, and nothing bad ever happened. They were all exactly who they portrayed themselves to be online, and I never had any cause for alarm. However, I also met my online community at conferences, meetups, dinners, and other events at which I wasn't alone and the event was sanctioned by a bigger brand.

I can also tell you that in the past, I've participated in many communities whose members weren't who they said they were. Though your members are most likely adults who can make their own decisions, it's a good idea to cover your butt. Make it known that you don't discourage community meetups, but if members are venturing out on their own and meeting in a group or by themselves, you're not responsible or liable. Encourage them to follow some best practices:

Consider sharing the following tips with your members:

- **Don't meet strangers in a secluded area.** Even if you have been talking to someone online for months, there's still a chance they're not acting with honorable intentions. Meet in a crowded place, somewhere a lot of people will see you. A bar, lively boardwalk or popular restaurant is a good choice for meeting someone for the first time.

- **Don't go back to someone's home.** Even if the other person seems trustworthy, don't go back to his house for a nightcap. Not only is it impossible to know exactly who or what is waiting for them, if anything, but no one wants to be too far from home or civilization if something unfortunate happens.

- **Bring friends.** If members are meeting another member alone, encourage them each to bring friends, even if the friends sit at another table while members meet alone. If two members are feeling a romantic connection, encourage them to double-date with trusted friends. It never hurts to have people around who have your back.

- **Tell friends.** If a single member insists on meeting another member alone and she's absolutely sure that it's a safe situation, urge her to tell people where she is. She should tell friends and family who she's meeting and where she's going. She also should post check-ins on location-based apps, such as Foursquare, Gowalla, and Facebook, and tweet updates from the road. It may sound silly to let so many people know where she is and what she's doing, but it's also a good idea for folks know where she is just in case.

  Those under 18 should bring a parent or let their parents know where they are at all times. Teens are especially vulnerable when meeting someone from online. Discourage "alone" meetings without parental permission or chaperones present.

✔ **Have an exit strategy.** If members meet alone, they should prepare an exit strategy if things don't turn out as planned. Encourage them to park their cars in well-lit parking lots that are close to the meeting place, where they'll be seen by plenty of people. They should memorize all exits and know how to get out quickly in case the situation turns bad or uncomfortable. Members should have their own transportation and not rely on someone they don't know to get them home.

✔ **Make sure that your cellphone is fully charged.** You don't want to have to hunt around for a payphone to call a friend or 911 if something happens or if you find yourself stranded. Always leave battery space for an emergency.

✔ **Don't give out phone numbers and addresses.** Don't give out personal details, such as a home phone number, address, place of employment, or school, unless you're 100 percent absolutely sure that you can trust the other party.

✔ **Don't drink too much.** Not only is it tacky, but you don't want to find yourself in a situation where judgment is impaired.

I'd like to stress again that I've never met anyone online who lied about who they were or their intentions. Everyone I met offline who came from an online community provided a valuable experience, and I'm glad I took the opportunity.

The circumstances in which I usually met people from online were primarily professional, though some good friendships resulted from those relationships. Just know there's safety in numbers and trust builds up over time. Don't discourage members from getting to know each other, but do make it clear which situations have your approval, and which don't. You might even want to put up a post in your community guidelines something about bearing no responsibility for unauthorized or unofficial meetings.

Part VII
The Part of Tens

The 5th Wave   By Rich Tennant

"I think you're just jealous that I found an online community that worships the yam as I do, and you haven't."

In this part . . .

In true *For Dummies* tradition, the Part of Tens offers top-ten lists filled with bite-sized information every community manager needs to be successful. I highlight a community manager's essential tasks and skillsets, and also showcase best practices so that you can be the best community manager you can be.

Chapter 17

Ten Essential Community Manager Tasks

1'm going to assume that this book isn't the only resource you're using to find out more about being an effective community manager. If you're reading up on what it takes to be a community manager or attending classes or lectures on community management, you're probably hearing a lot about the many hats worn by today's online community managers. The hat-wearing thing is a common metaphor because community managers aren't sitting at a desk handling one task at a time.

Even with the ever-changing roles, most community managers can expect to fulfill some core tasks.

Handling Community Correspondence

Being a community manager means being an effective communicator. Though there may be times you dread checking e-mail, know it's an important an essential part of your job.

You're going to handle a lot of e-mail. When word gets out that you're the one community members come to with questions and concerns, your inbox is going to be flooded. Though some days, e-mail is minimal, expect more days when your inbox seems almost bottomless. To make matters worse, your coworkers are going to forward e-mails that they feel fall under your department's jurisdiction, so be prepared to receive lots of inquiries, complaints, and stuff that has nothing to do with you at all. Also, you're going to find that the same questions are asked over and over.

But no matter how tired you are, and even if you're ready to pull your hair out after receiving the same question 100 times in the past hour, you have to respond to everyone with the same positive, professional, courteous tone.

You may be inclined to create a form letter for giving the same stock answer to frequently asked questions, but do reconsider. Form letters are impersonal and make your community members feel that they mean so little to you that you can't be bothered to create a brief, personal response. With the exception of a mass community announcement, you should avoid using a form letter if at all possible.

Set aside a time each day in which to handle member inquiries, complaints, and comments. Read everything to determine whether it should go to another person, receive an answer right away, or get further investigation. Anything that isn't concluded right away requires follow-up. Make sure to note any unresolved correspondence so that it doesn't end up falling through the cracks.

To cut down on the amount of e-mail you're receiving, you may want to post frequently asked questions on your Facebook page, blog, or community forum. Post a link to your FAQs on your blog's or website's Contact Us page so that members know to read the FAQs before writing to you with questions that you've already answered.

Planning Events

Online communities don't gather only online; they get together offline as well. As community manager, you may be tasked with setting up a variety of events.

If you're someone who enjoys planning parties and meeting people, you'll enjoy this aspect of your job. Not only will you have fun putting together meetups and tweetups, finding a venue, and inviting your community members, but you'll also have to attend the events you put together. In some cases, you may have to travel to plan parties in other locations. Traveling to meet and greet members of the community is often cited as a favorite part of the community manager's job.

Event planning isn't only fun and games, however, and not every community event is a party. You may also assist in putting together more serious functions:

  ✔ Conferences

  ✔ Lectures

  ✔ Fund-raisers

  ✔ Awards ceremonies

  ✔ Luncheons or dinners

Most likely, you'll be involved only in affairs that have to do with your community, not those that involve other departments. Also, not all brands host events for their communities. If there's an occasion for your brand and your members to meet offline, however, it'll probably fall to you to help put it all together.

For more on attending offline events, see Chapters 15 and 16.

Creating Content

If you're a creative person, you'll enjoy creating content for your community. In essence, any method you use to communicate with your members is content. It's up to you to provide news, updates, and general conversation to your community, and you can do so via several methods:

  ✔ **Newsletters:** Use weekly or monthly newsletters for brand news, updates, and discounts. Newsletters are e-mailed to members who opted in or gave permission to receive them in their e-mail. Newsletters are less conversational than blog posts and other web content, and they don't allow comments by members. Brands that use newsletters usually do so to drive sales.

  ✔ **Blog posts:** Brands use blogs for several reasons, the most important of which is to bring in readers who will comment on each day's contributions. These blog posts become part of the community and ideally drive sales. Blog posts have a more conversational tone than regular news articles, in the hope of stimulating discussion. Though brands often have staff writers, community managers also update blogs with news, anecdotes, and stories related to the community.

  ✔ **Videos:** Feel free to find fun ways to use video to share with your online community. Provide a behind-the-scenes look at what goes on internally. Introduce and interview staff members. Remember to film footage at conferences and meetups so that members can feel that they were there. Show how your product is being made, or give tutorials on how to use your product. The possibilities for video are endless.

  ✔ **Social-networking updates:** As community manager, you're tasked with community outreach via the social networks. All your social-media tools — such as Twitter, Facebook, and Google+ — are content.

Troubleshooting

If community members are having problems getting something to work properly, there's a good chance that they'll contact you. They don't always think about heading over to technical support. If you're a very public community manager and folks know that you're accessible, they reach out to you because they know you and trust you to help them with their requests. Some may even want to bypass the correct team of people because they think that they're more likely to get results if they go through you.

Troubleshooting can be anything from regenerating a wonky password to asking a complainant to jiggle a switch to see why his cable TV isn't working. It can involve internal issues as well, such as funky code in the corporate blog. Although seeing to these issues isn't necessarily your job, you may have to pitch in with technical help once in a while.

If you can't help the person who's asking for help, let him know that you're turning his complaint over to a different department — one that can better help with the problem.

Writing and Editing

Being a writer and editor isn't the same thing as being a content creator. Although you're required to create content for your community, you don't necessarily have to get out the formal tone or the red pencil when you're writing a blog post. As community manager, you need to be a great communicator and have a terrific command of grammar.

Because you're representing the community with your words, you have to be careful not to make any mistakes or typos that cause someone to call you out online. This happens all the time. One minute, you're sending out a newsletter, and the next minute, a member is ridiculing you on her blog for spelling a word wrong.

As the voice of your community and public representative of your brand, you have to submit the cleanest copy possible. When the writing is over, put on your editing hat.

Moderating and Mediating

Being responsible for all your content means that you're responsible for content posted by your community members. All the comments on forums and Facebook pages are a reflection not only of your brand, but also of you as a community manger. Sometimes, items posted by members of your community aren't appropriate. It's up to you to ask the offending member to edit the inappropriate content or even to remove it.

You're also tasked with stepping between members who are having an argument on your community pages. Soothe hurt feelings, defuse tempers, and bring the situation under control.

Though you may be inclined to side with a member of the community in an argument, you have to be fair and impartial, treating everyone with the same courtesy.

Your community should be a safe haven for all who attend. Make sure that it's a pleasant place for members to converse and enjoy one another's company.

Providing Customer Service

Dealing with customers is one of your more pleasant tasks. You'll find that most of them are good-natured and get upset only if they feel like they're getting the runaround. At times, however, customers are angry and treat you as though everything is your fault. Don't get angry back and don't fly off the handle. It's when you react in anger that the real trouble starts.

Always treat your community members in the same manner that you want to be treated. When there's mutual respect, everyone is at ease, even in a difficult situation.

Nowadays, many customers use the social networks to talk about their issues with a particular brand. Don't be surprised when people contact you directly by reaching out to you on Twitter, posting a message on your Facebook page, or sending you an e-mail. Because you're the public face of the community, you have name recognition, and people will reach out to you when there's an issue. You'll find that members of your community feel more confident about dealing with a familiar and trustworthy person than about calling a department where they don't know anyone.

For more on handling customer service, see Chapter 6.

Serving as a Liaison

You're not only the voice of the community, but also the voice of the brand. You report community news and updates on behalf of the brand while reporting customer service issues and feedback on behalf of the community. In other words, you're a two-way messenger.

You're advocating on behalf of two separate parties. You have to make sure that the members of your community are heard and receive a fair shake. You also have to show transparency on behalf of the brand.

Social Networking

The social-networking aspect of the job inspired many people to become community managers. Though it's a small part of the job, using networks such as Google+, Facebook, Twitter, and LinkedIn is vital.

Back in the day, long before people were socializing online, it was very rare for customers to have a conversation with executives from a brand unless it was in the form of an impersonal letter. Now they can reach out to the people behind the brand and get a real-time response. When you or someone from your team responds, it means the world to your members, especially if they can have conversations that aren't even remotely related to the brand. They appreciate the human element of knowing that you're there for them, even if it's just to say "Hi."

Marketing

Because you know so much about what makes your community tick, you're a regular fixture in marketing meetings and marketing-team planning sessions. The team members want your input because you know so many details that they don't, such as these:

- The median age of your members
- The common locations where your members reside
- The topics and campaigns that receive the biggest responses
- The best search terms that leading to your website and community pages
- What your community members are saying about you online
- What your community members are writing to you about in their e-mails

You're managing your community's stats and use, and have valuable information regarding their habits. Marketing needs the same information to better plan sales and promotions. In fact, it shouldn't put together any campaign without your input.

For more on working with stats and numbers, see Part V.

Chapter 18

Ten Must-Have Skills for Community Managers

*P*eople who aren't familiar with all the roles of an online community manager are surprised to find out that community managers do much more than hang out on Twitter all day. Also, aspiring community managers who see only the public side of the job are often surprised at all the different roles of a community manager. Make no mistake; this job requires skill in many different areas.

In this chapter, you discover ten vital skills a successful community manager must have.

People Skills

Because community management is a public job and because you have to deal with people on a daily basis, being a community manager requires skills far beyond that of a general education. Some of the skills are learned, and some of the skills are innate, but all are necessary.

Not everyone has what it takes to be a community manager, not only because of the many tasks and duties a community manager has to handle, but also because of the skillset. It takes a special person to run a community.

The ability to deal with people is a skill that many people don't have. It's not easy to treat all people the same way whether you agree with them or not, and it's certainly not easy to keep a pleasant, even tone with people who are making you so angry that you want to tear your hair out. Still, that's what the job requires. There are absolutely no occasions on which you should be cross with a community member.

Having people skills doesn't mean being Polly Perky all the time, though. Although you're expected to remain positive and upbeat, you also have to be respectfully firm when a member makes an unreasonable request or you can't give him what he wants.

Your people skills take you through a variety of circumstances and situations (see Figure 18-1). Not all situations are positive, so you have to be able to handle all of them without flying off the handle, calling people names, or slamming down the phone. It's the corporate equivalent of a doctor's bedside manner.

Figure 18-1:
Use your
people skills
to have
lively con-
versations
with your
community
members.

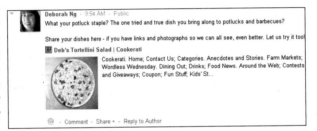

These traits will serve you well as a community manager:

- ✔ Polite.
- ✔ Respectful.
- ✔ Calm.
- ✔ Fair.
- ✔ Firm.

If you're known for being brutally honest or using swear words to illustrate a point, you probably should work on those people skills a little more. You're not there to make folks feel chastised, hurt, or offended. Rather, you should strive to make everyone feel comfortable, even in uncomfortable situations.

A Way with Words

Words are powerful tools. They sell, command, direct, and suggest. How you use words has a bearing on how well you and your community members get along, as well as how well your customers respond.

Having a way with words is more than simply writing a sentence. Part of your job is attracting people to your community and you're not going to do that with bland writing. Not only do you have to attract the attention of the search engines, but you also have to attract the people who land on your community pages via search engines or other means.

People read differently online than they do offline, but they also have short attention spans. They scan the computer screen rather than become truly absorbed in content. Your words have to keep their attention for longer than five seconds (see Figure 18-2).

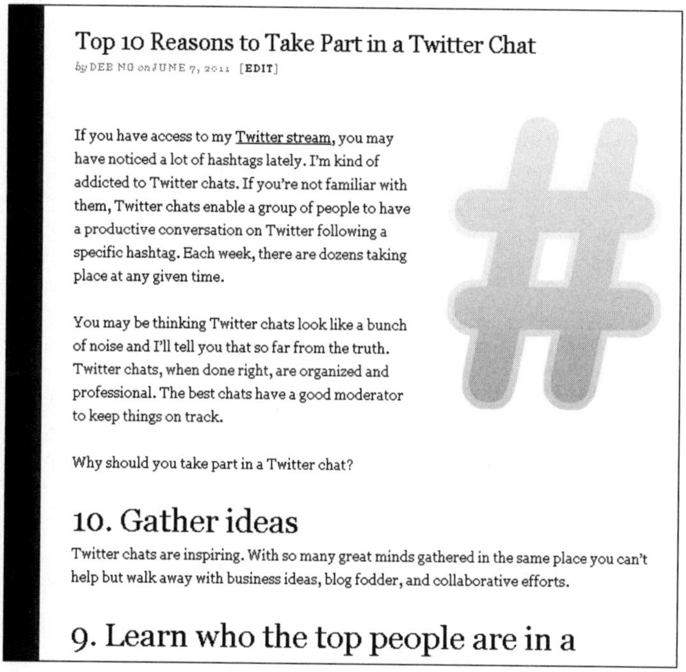

Figure 18-2:
Use eye-catching headlines to draw in visitors and community members.

Top 10 Reasons to Take Part in a Twitter Chat
by DEE NG on JUNE 7, 2011 [EDIT]

If you have access to my Twitter stream, you may have noticed a lot of hashtags lately. I'm kind of addicted to Twitter chats. If you're not familiar with them, Twitter chats enable a group of people to have a productive conversation on Twitter following a specific hashtag. Each week, there are dozens taking place at any given time.

You may be thinking Twitter chats look like a bunch of noise and I'll tell you that so far from the truth. Twitter chats, when done right, are organized and professional. The best chats have a good moderator to keep things on track.

Why should you take part in a Twitter chat?

10. Gather ideas
Twitter chats are inspiring. With so many great minds gathered in the same place you can't help but walk away with business ideas, blog fodder, and collaborative efforts.

9. Learn who the top people are in a

Keep these points in mind as you create content:

- Use eye-catching headlines.
- Write in a conversational tone.
- Make your writing open-ended so that folks respond.
- Use anecdotes.
- Keep community members engaged by asking interesting questions and discussing the responses.
- Use a kind, positive tone.
- Don't be afraid to inject humor into your discussions.

Networking Skills

Whether you call it schmoozing, chatting up, or mingling, you're required to spend time networking offline at professional events and online via social-media tools. Networking with confidence is a skill that many professional people haven't mastered.

Most people confuse networking opportunities with selling opportunities, but those who network the right way can drive sales without a single pitch. You're not necessarily networking for the sale, however. You're networking to meet people and build relationships. You're networking to find out about people who are in your community and in similar communities and to bring them all together. You're also gathering information for your marketing and product development teams. The more they know about the people who use your products or services, the better able they are to create the things that those people want to use.

Many times, networking isn't about work or business. Because most networking events include people who have something in common, you're there to gain new clients, followers, community members, or sales. But have a conversation that isn't about any of that stuff, and see where it takes you. Chances are that you'll achieve your networking goals better if you don't push your business on everyone there.

The best networkers know that the conversation isn't about them. Instead, they ask questions and find out as much as they can about the people they're talking with. They use *I* and *me* as little as possible to make it more about *you*.

Technical Abilities

You don't have to know heavy coding, but it helps to be a little tech-savvy, mostly to be independent and fix things without having to call in the cavalry. It helps to know a little HTML in case your blog is acting funny and to know some basic commands so you can to delete or edit a post.

You should also know how to set up a Facebook landing page, add your brand's logo to your Twitter account, and give the company newsletter a professional look. You should be able to read your stats or statistics page and know what each metric or measurement is telling you (see Part V). You should also know how to act on those results.

You don't need to master Computer Science to be an online community manager, but you should have a basic working knowledge of the various tools and techniques needed to make your job a successful one.

Communication Skills

Because you perform so many tasks and work in conjunction with different departments, there are many opportunities for communication breakdowns. Also, because you may work remotely from home, there's an even bigger opportunity for members of the teams to be out of the loop.

Being a good communicator is essential to this job:

✔ Create a weekly or monthly report for the departments you work with so that there are no surprises.

✔ Request regular updates from other departments so that you don't find yourself left out when projects or promotions are introduced.

✔ Report any known issues with your community to the proper channels as soon as possible. Don't ever let an incident escalate out of control because you didn't want to make waves.

✔ Follow up on every complaint or request from a team or community member. Even if you delegated a request to another department to handle, follow up to make sure that the issue is resolved.

Being a good communicator means you keep your team apprised of new developments and stay on top of the different departments to make sure you're not missing any key details. Don't put the onus on other people to give or receive information.

Multitasking Ability

Not only do you have to wear a lot of hats as a community manager, but sometimes you also feel that you're wearing them all at the same time. On any given day, you can expect to have at least half a dozen computer windows open at the same time. You may have the best intentions and set up times for everything. Perhaps you schedule social networking for one hour and responding to e-mail the next.

I have news for you: It never works that way. Things happen. You hear TweetDeck pinging, and you can't wait to see who's calling out to you on Twitter. Your e-mail is beeping as well. Your phone rings, and your boss is on Skype. Although your perfect scenario is to be able to focus on one task at a time, sometimes you have your hands in several pots at the same time.

Figure out when you're the most focused. Some people work best first thing in the morning; others do their best work immediately after returning from lunch. Think about the time you work best and schedule the tasks that require your complete attention for that time. Save e-mail, social networking, Skype chats, and other tasks for the times when you're most unfocused. Sometimes you can't help multitasking, but you can try to work multitasking times into your schedule so that you can put your all into the most important tasks.

Flexibility

The stubborn need not apply for a community manager gig. You can't be set in your ways and manage an online community. Flexibility in this job requires the ability to

- Try different things
- Adjust to the needs of your community
- Set up calls and meetings that fit someone else's schedule
- Change deadlines if necessary
- Fill your time in case duties are delegated to someone else, or meetings or phone calls are canceled
- Take on additional tasks if asked to do so

Make no mistake — being flexible doesn't mean that you should let everyone walk all over you or show disrespect to your deadlines or time. It means that you can see to people's needs and don't mind switching an appointment time or changing a few words around to suit someone else. It also means that you can break your focus and multitask if you're called on for another task. Flexibility simply means that you're willing to adapt to different situations and don't mind changing times and dates if doing so makes things easier.

Focus

All community managers like to spend time on the social networks chatting with their members. Also, they all like reading and commenting on blogs, and performing other social tasks to foster good community relations. Although the fun stuff is necessary, it's also distracting.

Sometimes, you need to shut out the world and concentrate on the important stuff so that you can get the job done. Keep these pointers in mind as you hone your focus:

✔ **Scheduling is key.** The secret to staying focused is having specific times of day when you handle everything. Take the tasks that require the most focus and do them for your first couple of hours. Then schedule e-mail for the next hour and phone calls for the first thing after lunch. After that, take to the social networks. If every task has its own time, you're less likely to get distracted by different tasks.

✔ **Use the fun stuff as a reward.** Try handling the most unattractive tasks first to get them out of the way. Use the stuff you like best as a reward. If your least favorite task is writing the community newsletter, and your favorite task is monitoring the social networks, do the newsletter first while telling yourself that the sooner you get it done — and get it done right — the sooner you can chat up your community members.

✔ **Block out noise.** If you work in a cubicle in a noisy office, you have trouble focusing because of the noise. Phones ring, coworkers chitchat, and you have to cope with office sounds. Having good focus means being able to block out these sounds and attack the matter at hand. If noise is a problem, see whether your company grants permission to wear noise-reduction headsets or listen to low music as long as you can still hear if you're being paged.

✔ **Say "No" or "Later" when necessary.** Although being flexible is important, you also have to let people know when you can't be disturbed. If a coworker is asking you for help with something that you're not obligated to do, you can politely decline. If you have too much on your plate, you can nicely mention your to-do list without sounding whiny. If someone comes to you with a task or request for help, you can also say that you're in the middle of something and can't stop, but you'll be happy to help when you're free.

Drive

Not everyone has the determination to land his dream job and be the best at that job that he can possibly be. You can't just go through the motions with this job, especially because communities can be so competitive. Your job is to grow your community, keep new members coming, and make sure that the existing members are appreciated as well. You have to keep people engaged so that they continue to see you and your brand in a positive light.

You can't rest on your laurels or take days off from your community. If you stop engaging, your community will dry up. If you stop the outreach on the social networks, you won't have new members coming in. If you don't plan offline events, the people who don't spent time online won't know about your brand's community efforts. This isn't a job for the lazy or unmotivated. You have to have the drive to bring in traffic and promote your community every single day.

Business Development Acumen

In a way, you're the most important person in your company. Without you and your input and data, the other teams don't know how to serve your customers and community members properly. Even though you're not officially part of the business development department, you're the one person that this department can't manage effectively without.

Because you're receiving feedback from your community on a regular basis, you're best equipped to tell the business development how the people who use your products and services feel about them. If any aspect of what your brand creates isn't working, you're the one who hears about it. Also, it's up to you to offer surveys to collect information from customers and community members.

Because you spend so much time talking to your members, you know things that the rest of your team may not:

- **The median age of your community:** After conversing with members over time, you find out how old they are.

- **The location of your members:** You find out where members live and whether more of them live in one area than in other areas.

- **Their hobbies and interests:** Community chats often go off topic, and this is okay, because you want to find out about your members' interests — the things they like to do during their down time.

- **Careers:** You know what some of your members do for a living.

- **Income:** Unless you come out and ask, you won't know for sure, but some indicators let you know the income levels of your members. If they talk about their in-ground swimming pools and country-club memberships, it's a good guess that they're upper-income. If they talk about clipping coupons, saving money, and not being able to afford certain services, your members are in a lower- or middle-income bracket.

This information may seem to be unrelated to your brand, but I can assure you it's very important. Without knowing some of the deeper personal details about your community, you won't be able to reach them on a deeper level. Knowing how they roll means that your brand can create the products and services they'll respond to best at prices that they can afford.

Chapter 19

Ten Best Practices of a Community Manager

In This Chapter

▶ Being a neutral party

▶ Being accessible to your community

▶ Setting the right tone

Your success as a community manager is contingent upon your actions. If you go through the motions and put in the bare minimum of effort, you'll achieve the same results in return. If you have a good work ethic and follow some best practices, you'll achieve even better results. It's not enough to go to work every day and talk to people online. Your habits and work ethic are what set you apart from the rest.

To succeed as a community manager, you have to go beyond skill. Your habits also have to stand out.

Staying Impartial

As a community manager, you have to be fair. In fact, that should be the number one rule of community management. Even if you don't like a person or don't agree with him, you have to be fair. You can't side with your friends simply because they're your friends or roll with the popular kids because they're more fun. Everyone in your community have to be treated with equal respect.

Being impartial goes far beyond moderating community comments, though that's a big part of it. It's also inviting a diverse group of people into your community. It's making sure that you have a true community and not a clique.

Your community looks at you to be the voice of reason. Though they're most likely adults and old enough to fight their own battles, you may have to step in and guide a heated argument back to a productive discussion without choosing sides or singling out one person.

Being impartial doesn't mean that you shouldn't ask abusive people to leave the community. Treating everyone with equal respect also means providing a safe haven where members can socialize without being bullied or putting up with profanity or vulgarity. If one person is called out for a community violation, you can't let others go for the same infraction, even if you like them better. Impartiality puts everyone on equal footing, allowing them to be themselves and communicate with ease.

Having a Regular Presence in Your Community and Others

The worst thing you can do is be an absentee online community manager. Your community-building efforts are all for naught if you're not a familiar face at all your online haunts. People want to see you. In many cases, they joined the community because of you. You're the voice of reason and the glue that holds it all together. If you're never around, things start to fall apart. Have a regular presence each day, even if you're just saying hello (see Figure 19-1). Your presence matters a lot more than you think.

Figure 19-1:
Your community feels assured knowing that you're there each day.

@debng
Deborah Ng

Good morning, world! How's Friday looking?

8 hours ago via Seesmic Desktop   ☆ Favorite ↰ Reply ⬛ Delete

About Help Blog Status Jobs Terms Privacy Advertisers Businesses Media Developers Resources © 2011 Twitter

Here are a few things you can do to help you establish a regular presence:

✔ **Lead discussion topics.** Your community should have a fresh supply of discussion topics each day, whether it's a forum, an e-mail group, a Facebook page, or Twitter. Even if it's the type of community where the people generate their own topics, you still can't leave it to run by itself. Posting your own daily discussion topic lets members know that you're there and paying attention. It also shows that you enjoy participating in the community and aren't there just because you're being paid.

✓ **Interact and engage.** Most brand-related communities exist so that customers and members can interact with the brand. Customers put their trust in brands that have accessible people working for them. They like being able to reach out on Twitter and ask questions or discuss issues. Having an active community manager dispels the myth of the big corporate executive sitting behind his desk chewing on a cigar, not having time for the "little people." Your active presence ensures faith in the bran because your customers know their thoughts are concerns are being heard.

✓ **Note problems or issues.** When you routinely monitor community discussions, you're aware of problems and issues. Sometimes, community members reach out to one another to see whether they're experiencing the same issues with your brand, website, or community. It pays to have an active presence so that you can observe these discussions, respond if necessary, and take action.

✓ **Receive feedback.** You know what happens if community members don't see an active brand presence? They assume that no one is around to receive their feedback. Yes, they can call an 800 number, and yes, they can e-mail their feedback, but customers want to reach out via the social networks too. The last thing they want is to offer feedback on a Twitter or Facebook page and get virtual crickets in response.

You also want to hang out in other communities. Other communities aren't competition; they're places to share, collaborate, and commiserate. It pays to visit blogs, forums, and Facebook pages and take part in Twitter chats so that you can

✓ **Build relationships with like-minded people.** The beautiful thing about online communities is members can join more than one, and many do. You may see the same people visiting several communities in the same niche. You want members of other communities to interact with your tribe as well-. Community is not about spamming someone else's forum. It's about having a conversation with people who have a common passion and hoping that they visit your community in return.

✓ **Raise brand awareness.** If a blogger is listing lemonade recipes, how cool would it be for someone from a lemonade brand to leave comments offering kudos or tips on making things with lemonade?

A daily presence goes a long way. Your community members give up their time to be there for you. Shouldn't you offer the same?

Responding to Inquiries in a Timely Manner

You know what happens when people reach out to you for answers and you don't respond?

- ✔ They denounce the brand on the social networks.
- ✔ They denounce you on the social networks.
- ✔ You gain a reputation for being unresponsive.
- ✔ You lose the trust of your community members.
- ✔ E-mail that could have been answered in five minutes is now so stacked up that it'll take you hours to go through it all.
- ✔ Stuff falls through the cracks.
- ✔ Your community members go to a more receptive community.

Don't ignore anyone who reaches out to you with a question, no matter how small you think it is. Your reputation is at stake, and your brand could take a hit as well.

Keeping a Positive Tone

It's up to you to set the tone for your community. If you're a regular presence, members are less inclined to sling mud or use profanity, and the community is a more positive place to interact. With no visible leader or personal authority, controversial topics and inappropriate comments can make their way through. Your community can certainly talk about thought-provoking issues, but it's better to step in a few times a day to make sure that things don't get out of hand.

Your community is a reflection of you and your ability to manage effectively. A positive community reflects on you positively, and a negative atmosphere shows that you don't have good control — or don't care.

To keep the tone positive:

- ✔ **Steer topics in the right direction.** Sometimes, it's okay if a discussion meanders away from the original topic. If the topic goes completely off track and members are confused or unsure what everyone is talking about, you have to guide it back on track with leading questions and comments.

✔ **Offer encouraging words.** Positive words yield positive results. Praise members for good deeds, offer good wishes on birthdays or other milestones, and let them all know that they have something special to offer. Don't suck up to members or offer false flattery, but when you're encouraging and supportive with your members, your members offer the same to you, the brand, and their community.

✔ **Use humor.** Everyone enjoys a good laugh. Inject fun into your community, and encourage your members to have fun as well. Slapstick can be annoying, but who doesn't appreciate a good sense of humor?

✔ **Don't tell the world your problems.** Nothing kills a mood like a sob story. Also, your personal problems have no place in community discussions. Keep your TMI (too much information) to yourself.

Being Supportive of the Brand and the Community

Because you spend so much time with your community, it's easy to forget you're employed for a more important reason: to advocate for your brand. The whole purpose of the community is to build relationships with customers and the people who use your products and services. So when members are bad-mouthing the brand or complaining about things that they don't like, remember that you're there for brand support.

Though you may agree with members of your community at times, if they're disparaging the brand, you have to show loyalty to your place of employment. If you don't, you community members will lose faith in you, and their relationship with the brand will be over.

By all means, advocate for the customers; you have to show your community members that you have their backs. Offer feedback to your brand on their behalf, and if you see unfair practices or issues that won't sit well with the community, have a discussion with your team on why that won't work. It won't do for you to cast your brand in a negative light, however.

Forging Relationships

When you spend time talking each day to the same people, you find out about them. Sometimes, you know more about your members than about how they use your brand. You may know about their kids, hobbies, or favorite types of books and movies. These details may seem to be sort of personal, but knowing them is a way to deepen discussion topics and add to your relationships with members. Although you don't want to offer intimate details about your life, it's okay to talk about your favorite music or actor. Sharing likes and dislikes is a great way to find common ground with your members.

The relationships you build do more than just create good discussion topics; they also create trust in you and in your brand. People like supporting brands that they feel good about, and you're the one who's tasked with bringing on those good feelings. If your community trusts you, you continue to find out more about them, and you can provide feedback to the brand so that it can create more of the products and services people want to use.

Thanks to the Internet and social media, brands now have the tools they need to learn about what people want and need. There are no more impersonal form letters or surveys to fill out or telephone recordings to deal with. Feedback is instant and it's made directly to the people who can do the most good. Having good relationships with your community means they don't feel shy about telling you how they use your community or your brand.

Promoting the Community

Your community rocks. All your members mesh, and when they brainstorm, they come up with amazing ideas. So why would you keep all that to yourself? To catch the attention of potential members, as well as the press, product reviewers, and other communities and community managers, you need to get a little shameless with the promotion, but not so shameless that you're spammy and annoying:

- Highlight your members' achievements in the blog, in the newsletter, and on the social networks.
- Bring community achievements to the attention of bloggers and the press.
- Participate in other communities' discussions to attract new members to your community.
- Attend events of interest to your community and brand and talk to the people who can most benefit from participating too.
- Hold Twitter chats and invite both members and nonmembers to attend.

Your community is your brand's greatest asset. There's absolutely nothing wrong with showing the world how it shines.

Being Passionate about the Community

Having a passion for the brand or niche is what makes the most successful community managers. It's because you're passionate that you love your job and want to do everything you can for your community. You love talking with everyone each day, and your knowledge of the topic or brand is apparent. You love what you do, and it shows.

Compare someone who loves his job with someone who's just going through the motions. The person who's going through the motions handles the bare minimum. He clocks in at exactly 9 a.m. and leaves at exactly 5 p.m. His favorite part of the job is leaving for the day.

Your community is better than that. It doesn't deserve the guy who can't wait to leave his job. Your members spend money on your brand and advocate it by joining your community or sharing your promotions with friends, so they deserve a community manager who's at his best each and every day.

Staying on Top of Trends

What are people buying? How are they communicating online? Are they spending more money or less? What foods, gadgets, or fashions are in or out? You need to know all that, whether it pertains to your community or not.

To stay on top of trends, know

- ✔ What's in and what's out so that you can hold a conversation without appearing old, out of touch, or just not hip to current situations.
- ✔ How people are spending their money so that you can determine how to set up promotions and discounts. It also enables you to work with the proper teams in setting up price points.
- ✔ The latest news so that you can create timely discussion topics.
- ✔ The latest trends in colors, which helps you design your websites, blogs, and community pages to stay current.
- ✔ The latest social-networking sites, which allows you to continue to interact with your existing members and attract new members.
- ✔ The latest tools and technologies, which makes your job easier.

It's also important to note trends within your community (see Figure 19-2). Are there fewer comments lately? Are your veteran members disappearing?

Are people coming to your community via a completely new set of search terms? Your community is going to have both upward and downward trends, and it's up to you to pinpoint trends and unearth the reasons for them.

Figure 19-2:
Staying on top of the latest trends enables you to keep up with your community and spot any potential issues.

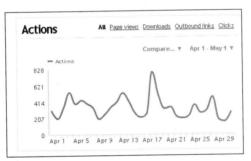

Continuing Your Education

Don't be afraid to learn something new. This may mean reading articles about your industry, the brand, and community management, and it can mean seeking education that better enables you to run your community.

It never hurts to know basic web or blog design and to stay on top of the latest techniques. Also, knowing about branding, marketing, customer service, public relations, and even basic psychology doesn't hurt. In every profession, the people who get ahead fastest are the ones who aren't afraid to learn.

Your brand may be interested in helping you on your journey. Many companies are willing to invest in their employees and pay for continuing education. If sending you to classes isn't in your company's budget, don't be afraid to invest in your own future and do it on your own.

Educating yourself doesn't necessarily mean sitting in a classroom taking notes. You can also attend conferences, webinars, and lectures; watch videos; and read books, magazines, newspapers, and web articles.

You know what looks bad? Watching discussions that you can't take part in or responding "I don't know" to questions. If you're hired as a community manager, and you don't know enough about the product or niche, you owe it to yourself to learn more and keep learning more so that you can hold your own in a conversation.

Index

• F •

• *M* •

• P •

Apple & Macs

iPad For Dummies
978-0-470-58027-1

iPhone For Dummies,
4th Edition
978-0-470-87870-5

MacBook For Dummies, 3rd
Edition
978-0-470-76918-8

Mac OS X Snow Leopard For
Dummies
978-0-470-43543-4

Business

Bookkeeping For Dummies
978-0-7645-9848-7

Job Interviews
For Dummies,
3rd Edition
978-0-470-17748-8

Resumes For Dummies,
5th Edition
978-0-470-08037-5

Starting an
Online Business
For Dummies,
6th Edition
978-0-470-60210-2

Stock Investing
For Dummies,
3rd Edition
978-0-470-40114-9

Successful
Time Management
For Dummies
978-0-470-29034-7

Computer Hardware

BlackBerry
For Dummies,
4th Edition
978-0-470-60700-8

Computers For Seniors
For Dummies,
2nd Edition
978-0-470-53483-0

PCs For Dummies,
Windows
7 Edition
978-0-470-46542-4

Laptops For Dummies,
4th Edition
978-0-470-57829-2

Cooking & Entertaining

Cooking Basics
For Dummies,
3rd Edition
978-0-7645-7206-7

Wine For Dummies,
4th Edition
978-0-470-04579-4

Diet & Nutrition

Dieting For Dummies,
2nd Edition
978-0-7645-4149-0

Nutrition For Dummies,
4th Edition
978-0-471-79868-2

Weight Training
For Dummies,
3rd Edition
978-0-471-76845-6

Digital Photography

Digital SLR Cameras &
Photography For Dummies,
3rd Edition
978-0-470-46606-3

Photoshop Elements 8
For Dummies
978-0-470-52967-6

Gardening

Gardening Basics
For Dummies
978-0-470-03749-2

Organic Gardening
For Dummies,
2nd Edition
978-0-470-43067-5

Green/Sustainable

Raising Chickens
For Dummies
978-0-470-46544-8

Green Cleaning
For Dummies
978-0-470-39106-8

Health

Diabetes For Dummies,
3rd Edition
978-0-470-27086-8

Food Allergies
For Dummies
978-0-470-09584-3

Living Gluten-Free
For Dummies,
2nd Edition
978-0-470-58589-4

Hobbies/General

Chess For Dummies,
2nd Edition
978-0-7645-8404-6

Drawing
Cartoons & Comics
For Dummies
978-0-470-42683-8

Knitting For Dummies,
2nd Edition
978-0-470-28747-7

Organizing
For Dummies
978-0-7645-5300-4

Su Doku For Dummies
978-0-470-01892-7

Home Improvement

Home Maintenance
For Dummies,
2nd Edition
978-0-470-43063-7

Home Theater
For Dummies,
3rd Edition
978-0-470-41189-6

Living the
Country Lifestyle
All-in-One
For Dummies
978-0-470-43061-3

Solar Power Your Home
For Dummies,
2nd Edition
978-0-470-59678-4

Available wherever books are sold. For more information or to order direct: U.S. customers visit www.dummies.com or call 1-877-762-2974.
U.K. customers visit www.wileyeurope.com or call (0) 1243 843291. Canadian customers visit www.wiley.ca or call 1-800-567-4797.

Internet

Blogging For Dummies,
3rd Edition
978-0-470-61996-4

eBay For Dummies,
6th Edition
978-0-470-49741-8

Facebook For Dummies,
3rd Edition
978-0-470-87804-0

Web Marketing
For Dummies,
2nd Edition
978-0-470-37181-7

WordPress
For Dummies,
3rd Edition
978-0-470-59274-8

Language & Foreign Language

French For Dummies
978-0-7645-5193-2

Italian Phrases
For Dummies
978-0-7645-7203-6

Spanish For Dummies,
2nd Edition
978-0-470-87855-2

Spanish
For Dummies,
Audio Set
978-0-470-09585-0

Math & Science

Algebra I
For Dummies,
2nd Edition
978-0-470-55964-2

Biology For Dummies,
2nd Edition
978-0-470-59875-7

Calculus For Dummies
978-0-7645-2498-1

Chemistry For Dummies
978-0-7645-5430-8

Microsoft Office

Excel 2010 For Dummies
978-0-470-48953-6

Office 2010 All-in-One
For Dummies
978-0-470-49748-7

Office 2010 For Dummies,
Book + DVD Bundle
978-0-470-62698-6

Word 2010 For Dummies
978-0-470-48772-3

Music

Guitar For Dummies,
2nd Edition
978-0-7645-9904-0

iPod & iTunes For
Dummies, 8th Edition
978-0-470-87871-2

Piano Exercises
For Dummies
978-0-470-38765-8

Parenting & Education

Parenting For Dummies,
2nd Edition
978-0-7645-5418-6

Type 1 Diabetes
For Dummies
978-0-470-17811-9

Pets

Cats For Dummies,
2nd Edition
978-0-7645-5275-5

Dog Training For Dummies,
3rd Edition
978-0-470-60029-0

Puppies For Dummies,
2nd Edition
978-0-470-03717-1

Religion & Inspiration

The Bible For Dummies
978-0-7645-5296-0

Catholicism For Dummies
978-0-7645-5391-2

Women in the Bible
For Dummies
978-0-7645-8475-6

Self-Help & Relationship

Anger Management
For Dummies
978-0-470-03715-7

Overcoming Anxiety
For Dummies,
2nd Edition
978-0-470-57441-6

Sports

Baseball
For Dummies,
3rd Edition
978-0-7645-7537-2

Basketball
For Dummies,
2nd Edition
978-0-7645-5248-9

Golf For Dummies,
3rd Edition
978-0-471-76871-5

Web Development

Web Design
All-in-One
For Dummies
978-0-470-41796-6

Web Sites
Do-It-Yourself
For Dummies,
2nd Edition
978-0-470-56520-9

Windows 7

Windows 7
For Dummies
978-0-470-49743-2

Windows 7
For Dummies,
Book + DVD Bundle
978-0-470-52398-8

Windows 7 All-in-One
For Dummies
978-0-470-48763-1

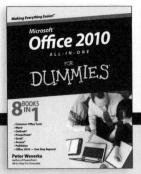

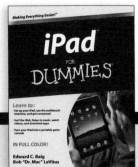

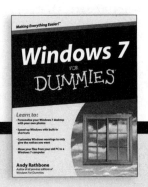

Available wherever books are sold. For more information or to order direct: U.S. customers visit www.dummies.com or call 1-877-762-2974
U.K. customers visit www.wileyeurope.com or call (0) 1243 843291. Canadian customers visit www.wiley.ca or call 1-800-567-4797.

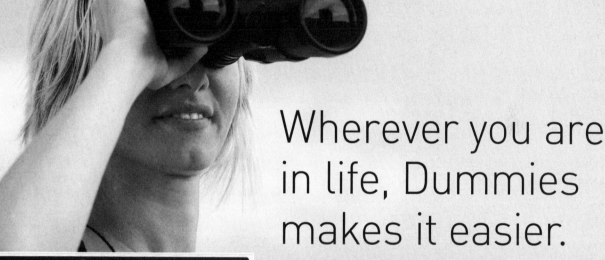

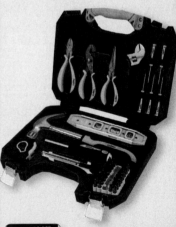